Religion, Law, and the Land

**Recent Titles in
Contributions in Legal Studies**

Innovation, Reaction, and Atrophy: The Impact of Judicial-Selection Method on Policy in State Supreme Courts
Daniel R. Pinello

Controversy, Courts, and Community:
The Rhetoric of Judge Miles Welton Lord
Verna C. Corgan

Constitutional Politics in the States: Contemporary Controversies and Historical Patterns
G. Alan Tarr, editor

Law and the Great Plains: Essays on the Legal History of the Heartland
John R. Wunder, editor

Judicial Entrepreneurship: The Role of the Judge in the Marketplace of Ideas
Wayne V. McIntosh and Cynthia L. Cates

Solving the Puzzle of Interest Group Litigation
Andrew Jay Koshner

Presidential Defiance of "Unconstitutional" Laws: Reviving the Royal Prerogative
Christopher N. May

Promises on Prior Obligations at Common Law
Kevin M. Teeven

Litigating Federalism: The States Before the U.S. Supreme Court
Eric N. Waltenburg and Bill Swinford

Law and the Arts
Susan Tiefenbrun, editor

Contract Law and Morality
Henry Mather

The Appearance of Equality: Racial Gerrymandering, Redistricting, and the Supreme Court
Christopher M. Burke

Religion, Law, and the Land

Native Americans and the Judicial Interpretation of Sacred Land

Brian Edward Brown

Contributions in Legal Studies, Number 94

GREENWOOD PRESS
Westport, Connecticut • London

Library of Congress Cataloging-in-Publication Data

Brown, Brian Edward.
    Religion, law, and the land : Native Americans and the judicial interpretation of sacred land / Brian Edward Brown.
        p. cm.—(Contributions in legal studies, ISSN 0147–1074 ; no. 94)
    Includes bibliographical references and index.
    ISBN 0–313–30972–8 (alk. paper)
    1. Indians of North America—Religion. 2. Indians of North America—Land tenure. 3. Freedom of religion—United States.
I. Title. II. Series.
KF8210.R37B76   1999
346.7304'32'08997—dc21   99–33830

British Library Cataloguing in Publication Data is available.

Copyright © 1999 by Brian Edward Brown

All rights reserved. No portion of this book may be reproduced, by any process or technique, without the express written consent of the publisher.

Library of Congress Catalog Card Number: 99–33830
ISBN: 0–313–30972–8
ISSN: 0147–1074

First published in 1999

Greenwood Press, 88 Post Road West, Westport, CT 06881
An imprint of Greenwood Publishing Group, Inc.
www.greenwood.com

Printed in the United States of America

The paper used in this book complies with the Permanent Paper Standard issued by the National Information Standards Organization (Z39.48–1984).

10 9 8 7 6 5 4 3 2 1

To Alexis and Justin,
with love

Contents

	Introduction	1
1	*Sequoyah v. Tennessee Valley Authority:* **The Tellico Dam and the Submersion of Cherokee Sacred Homeland**	9
	Cherokee Legal Arguments	16
	TVA Response	22
	Decision of the U.S. District Court for the Eastern District of Tennessee and Appeal to the Sixth Circuit	27
2	*Badoni v. Higginson:* **Navajo Religion, National Monuments, and the Colorado River**	39
	Response of the District Court	44
	Response of the Tenth Circuit Court of Appeals	50
3	*Wilson v. Block:* **Skiing the Slopes of a Sacred Mountain**	61
	Response of the District Court	68
	On Appeal to the U.S. Court of Appeals for the District of Columbia Circuit	76
	Decision of the Court of Appeals	87

4	*Frank Fools Crow et al. v. Tony Gullet et al.:* **State Tourism on Sacred Land**	93
	Analysis and Decisions of the Federal District Court	100
	On Appeal to the Eighth Circuit	109
5	*Lyng v. Northwest Indian Cemetery Protective Association:* **The Supreme Court and the Triumph of Property over Religion**	119
	Decision of the U.S. District Court	132
	Decision of the U.S. Court of Appeals for the Ninth Circuit	140
	Decision of the United States Supreme Court	149
	Epilogue	171
	Notes	179
	Bibliographical Index	191
	Index	193

Introduction

In 1988 two radically distinct conceptions of land found formal expression within the broad forum of American political life. Neither conception was new, since both were rooted in ancient patterns of human relationship to the earth. The coincidence of their coming in the same year, however, sharpened their mutual contrast and identified their relative dominance at the close of the twentieth century. On the one hand, the Wise Use Movement was officially launched in August 1988 by the Center for the Defense of Free Enterprise in Reno, Nevada. Representing the interests of ranchers, miners, loggers, gas and oil drilling operatives, real estate developers, and hosts of recreational vehicle owners, the Wise Use Movement has come to advocate an agenda that includes the lifting of all restrictions on the development of private property; the opening of all national parks, national wildlife refuges, wilderness areas, and all other protected lands to mining and oil and gas drilling; the encouragement of off-road vehicle use in areas of public lands where it has been prohibited; the clear-cutting and replanting of all ancient forests; and the amendment of the Endangered Species Act to exclude species deemed non-adaptive to human-induced changes in their natural habitat.

Attracting substantial corporate funding and providing common identity for otherwise disparate interest groups, the Wise Use Movement is a recent political expression of an otherwise inveterate conceit that sees land solely in terms of human exploitation. In its reductive vision, such a perspective is blind to the inherent value of land other than what it may yield for human use. As both legacy and perpetuation of an antiquated cosmology that minimized the moral significance of the natural world as so many insensible components of a similarly inanimate mechanism, the wise use agenda speaks only the language of resource use and management. Its rhetoric, invidiously polarizing the priority of human economic activity against any concern for the protection and well-being of other living creatures, is without ethical complication. Since nature's value is always subsidiary and derivative from the uses to which humanity applies it, problems do not arise from any recognition of and respect for the innate worth and integrity of living beings. Rather, conflicts arise from the competing claims of varying human interests over the disposition of a natural world rendered wholly domestic and servile through the hoary convention of property. For ultimately, the agenda publicized in 1988 under the guise of "wise use" was but a strident reassertion of proprietary interest as the fundamental conception defining human relationship with land.

Whether it be the voice of a single individual, a unified special interest group, corporate entity, or whole industry, the insistence against government restrictions on the use of land, although fueled by a suspicion of expansive bureaucratic regulatory regimes, is grounded in a more elementary assumption. Land exists in a condition of servitude; it ultimately belongs to someone who enjoys control over the allocation of resources contained within its boundaries. As small parcel or vast acreage tract, the traditional designation of land as "the holding" of individual people, corporations, or governing entities indicates the customary notion of land as property. To hold land as property is to own it as lord (hence "landlord"), exercising an exclusive authority to possess, enjoy, use, and dispose of it at one's will. The extent to which land remains under the exclusive status and valuation as property, its reality as the community of living beings capable of evoking respect and care is diminished and threatened. It is this fundamental orientation toward land as property that animates the wise-use agenda. At a moment in human civilization that witnesses an emergent awareness of and concern for the earth as the planetary integrity of land, water, atmosphere, and the innumerable communities of living beings that inhabit them, the wholesale repudiation and aggressive challenges to efforts for the protection of the environment by wise-use proponents expresses the tenacity with which the proprietary mentality yet holds sway. But such a perspective is not limited to the blunt antagonism of wise-use organizations alone. The extent to which property remains the dominant conception for the characterization and disposition of land became apparent in one of the most consequential and disturbing decisions handed down by the Supreme Court in 1988.

In *Lyng v. Northwest Indian Cemetery Protective Association*,[1] the highest court in the United States embraced the paradigm of land as property through its injudicious rejection of a claim raised by Native American tribal peoples alternatively arguing the sacred character of land. The *Lyng* decision was the final judicial determination of an issue that had been at the heart of several cases brought by different Indian tribes throughout the 1980s. Together, they represent the unique convergence of arguments for constitutionally protected religious freedom on the one hand and the sacredness of land on the other. The cases alleged that particular decisions made or contemplated by federal land management agencies would not only desecrate the land in question, but in that very process, interfere with and deprive the respective tribes of their right of religious exercise.

More specifically, the Indian plaintiffs based their claims primarily upon the religion clauses of the Constitution's First Amendment that "Congress shall make no law respecting an establishment of religion, or prohibiting the free exercise thereof . . .". The amendment's two clauses bar governmental action when that action either entangles the government in the establishment of a religion or when that action threatens the free exercise of religion. In each of the tribal cases, land held by the government had long been the traditional site of religious belief and practice for particular tribes within the respective region. The Indian plaintiffs argued that governmental development of the land in question would alter the land's sacred character, thus, essentially interfering with tribal religion and infringing upon their First Amendment freedom of religious exercise. The extent to which the courts would have recognized and upheld the Indian claims to religious liberty would have simultaneously recognized the sacred modality of land. Significantly, no court of final hearing sustained the Indian claims.

Thus, in 1980 in *Sequoyah v. Tennessee Valley Authority*, 620 F.2d 1159 (1980), the United States Court of Appeals for the Sixth Circuit found that the flooding of the Tellico Dam on the Little Tennessee River did not infringe on the Cherokee Indians' First Amendment right of free exercise of religion. Similarly, in the same year, the United States Court of Appeals for the Tenth Circuit in *Badoni v. Higginson*, 638 F.2d 172 (1980), refused to find a First Amendment free-exercise violation of the Navajo Tribe that would result from the government's building of the Glen Canyon Dam in southern Utah and the subsequent flooding of the area around the Rainbow Bridge National Monument by Lake Powell.

Again, in 1982 the United States District Court for the District of South Dakota rendered a decision in *Crow v. Gullet*, 541 F. Supp. 785 (1982), that members of the Lakota and Tsistsistas Nations were not protected under the free-exercise clause of the First Amendment from the state's construction of a paved access road and parking area at Bear Butte in the eastern edge of the Black Hills. Later, in 1983 the United States Court of Appeals for the District of Columbia Circuit held in *Wilson v. Block*, 708 F.2d 735 (1983), that a government decision to permit private interests to expand and develop a ski area on the San Francisco Peaks in Arizona's Coconino National Forest did not violate any First Amendment rights of Navajo and Hopi Indian tribes.

But in what appeared to be a reversal of the trend, a 1983 decision by the United States District Court for the Northern District of California did conclude in *Northwest Indian Cemetery Protective Association v. Peterson*, 565 F. Supp. 586 (1983), that government plans to permit timber harvesting in, and to construct a six-mile road through the Chimney Rock area of California's Six Rivers National Forest would in fact violate the constitutionally protected religious rights of the Yurok, Karok, and Tolowa Indians. On appeal, the district court's decision was upheld in 1986 by the United States Court of Appeals for the Ninth Circuit (*Northwest Indian Cemetery Protective Association v. Peterson*, 795 F.2d 688 [1986]). The government, however, petitioned the United States Supreme Court to hear the case on writ of certiorari. The Court accepted, but in a lamentable failure of First Amendment jurisprudence relating to the Free Exercise Clause, reversed the two lower courts' decisions and refused to acknowledge any constitutional harm to the Indians' exercise of their religious beliefs that would result from the government's use of the land. The Supreme Court's shocking insensitivity in failing to protect against a government action that it conceded would "virtually destroy the Indians' ability to practice their religion,"[2] represents a serious flaw in Constitutional analysis. Just as disturbing was the Court's unwillingness to address the profound issue at the heart of these conflicts. In his rigorous dissent, Justice William J. Brennan Jr. correctly identified the convergence of Indian religious liberty and the notion of land. The majority's refusal to recognize that the Indians would suffer a constitutionally protected injury reflected its allegiance to the concept of land as property: to accord the tribes freedom of religious exercise would threaten the government as landlord. *Lyng v. Northwest Indian Cemetery Protective Association* and the lower court decisions that preceded it signify the confrontation of divergent paradigmatic attitudes toward land. As Justice Brennan noted in his dissent, the cases "represent yet another stress point in the longstanding conflict between two disparate cultures—the dominant western culture, which views land in terms of ownership and use, and that of Native Americans, in which concepts of private property are not only alien, but contrary to a belief system that holds land sacred."[3]

This book examines *Lyng* and its predecessors to document the consistent judicial failure to accord constitutional protection to tribal religious belief and practice with respect to land. The discussion of each case will review the record to identify the particular sacred site involved and the circumstances that led to the respective tribes' attempt to enjoin government actions that threatened to desecrate the land. No further analysis of the Indian beliefs will be made beyond the testimony provided by the different tribes to substantiate their claim of a constitutional violation against their religious freedom. Attention will be paid to the legal arguments made by the Indian plaintiffs and the government defendant and the reasoning of the courts for their final determination in each of the cases. The book will identify a persistent judicial burden imposed upon the Indian claims by the variously subtle or more pronounced cultural predisposition toward religion. The non-Native notion that religion is separable and essentially discrete from land, reduced to a core of beliefs and behavior that are ultimately distinct from the customary and traditional mores and practices of a particular society, often blunted the courts' sensitivity to the extent of the spiritual and cultural harm from which the tribes sought protection. With an implicit categorization of religion as primarily the conceptual faith to which one subscribes rather than an integral way of being and living, several of the district and appellate courts were less disposed to countenance a harm to Indian religion from proposed government land alterations.

Yet the judicial predisposition to an intellectually constricted notion of religion was not as injurious to the Indian claims as was the courts' allegiance to land as property. In the *Lyng* case, the Supreme Court successfully corrected the truncated notions of religion entertained by certain of the lower courts. The Court fully recognized and understood the tribal perception of land as inherently sacred, the numinous reality that sustained the Northwest California tribes with restorative energy and healing power, evoking their acknowledgement and response in the meditational prayer and ritual ceremonies that defined their religious life. Indeed, through Justice Brennan's dissent, the very subjectivity of land in tribal belief as "a sacred, living being . . . unique [with] specific sites possess[ing] different spiritual properties and significance" was judicially noted. It was further acknowledged in the majority opinion that if the United States Forest Service (an agency of the federal government) were to proceed with the building of a road through the contested area, it would have devastating effects on the practice of tribal religion. But instead of proceeding to the next step in its own established analysis for such cases when government action threatens the exercise of religion, the Supreme Court irresponsibly freed the government of its obligation to prove a compelling state interest of sufficient magnitude that would justify the consequent religious harm.

It was incontestable from the record of the California district court and the circuit court of appeals that the government would have failed the test.

It had clearly been shown that the proposed road would be of scant or no benefit and could not qualify as the requisite paramount interest necessary to override the constitutionally protected religious right to leave the land undisturbed. Having ignored its own procedure, thereby relieving the government of an obligation it was incapable of sustaining, the Supreme Court compounded its wrong by an injudicious policy determination concerning public land. In doing so, it disclosed the profound and prejudicial tenacity that the notion of property yet exercises over the legal as well as popular imagination. For although it accepted the authenticity of the Native American belief in the religious character of land, the Supreme Court impermissibly ruled that "such beliefs could easily require *de facto* beneficial ownership of some rather spacious tracts of public property.... [T]he diminution of the Government's property rights ... would be far from trivial.... Whatever rights the Indians may have ... those rights do not divest the Government of its right to use what is, after all, *its* land."[4] Fearing that the tribal claim could potentially strip the government of its unchallenged role as landlord to dispose of its property as it wished, the Supreme Court distorted the nature of the relief sought by the tribes and, as Justice Brennan wrote, "sacrifice[d] a religion at least as old as the Nation itself [for] a six mile segment of road [having] only the most marginal and speculative utility."[5]

But the harm wrought by the *Lyng* case extended far beyond the immediate California tribal plaintiffs. The application of its broad ruling effectively condoned the dismissal of the Indian claims made by the lower courts in the *Sequoyah*, *Badoni*, *Crow*, and *Wilson* cases. Although *Lyng* might have clarified the integral connection between land and tribal religion that had been obscured in those cases, its unqualified embrace of governmental property interests would have dictated the same results on the sweep of one uniform rationale.

Beyond that retrospective reach, *Lyng* stands as the controlling precedent that threatens the survival of all traditional American Indian communities whose sacred sites are on public land and off Indian reservations. In abdicating its responsibility to enforce the First Amendment rights of the Indian plaintiffs in *Lyng*, the Supreme Court has effectively exposed Native American tribal cultures to the expediencies of government land management agencies. Since the unique identity of the different Indian tribes is so often coherent with the land that animates and sustains their religious beliefs and practices, bureaucratic decisions to alter land sites are intrusive invasions of tribal self-understanding; the dissipation of tribal identity is the inherent consequence of land desecration. But with its ruling, the *Lyng* Court refused to countenance a religious valuation of land. Instead, the Court reduced public land to a purely administrative entity over which governmental agencies should enjoy near complete discretion. The Court's characterization of land disposition as purely "internal procedures" of the respective governmental agencies indiscriminately placed those agencies beyond constitutional scrutiny, investing them with a power to more easily ignore or circumvent environmental protections that would otherwise preserve public lands from development.

Forfeiting its role as guardian of religious liberty by unworthily becoming the advocate of governmental proprietorship over land, the Supreme Court through its *Lyng* decision in 1988 thus facilitated the emergence of the "wise-use" agenda later that same year. The case not only reflected the prevalent inclination to view land as property, but powerfully consolidated that ancient bias. In its refusal to accord constitutional protection to tribal belief and practice, the Supreme Court ultimately prevented religion from celebrating, reverencing, and thus effectively liberating land as a sacred reality to be protected and preserved, not merely owned and exploited.

1

Sequoyah v. Tennessee Valley Authority: *The Tellico Dam and the Submersion of Cherokee Sacred Homeland*

On October 12, 1979, Ammoneta Sequoyah, a Cherokee medicine man and descendant of the eighteenth-century silversmith, painter, warrior, and creator of the Cherokee writing system, brought suit against the Tennessee Valley Authority (TVA). In his complaint, filed in Knoxville with the United States District Court for the Eastern District of Tennessee, Sequoyah was joined by two other individual Cherokee plaintiffs as well as the Eastern Band of Cherokee Indians now settled in North Carolina and the United Ketooah Band of Cherokees from Oklahoma. Sequoyah and the other Cherokees sought the protection of the court to prevent the TVA from impounding the waters of the Little Tennessee River with the construction of the Tellico Dam. The tribal parties argued that the dam would flood their sacred homeland along the Little Tennessee River, inundating and destroying sacred sites, medicine gathering sites, holy places, and innumerable ancestral grave sites, and would otherwise "disturb the sacred balance of the land" by stopping up the last free-flowing stretch of what was acknowledged to be the largest and best trout-fishing water east of the Mississippi River. But before examining the legal basis of the Cherokee claim, the history of the long-contested project with its reprehensible distortion of the legislative process needs to be understood.

The Tellico Dam had its hypothetical conception as early as 1936, when the TVA identified all the potentially dammable sites in the Tennessee Valley system. It did so on the basis of the original 1933 mandate for the TVA to maintain and operate properties then owned by the United States in the vicinity of Muscle Shoals, Alabama, in the interest of national defense, for agricultural and industrial development, and to improve navigation and flood control on the Tennessee and Mississippi River basins.[1] Until 1966, however, the Tellico site received low priority as the TVA proceeded to build hydroelectric dams and flood-control structures among some seventy other originally identified locations throughout the Tennessee Valley. But by 1960, with more than sixty dams built, the TVA fastened onto the only remaining area of the Little Tennessee River that still flowed unimpeded for some thirty-three miles at its mouth into the Big Tennessee. As anticipated, the TVA acquired 38,000 acres for the Tellico project. More than 16,000 acres were eventually inundated by the dam, and the remaining acreage was slated for development having industrial, commercial, residential, and recreational applications. The project, however, would sacrifice more than seven hundred farms of some of the most fertile, prime growing land in the entire country and restrain the last stretch of free-flowing river favored by regional fishermen and canoeists. In addition, the impounded water, projected as a vast recreational lake and shoreland development by the TVA, would submerge Chota, the ancient Cherokee capital, along with the historic Cherokee villages of Citico, Toqua, Tomotley, Mialaquo, Tuskegee—the birthplace of Sequoyah, and Tanasee, from which the state of Tennessee derived its name. Although Cherokee villages once covered the Southern Appalachians with hunting grounds extending across Tennessee, Kentucky, Alabama, and Georgia, one of the densest concentrations of Cherokee life and culture had flourished in these and other villages now slated for submersion. Moreover, given the Cherokee custom of burying the dead near the places where they had lived, the entire 16,000 acres to be flooded contained the grave sites of thousands of Cherokee ancestors.

Local resistance by those whose historical roots and way of life would be destroyed by the Tellico project were not enough to stop the powerful linkage between the TVA, the pork-barrel congressional committees, local politicians, and land speculators. Congress appropriated funds for the project in 1966, and the concrete portion of the dam was completed by 1968. But before earthen dikes could be positioned for the actual impoundment of the river, a lawsuit was initiated by the Environmental Defense

Fund that halted the project until the TVA adequately complied with the National Environmental Policy Act's requirement for a statement of the project's negative consequences. Yet in 1973 when work could have resumed, the discovery of a small endangered perch, the snail darter, initiated further litigation. According to Section 7 of the Endangered Species Act, federal agencies are prohibited from taking any action that jeopardizes the existence of an endangered species or modifies a critical habitat. The Tellico project would do both. The snail darter was found living in the midst of the project area, and it required a clean-flowing river habitat that the dam would destroy. Local citizens again acted and filed suit in 1975 to enjoin completion of the Tellico dam, this time on the grounds that it would violate the Endangered Species Act.

The issue was finally determined in 1978 by the Supreme Court, which ruled in *Tennessee Valley Authority v. Hiram Hill et al.*[2] that even if the dam was purported to be ninety-nine percent completed, it was in clear violation of Section 7 of the Endangered Species Act and must be halted. Congress responded to the decision by holding three series of hearings in the relevant substantive committees to consider whether to reverse the application of the Endangered Species Act as applied to the Tellico project. Three times the committees concluded that an exemption for the dam would be inappropriate. But in late 1978, Congress did agree to authorize a general exemption procedure to the strict mandates of Section 7 of the Endangered Species Act, by creating a cabinet-level review board (dubbed "the God Committee") that might allow the extinction of a species if certain requirements were met. In response to the TVA's request that the Tellico project be exempted, the committee unanimously denied it on specifically economic grounds. The committee concluded that the dam would operate at an annual deficit of some $750,000; that it would not contribute significantly to energy production in the area; that it did not meet current dam safety standards; and that there were significant non-dam alternatives that would preserve the rich agricultural soils of the river valley, the historic archeological record of more than 10,000 years of human occupation, and the recreational and tourist values of the free-flowing river itself. The committee's decision on January 23, 1979, appeared to have fully exposed the destructively wasteful distortion that the TVA's plan would have inflicted on the water and land at the mouth of the Little Tennessee River Valley. Preserving the integrity of that particular bioregion, the decision simultaneously protected the religious beliefs and practices of the Cherokees who had opposed the dam throughout the lengthy process of resisting the TVA.

But if congressional intent to finally terminate the Tellico project had been clearly established, vested interests in the completion of the dam were still active. On June 18, 1979, in an insidious manipulation of the legislative process, Representative John Duncan from Tennessee, with the knowledge and approval of his counterpart in the Senate, Howard Baker, inserted a rider onto an ongoing energy and water development appropriations bill explicitly overriding the Supreme Court decision in the *Hill* case and ignoring the findings of the God Committee by directing the TVA to complete and operate the Tellico Dam. Duncan's amendment was introduced in flagrant violation of House rules against attaching substantive legislation onto appropriations bills without sufficient notice to all congressmen. Since the amendment had not been printed in the Congressional Record, nor read and described on the House floor, it was not debated and was passed by a voice vote at a time when only some fifteen representatives were on the floor.[3] The whole treacherous process took only forty-two seconds and reinstated a ruinous flooding scheme that had been thoroughly discredited by the intense scrutiny of public litigation and otherwise legitimate congressional review proceedings.

Many Congressmen were incensed not only at the deceitful parliementarian maneuvering Duncan used to introduce the amendment, but at the broad sweep of its language, seeking, as it did, to place the dam project beyond all legal constraints. The amendment read:

> Provided, that notwithstanding the provisions of 16 U.S.C. Chapter 35 [i.e., the Endangered Species Act] *or any other law*, the corporation [i.e., the Tennessee Valley Authority] is authorized and directed to complete construction, operate and maintain the Tellico Dam and Reservoir project for navigation, flood control, electric power generation and other purposes, including the maintenance of a normal summer reservoir pool of 813 feet above sea level. (emphasis added)[4]

An attempt in the House to delete the offensive overreaching amendment was nevertheless defeated. Initially, the Senate voted to repudiate it, but members ultimately relented when it became clear in the Conference Committee that the House would approve the entire Energy and Water Development Appropriations Bill only if the Tellico amendment were included.[5] The bill became effective on September 25, 1979, when President Jimmy Carter, noting his objections to the Tellico amendment, nevertheless signed it into law.

With the TVA losing little time to execute its newly revived mandate to flood their sacred homeland, the Cherokees who had objected to the project from its inception and had witnessed the futility of resisting the dam through endangered species protection as well as cost-benefit economic analyses, now raised their complaint to formal constitutional status. Seeking a declaration of their rights from the federal court in Knoxville, the Cherokees also filed for a temporary restraining order or preliminary injunction to halt the TVA from any further action to complete the dam or to further excavate Cherokee and other Indian graves within the Tellico project area until the court made a final determination after a full hearing on the merits of the case. Since the TVA had already dug up and removed the skeletal remains and burial artifacts of more than 1,000 Indian dead, the Cherokees sought to enjoin any further disturbance to their ancestors whose abiding presence within the earth contributed to the reverence with which their descendants held the Little Tennessee River Valley.

According to Cherokee belief, the dead invigorate the ground where they lie, bringing to it and preserving within it the wisdom that they learned during life. The land is strengthened by all those who were themselves originally nurtured by it.[6] Moreover, since it was customary for the Cherokees to bury individuals close to or within their dwellings to remain near their families, and given the density of the Cherokee population over the centuries within the Little Tennessee River Valley, the land was properly understood as the community of forefathers and mothers who yet rest within it.[7] The infiltration of waters from the dammed river into the graves of their deceased tribal relatives was a desecration the Cherokees sought to prevent with their suit, along with the demand for the ceremonial reinternment of those who had been removed by the TVA and remained stored in the museum basement at the University of Tennessee.

The endangered river valley was also revered because it contained sites such as Chota, "the Rome and Jerusalem of the Cherokees"[8] their religious and political capital, where the eternal and sacred fire of the Cherokee nation had once been kept burning and in whose temple had been kept the sacred artifacts of Cherokee religion. It was the place where major Cherokee ceremonies had been conducted as well as the seat of the principal Cherokee chief and the Cherokee National Council. Considered so hallowed that no blood could be shed within its boundaries, Chota became a sanctuary even for murderers who sought safety within it.[9]

But if the reserve of their ancestors and the preservation of and access to Chota and other village sites of historical and cultural significance were dimensions of the religion that the Cherokees sought to protect, the heart of their complaint was the notion that the waters and land of the river valley were themselves sacred, holy realities that would be destroyed by the impending Tellico project. Noting that the constitutional right that they asserted under the First Amendment had been crafted by tinkers of a very different religious orientation, the Cherokees identified their "reverence [for the] land solely because it is deemed holy or sacred."[10] Drawing an analogy to the experience of the Jewish, Christian, and Islamic traditions with the sacred sites of Jerusalem, Bethlehem, Mount Sinai, and Mecca, the Cherokees nevertheless spoke of the numinous character of the river valley possessing an ultimate significance in itself beyond its mere historical association with any specific people, places, or events. Unlike the Jewish, Christian, and Islamic places and cities popularly held sacred as the sites where the divine entered into human affairs and where patriarchs, saviors, and prophets lived and taught, the holiness of the Cherokee river valley was self-referential. Although it was not elaborated at length, and was supported in general terms by the combined impression of the accompanying affidavits, the Cherokees enunciated an explicit understanding that the sacred character of the river valley was not derivative from any human activity within it. Rather, the river valley itself was the primordial reality investing life-enhancing energy, which sustained a meaningful existence for the human community that it nurtured. In the words of the Cherokee memorandum accompanying their complaint:

> It is difficult to translate into Anglo-American concepts the meaning of a sacred place to American Indians. It is not merely the symbol of something sacred or merely a place to bring forth memories of past persons or events. It is *itself sacred*, itself the source of sacred power.[11]

It was clear, then, that the Cherokees were arguing that "the flooding of the Little Tennessee River Valley [would] *in an immense and immeasurable way*, infringe upon [their] basic right to practice their ancient religion"[12] because it would disturb the rest of their ancestors and contact with them; prevent pilgrimages to Chota and other sites of traditional Cherokee habitation; prevent the gathering of certain plants used by medicine men for healing; or render certain religious ceremonies unperformable by stopping up and "deadening" the purifying flow of the living river.[13] The Tellico project would do more than obstruct those religious practices of traditional Cherokee belief. More essentially, the flooding of the river valley, submerging the rich life-sustaining topsoil, altering the configuration of the land with the impounded waters, and hastening the extinction of at least one endangered fish species, would destroy the valley and thus desecrate the reality at the heart of Cherokee religion.

The unambiguous harm that would be inflicted on Cherokee religion by the government-sponsored project to flood the river valley had an added severity that becomes apparent through the testimonies of the Cherokees whose affidavits accompanied the complaint. Alluding to the destructive flood that threatened their ancestral home, Cherokees repeatedly referred to their own ensuing destruction as a people. One of the prophecies (translated in the Cherokee language as "sacred explanations") that was integral to their religious self-understanding foretold the calamitous impact of white civilization with its trains, planes, highways, and drainage and irrigation projects that would upset the delicate balance of nature.[14] Another spoke of the time when the Little Tennessee River Valley would be flooded so that the graves of the Cherokee ancestors would look up "through the water like a wall of glass."[15] But, the prophecy continued, as long as the river continued to flow past Chota and the other ancestral towns, the Cherokees would remain as a viable ethnic group, retaining their culture, language, and heritage.[16] Ominously, the Tellico project threatened contemporary Cherokees with the forewarned condition that would bring their demise. The prophecy is another illustration of the profound coherence between Cherokee self-identity and the river valley. A consistent refrain running throughout the affidavits is the sense of profound disorientation that the Cherokees would suffer with the disappearance of their religious homeland. "When this place is destroyed, the Cherokee people cease to exist as a people. . . . The white man has taken nearly everything away from us, our heritage, culture, traditions, and our way of life that is our religion . . . and I'm afraid of what will become of us and our children if we allow the TVA to cover our sacred land with water. . . . I don't know what will happen to the Cherokee people if this area is flooded. This is still Indian land even if TVA says they have a deed for it. . . . [A]s the water backs over the once Cherokee land, our people will feel a great pain. The earth will cry . . . as water covers this beautiful, fruitful valley, members of our tribe will be in silence. . . ."[17] The psychic trauma that would be inflicted on the Cherokees, manifesting itself in a loss of self-esteem and accompanying depression,[18] would be symptomatic of their self-identification as a community animated by their relationship with the Great Spirit disclosing itself to them in the waters and land of the river valley. Such was the coherence between land, religion, and people that the destruction of one imperiled the abiding presence of that which bestowed ultimate meaning on the lives of the other. Recalling an etymological derivation of "religion" as suggesting an experience of being "tied up" or dynamically related to what is perceived as sacred, the religious significance of the river valley as mediating the presence of the Great Spirit is clear from the words of one of the named plaintiffs:

> I realized that it was understood by all our people that this location was our connection to the Great Spirit. All my people know it's there. The Government has tried for many years

and by many different methods to take this away from us. But this is one thing they cannot take from us. By knowing who you are, this is the power of our people. When we go to Tellico, even for a visit, the realization that this is our connection to our own ancestors and to the Great Spirit, all comes back to us, and it's like going home. Each of us comes back a better person, a better Cherokee, for having gone there. If the Tellico Dam is completed all this will be lost to us forever.[19]

CHEROKEE LEGAL ARGUMENTS

The Cherokee had unambiguously identified the nature of their religious belief and practice and had shown that the Tellico Dam project would submerge ancestral graves, prevent access to medicine gathering sites, render ceremonial practices unperformable, and obliterate the physical vestiges of Cherokee history and culture in the Little Tennessee River Valley basin. Not only that, but the dam, with its ensuing flood, would so distort the water and inundate the land, it would destroy the sacred reality at the heart of Cherokee religion. The Cherokee sought to prevent the government-sponsored destruction by invoking the Free Exercise Clause of the First Amendment, arguing that the surreptitious rider attached to the Energy and Water Appropriations Act of 1978, which mandated the completion and operation of the Tellico Dam project, was unconstitutional. The dam would not only infringe upon Cherokee religious practices, but would, in fact, annihilate the life of the river valley whose sacred character evoked and gave meaning to those practices. The submerged river valley violated the very essence of Cherokee religion and attacked the integrity of Cherokee self-understanding. Congressional authorization for this kind of religious devastation effectively contravened the spirit of the First Amendment that says Congress shall make no law prohibiting the free exercise of religion.

To further substantiate their claim, the Cherokees invoked the recently passed American Indian Religious Freedom Act, which had generically affirmed that "traditional American Indian religions, as an integral part of Indian life, are indispensable and irreplaceable" and that "religious practices of the American Indian . . . are an integral part of their culture, tradition and heritage, such practices forming the basis of Indian identity and value systems."[20] The act acknowledged that federal government policy, stemming from insensitivity and inflexibility, had often infringed upon the religious freedom of traditional American Indians, including denial of access to sacred sites, the prohibition of sacred objects, and the interference with ceremonial practices.[21] The act resolved that "henceforth it shall be the policy of the United States to protect and preserve for American

Indians their inherent right of freedom to believe, express and exercise the traditional religions of the American Indian, Eskimo, Aleut, and Native Hawaiians, including but not limited to access to sites, use and possession of sacred objects, and the freedom to worship through ceremonial and traditional rites."[22]

The Cherokees cited the act to further buttress their claim under the First Amendment that the free exercise of their religion would be unconstitutionally abridged by the government-authorized Tellico Dam project. Although the American Indian Religious Freedom Act didn't expand the constitutional protection afforded by the First Amendment, it was clear Congressional recognition that religious freedom had been wrongfully denied Indian tribes in the past and that it was the intent of Congress to prevent such constitutional harm in the future. The clandestine maneuvering and marginal awareness that permitted the Tellico rider to pass as an amendment to the Appropriations Act and would prove so ruinous to Cherokee religion and culture exemplified the very governmental insensitivity and infringement that Congress repudiated in the American Indian Religious Freedom Act.

Not only would the Tellico amendment violate the First Amendment and conflict with Congress's public resolve to protect and preserve American Indian Religious freedoms, but the Cherokees argued, the amendment's sweeping language and the very stealth with which it was attached to, and found passage through, the Energy and Water Development Appropriations Act made it highly suspect. The amendment mandated the TVA to complete the construction and commence the operation of the Tellico Dam "notwithstanding the provisions of 16 U.S.C. Chapter 35 or any other law."[23] The latter phrase, in its all-inclusive scope, effectively placed the TVA and its dam beyond the constraints even of the Constitution! The Cherokees didn't challenge the authority of Congress to repeal the Endangered Species Act (statutorily designated in the amendment simply as 16 U.S.C. Chapter 35), as it applied protectively to the snail darter to halt the dam. But the attempt to indirectly repeal constitutional and other legislated protections, allowing the TVA to complete, operate, and maintain the project with total disregard for obligations, standards, and procedures imposed by otherwise legitimate laws, was a tactic that had been recently reviewed and criticized by the Supreme Court. In *TVA v. Hill*[24] the Court addressed the argument that since Congress had continued to appropriate money for the Tellico Dam, those appropriations had, by implication, repealed the Endangered Species Act as applied to the project. In rejecting that notion, the Court held that attempts to repeal or alter substantive legislation through appropriations measures was against sound public policy as well as specific rules of Congress. Citing the House of Representatives Rule XXI (2) that any provision in any general appropriations bill that attempted to change existing law would be out of order,[25] the Court affirmed its own disapproval for such an evasion of the full legislative process. The purpose of an appropriations measure is limited to providing funds for specific authorized programs. In that process, Congress is simply not prepared to consider the substantive implications of major legislation that needs to be fully scrutinized through fora allowing thorough analysis, discussion, and debate. "When voting on appropriations measures, legislators are entitled to operate under the assumption that the funds will be devoted to purposes which are lawful and not for any purpose forbidden. Without such an assurance, every appropriations measure would be pregnant with prospects of altering substantive legislation, repealing by implication any prior statute which might prohibit the expenditure."[26]

The Cherokees argued that the harm against which the Supreme Court generalized in the *Hill* case was the precise offense that threatened their religious freedom through the Tellico amendment. The outraged response of many in Congress to the deceitful manipulation of disguising the discredited Tellico project as an unannounced, unpublished, undebated rider to the general appropriations bill for water and energy was clear evidence that the amendment should be very narrowly construed. Under the treacherous circumstances of its passage, retrospectively repudiated by many in Congress, the amendment could be interpreted as doing nothing more than exempting the Tellico project from the requirements of the Endangered Species Act. The "any other law" alluded to in the amendment could not be interpreted to signify congressional intent to repeal anything more than laws such as the Endangered Species Act that would directly prohibit the implementation of the dam project. Certainly, the amendment could not be read to abrogate fundamental constitutional rights. The policy resolve of the American Indian Religious Freedom Act and the elemental protection of the First Amendment could not be legislated away through the machinations of a rider to a general appropriations bill.

The Cherokees correctly stated that when conflicts arose from governmental activities that threatened the freedom of religious exercise, protected by the First Amendment, there existed a clearly established test to guide the judicial resolution of the competing governmental and religious interests. It was that test that had to be applied by the district court in its review of the Tellico project and the Cherokee religious liberty that it jeopardized. It was a test the TVA could not pass. Once a substantial infringement upon religion by governmental action has been demonstrated, there must be a showing of a "compelling state interest" to justify the ensuing religious deprivation. The Cherokees correctly relied on *Sherbert v. Verner*[27] and *Wisconsin v. Yoder*[28] as the Supreme Court precedents that had identified and applied the principle.

In *Sherbert*, a Seventh-day Adventist had been discharged by her South Carolina employer because she refused to work on Saturday, the Sabbath day of her faith. When she was unable to obtain other employment because she would not take Saturday work, she filed a claim for unemployment compensation benefits. In denying them to her, the South Carolina Employment Security Commission argued that she had voluntarily made herself unavailable for work. That decision was ultimately upheld by the South Carolina Supreme Court, which ruled that the state statute denying the woman unemployment benefits did not, in itself, restrict the woman's freedom of religion, nor did it prevent her from exercising her freedom to observe her religious beliefs.

On appeal, the United States Supreme Court disagreed and reversed the judgment, holding that the state's denial of unemployment benefits effectively imposed a fine upon the woman for her Sabbath-day belief, forcing her to choose between following the precepts of her religion and forfeiting benefits, on the one hand, and abandoning one of the precepts of her religion to accept work, on the other. In looking for some compelling state interest that would justify South Carolina's rigid enforcement of the eligibility provisions for unemployment benefits that would justify the substantial infringement upon the Seventh-day Adventist's belief, the high court found none. It was not enough for South Carolina to assert that its policy was necessary to prevent the filing of fraudulent claims by unscrupulous people feigning religious objections to Saturday work. The state interest that could justify the religious infringement could not be merely rational, but compelling. The permissible limitation of the constitutional freedom of religion would be warranted by "only the gravest abuses, endangering paramount interests."[29] Even if a showing had been made by South Carolina that potential spurious claims from fraudulent religious objections might threaten to dilute the unemployment compensation fund or hinder the scheduling by employers of necessary Saturday work, the Supreme Court would insist that the state "demonstrate that no alternative forms of regulation would combat such abuses without infringing First Amendment rights."[30]

The Supreme Court continued to indicate the high standard imposed by "the compelling interest test" when it struck down Wisconsin's compulsory education law as applied to Amish parents in *Wisconsin v. Yoder*.[31] There, the parents claimed that sending their children to public school beyond the eighth grade was contrary to the Amish religion and way of life. The parents saw public high school as an environment exposing their children to competitiveness, conformity to non-Amish styles of dress and manners, technical knowledge instead of wisdom, and deprivation of their contact with the Amish community and the soil, which they farmed as part of their religious way of life. Although the Supreme Court acknowledged that "[p]roviding public schools ranks at the very apex of the function of a State,"[32] the important state interest in universal compulsory education was not absolute to the exclusion or subordination of religious and other fundamental rights. After close examination, the Court concluded that although Wisconsin's education law was applied uniformly to all citizens of the state, it nevertheless threatened to undermine the Amish community and its religious practice. Holding that "a regulation neutral on its face may, in its application, nonetheless offend the constitutional requirement for governmental neutrality if it unduly burdens the free exercise of religion,"[33] the Court found that none of Wisconsin's otherwise legitimate concerns were of sufficient magnitude to override the right of the Amish to be granted an exemption from the regulation on religious grounds.

With the identification of the compelling interest test established, the Cherokees presented a careful review of the statutory duties of the Tennessee Valley Authority to demonstrate on all counts that the Tellico project could never satisfy the standard. It was already abundantly clear from the legislative history that Congress did not consider the dam of sufficient importance to complete, even if only to justify the more than $100 million that had already been expended on its construction. After the Supreme Court's invitation in its *Hill* decision for Congress to make an explicit exemption for the project from its prohibition under the Endangered Species Act, the relevant substantive congressional committees refused to do so on three occasions. Later, when the project was formally considered by the cabinet-level review board ("the God Committee"), it was unanimously rejected on specifically economic, rather than ecological, grounds. If there were any compelling interest in the Tellico dam, it was to terminate, not complete it. It survived only through the parliamentarian ruse of attaching it as an amendment to the appropriations bill.

But to further expose the untenable position for a project that would be ruinous to the river valley and to their religious culture, which held it sacred, the Cherokees demonstrated that the dam advanced none of the statutory purposes for which the TVA had been authorized. No compelling justification for the Tellico project existed on the grounds of national defense, agriculture and industrial development, improved flood control and navigation, or the generation of electricity. On the point of supporting the national defense of the country, the TVA had never made any pretense that the dam did so. As to advancing agricultural development, the dam would do the very opposite, resulting in the destructive submersion of some 16,000 acres of the most fertile lands in the country, condemning more than 700 farms in the process. Any industrial development to be realized from the agricultural devastation was highly speculative, based on a purely hypothetical model industrial city to be called Timberlake, theoretically attracting a series of factories requiring hundreds of acres for development. It was, then, grandiose real estate conjecture rather than any compelling industrial necessity that would doom the river valley and Cherokee religion. The devastation of rich growing soils, designated by the United States Department of Agriculture as "prime farm land," to make way for an artificial shoreline around which some imagined industrial park would materialize was a wasteful scheme in which the TVA ignored the established benefit of preserving agricultural development for the fantasy of a dubious real estate development. The technocratic manipulation of land, which had become routine for the TVA, indifferent to the profound animation revered by the Cherokees, merely substituted one exploitive use of the land for another. No compelling state interest existed to justify the capricious destructiveness of such a mentality.

Similarly, the record exposed the empty pretext that the dam would serve compelling flood control and navigational purposes. During the period when the Tellico project was being considered for exemption from the Endangered Species Act, Cecil D. Andrus, secretary of the interior, who had direct responsibilities for and jurisdiction over dam safety matters, had advised Congress that the Tellico dam didn't meet current standards for dam safety. Indeed, he warned that under maximal flooding conditions the dam could cause more significant destruction than if it had not been built! Adding to that, Charles Schultze, then chairman of the Council of Economic Advisers and a fellow member of the same committee headed by Secretary Andrus, said, "Here is a project that is 95 percent complete, and if one takes just the cost of finishing it against the [total project] benefits, and does it properly, it doesn't pay, which says something about the original design."[34] Likewise, any navigational impact that the project might have had was marginal since there were twenty-four other reservoirs within a fifty-mile radius of the Tellico site. In fact, since the dam would have choked off the last remaining stretch of high-quality fishing and recreational flowing water on the Little Tennessee River, a more persuasive argument could be made to leave the river in its last remaining natural condition.

Finally, there was nothing to compel the construction of the dam on grounds of electrical power generation, which was not even a primary statutory responsibility of the TVA. According to a report of the General Accounting Office published in 1977, the energy output of the Tellico dam was projected to be of only marginal significance. Yielding less than one one-thousandths of the TVA's total energy output, Tellico's value as an energy resource was negligible and could never justify a project that the Office of Management and Budget had rejected as operating at an annual deficit of almost a million dollars.[35]

If South Carolina's interest in administering a uniform unemployment benefits policy and Wisconsin's interest in ensuring universal education for its citizens were not sufficiently compelling to justify infringing on Adventist and Amish religions, the TVA's interest in the Tellico project was minimal. On every count the government was incapable of showing a paramount concern that would compel the destruction of the river valley life and Cherokee religious culture rooted within it. Raising significant questions of material fact, the Cherokee complaint had argued persuasively that legislative impropriety and Congressional hostility, consistent deficit spending, agricultural devastation, endangered species extinction, questionable flood control safety, lost recreational value, and scant energy production left the Tellico project without the requisite compelling state interest to justify the harm it would inflict on Cherokee belief and practice.

TVA RESPONSE

The serious issue raised by the Cherokees that land was sacred and holy in itself and worthy of constitutional protection through those who revere it was never engaged by the TVA, which persisted in referring to land solely in terms of property. The fundamental legal status of land went no further than the question of ownership. Land as numinous, as participating in and revelatory of ultimate reality, and therefore, land as possessing religious significance and value went unacknowledged. The possessory interest in land as property was the sole and controlling value that the TVA recognized. It was a perspective that was to be reiterated throughout all of the cases, ultimately sanctioned by the Supreme Court as the determinative principle over any claims of a religious nature.

In its brief, responding to the Cherokee complaint, the TVA made no mention of the circumstances facing the Cherokees in the early years of the nineteenth century: persistent designs on Cherokee territory in North Carolina, Georgia, Alabama, and Tennessee by white settlers and farmers, matched by pressure from the federal government on the Cherokees to exchange those eastern lands for promises of western acreage. Hoping to assuage the avaricious demands and be left in peace, the Cherokees agreed to give up some four million acres in 1819. But sixteen years later, harassed and threatened by the state of Georgia, and receiving no assistance from President Andrew Jackson, who openly sought their removal, Cherokee representatives committed their nation to surrendering all of their remaining lands east of the Mississippi. Reluctant to leave, the majority were rounded up and forcefully evicted by the army of General Winfield Scott during the winter months of 1838–1839. On the long march to their ultimate destination in Oklahoma, one in four Cherokees fatally succumbed to the brutality of fatigue, hunger, cold, and disease.

The infamous Trail of Tears and the government's responsibility for it was completely glossed over in the TVA brief, which summarily noted that the Cherokees had ceded the Tellico region by treaty and that their former lands had been held in private non-Cherokee ownership until the TVA began to acquire it for the dam project. "By then, all surface traces of Cherokee occupation had been erased by flooding, farming, erosion, and vandalism."[36] According to the TVA, then, treaties had severed Cherokee legal claim to the land and more than 125 years of non-possession had expunged any residual Cherokee property interests in the river valley. For the TVA, it was legally insignificant that the Cherokees retained a spiritual sensibility for the land and waters of the valley as their ancestral homeland where their connection to the Great Spirit was singularly experienced. The radical alteration of the river valley with the damming of the flowing waters and the subsequent inundation of the land wasn't legally injurious to Cherokee religious belief, since the government, not the Cherokees, now owned the land. With no elaboration and the support of only one federal district court decision, which was then being appealed,[37] the TVA merely asserted that the Constitution afforded no protection for religious belief and practice respecting land absent a property interest in it. With neither deed nor possession, the Cherokees had no constitutionally cognizable claim to prevent the government "from exercising normal incidents of ownership,"[38] which extended to eradicating the natural features of the land-water property. For the TVA there was nothing sacred about land itself, and any claim to that effect would be given constitutional consideration only by virtue of the claimant's status as landowner. The Constitution recognizes no ultimate significance in land itself beyond what may be imputed by one who holds legal title to it; not land itself, but only its condition as property, grounds the constitutional protection that may be afforded it under a claim of its religious significance.

The TVA argued that since the Cherokees were no longer owners of the river valley lands that had become the property of the federal government, they could not sustain the claim that they would suffer an infringement on their religious freedom from actions the government was taking on its property. Because the government inflicted no religious harm on the Cherokees, there was no need to engage "the compelling interest test," which was necessary only after some religious deprivation had been demonstrated. Whether the Tellico dam was of sufficient importance to justify it need not be entertained, since the Cherokees, without the requisite property interest, had not passed the threshold of showing legal harm to their religious freedom. The TVA argued that on the basis of this interpretation of religious freedom conditioned by property right, the federal district court should dismiss the Cherokee complaint or grant summary judgment for the TVA. As a matter of law, or the TVA's reading of the law, nothing further had to be said.

Nevertheless, the TVA proceeded to disparage the authenticity of the Cherokee claim by making an inappropriate issue of a formal tribal division. In an attempt to impugn their tribal integrity, the TVA implied that because the two bands of Cherokee plaintiffs, the Eastern Band from North Carolina and the United Ketooah Band from Oklahoma, were not joined by the majority Cherokee Nation of Oklahoma in their suit, the plaintiffs' religious claims were not genuine. Attention was drawn to the testimony of John Ross, the principal chief of the Cherokee Nation as well as a well-to-do bank president and Oklahoma attorney whose campaign for the U.S. Senate had received the pledged support of Howard Baker from Tennessee, a principal backer of the Tellico project.[39] Not a medicine man, Ross the banker, lawyer, and political candidate testified that "the village sites in the lower Tennessee River are important to the cultural history of the Cherokee Nation, but are not a part of its religion."[40] But Ross, whose status was essentially political and administrative and who had not identified himself as a traditional Cherokee and could not speak the traditional Cherokee language was in scant position to make any such conclusory pronouncement concering the traditional religious beliefs of the approximately 15,000 Cherokee plaintiffs.

The Eastern Band of Cherokees who had remained in hiding in the Great Smokies to avoid the Trail of Tears eviction to Oklahoma and to be near their ancestral homeland settled with other Cherokees in the region of Cherokee, North Carolina. This Eastern Band of Cherokees, considering themselves distinct from the Oklahoma Cherokees, and being a federally recognized tribe had, in fact, remained within some fifty miles of their traditional river valley homeland, where they continued to hold their traditional beliefs about its sacred character. It was not legally significant that the Oklahoma Cherokee Nation chose not to become a party to the suit.

The protection of religious beliefs and practices under the First Amendment has never been conditioned by the number of people claiming the protection, and an individual has the right to complain of a constitutional violation even if other potential class members acquiesce to the infringement on the right in question.

Finally, the TVA asserted that any religious claims that the Cherokees were making should be barred by the doctrines of laches and estoppel. Laches is the neglect for an unreasonably and unexplained time under circumstances that otherwise would have permitted it, to do what in law should have been done; generally, the failure to act on one's claim causes a prejudicial change for another party. Here, the TVA charged that the Cherokees knew in 1965 that the Tellico planned to flood the river valley. In 1972 when the project was detained for the TVA's failure to file an environmental impact statement, the Cherokees, although publicly opposed to the project, didn't advance any religious claims. Then in 1977 work was halted by the question of the Endangered Species Act's application to the snail darter. When the TVA petitioned the Supreme Court to review the issue, the Cherokees filed a brief as an *amicus curiae* in opposition to the project, discussing the importance of the Little Tennessee River to Cherokee history and culture without raising explicit religious claims. For that reason, the TVA argued that they should be estopped from raising their complaint after some thirteen years since the project had begun and the expenditure of more than $110 million.

What the TVA ignored, however, was the settled rule that when a party appears as an *amicus curiae*, as the Eastern Band of Cherokees did in the *Hill* case, it is constrained to address itself only to the issues raised by the parties to the particular litigation. Thus, the Cherokees could give their views about the importance of halting the Tellico project only on the grounds of strictly adhering to the protection of the Endangered Species Act; a discussion of their religious freedom concerns would have been irrelevant to the issue heard by the *Hill* Court.

As to the charge that the Cherokee plaintiffs were tardy in bringing their First Amendment claim and should therefore be estopped from further proceeding, the TVA conveniently overlooked both fact and law in its invocation of laches and estoppel. The Cherokees had made their claims known to the TVA, attempting to protect their religious and cultural rights through petitions, protests, support of other litigations, participating as *amicus curiae* (as in the *Hill* case), issuing tribal council resolutions against the project, and holding consultations with the TVA.[41] But much more directly, the Cherokees had instituted their suit attacking, on religious grounds, the constitutionality of the Energy and Water Appropriations Act, which had been signed by President Carter on September 25, 1979, within seventeen days, on October 12, 1979. The Cherokee response was more than timely, free of any charge of unreasonable or unexplained delay that had caused disadvantage to the TVA. Thus, the doctrine of laches was completely unfounded. Similarly inapposite was the invocation of estoppel, which generally requires the intentional deception of one party by the other through concealment or false representation as to the true statement of facts to the detrimental reliance by the other party. Neither deceit nor inaction could be attributed to the Cherokee response.

As early as 1965, the Cherokees presented a formal petition to Justice William O. Douglas, stating their opposition to the project. Again in 1966 a similar plea was made to Congress in which they expressed their active opposition, stating their fear of a "final desecration of their ancient homeland if Tellico Dam is built."[42] Again, the Cherokees joined suits, decided in 1972 and 1974,[43] complaining that a number of "historic and sacred Cherokee village sites would be destroyed by the Tellico Project," including among others "Chota, the sacred capital of the Cherokee Nation."[44] They contended that the project, by flooding the sacred homeland of the Cherokee Nation, would destroy it and would violate their right to preserve one of the great American Indian tribes as well as other outstanding historical, archeological, and environmental values of the area.[45] They once again made their opposition clear in their *amicus curiae* brief for the *Hill* case of 1978 as already noted. Thus, the record preserves an active opposition by the Cherokees to the Tellico project that simply does not support the delay that would justify any dismissal under laches nor a deceit that in some way had been relied upon by the TVA to its disadvantage; the elements necessary for an estoppel claim against the Cherokees did not exist. One technicality seized upon by the TVA to discredit the Cherokee suit was the fact that in the *Sequoyah* case the Cherokee plaintiffs for the first time explicitly claimed that the actions of the TVA in its Tellico project were violations of the Free Exercise Clause of the First Amendment. The TVA complained that in their past protests against Tellico, the Cherokee plaintiffs spoke of protecting their cultural history or the archeological value of their homeland without specific reference to protection of religion and that they should now be prevented from raising this new issue. This issue, however, was not new, but reflected the tribal experience of an integrity of worship that was not readily delineated from social, political, cultural, and other areas of Indian lifestyle. Chief Oren Lyons of the Onondaga tribe referred to this phenomenon when he wrote that "[r]eligion, as it has been and is still practiced today on the reservation, permeates all aspects of tribal society. The language makes no distinction between religion, government, or law. Tribal customs and religious ordinances are synonymous. All aspects of life are tied into one reality."[46] The testimony of Mr. Barney Old Coyote of the Crow Tribe of Montana before the Senate Select Committee on Indian Affairs in 1978 also is instructive on this point. "The area of worship cannot be delineated from social, political, culture, and other areas of Indian lifestyle, including his general outlook upon economic and resource development. . . . [W]orship is . . . an integral part of the Indian way of life and culture which cannot be separated from the whole. The oneness of Indian life seems to be the basic difference between the Indian and non-Indians of a dominant society."[47] Unfortunately, the tendency for the law to draw linguistic distinctions and make legal determinations based on them, ignoring the evidence of a cultural pattern that does not reflect those distinctions, is typical of the TVA's invidious separation of Cherokee religion and cultural history. According to the TVA, the Cherokees sought relief from harm to Cherokee land, custom, and tradition and must be denied their claim since that did not fit the definition of religion for which the First Amendment might afford protection in the narrow construction of the TVA's reading. Tragically, this reading persisted up through the United States Court of Appeals for the Sixth Circuit.

DECISION OF THE U.S. DISTRICT COURT FOR THE EASTERN DISTRICT OF TENNESSEE AND APPEAL TO THE SIXTH CIRCUIT

In a decision without elaboration, Judge Robert L. Taylor Jr. dismissed the Cherokee complaint, in effect granting summary judgment for the TVA. Ignoring the irreparable injury to the Cherokee religious belief and practice that the damming of the river and subsequent flooding of the sacred valley would cause, ignoring the serious constitutional question raised by the Tellico amendment to the Energy and Water Development Appropriation Bill, as applied to the First Amendment protection of the Cherokees, Judge Taylor's adoption of the bill was literal and unquestioning.

For Judge Taylor, the language of the amendment, exempting the Tellico project not only from the strictures of the Endangered Species Act, but from "any other law," was comprehensive and unequivocal. His memorandum engaged no evaluation of the issue as raised by the Cherokees, but merely acquiesced to the legislative mandate. "Congress has clearly and expressly exempted the Tellico Reservoir from any law repugnant to its completion."[48] He proceeded to rule that an essential element to any First Amendment claim had to involve some form of governmental coercion of actions that were contrary to religious belief, such as some form of pressuring or forcing individuals not to participate in religious practices. Adopting this excessively narrow and restrictive reading of the First Amendment, Taylor found nothing coercive of Cherokee belief or practice from the impoundment of the Tellico reservoir. Absurdly, the government was free to destroy the life of the river valley, the very object of religious significance for the Cherokees, with utter impunity, inflicting no religious harm because it wasn't forcing the Cherokees to believe or participate in religious beliefs or exercises offensive to them; the government could forever alter the religious reality that animated Cherokee belief and practice without infringing on the First Amendment's protection of religious freedom!

But a plain reading of the amendment that "Congress shall make no law ... prohibiting the free exercise [of religion]" simply does not sustain the restrictive reading Taylor imposed on it. Clearly, Congress cannot legislate any state action requiring the overt negation of a religious belief or practice. The Constitutional protection, however, extends beyond that minimal range. Violations of the Free Exercise Clause, for example, have been found when statutes have merely interfered with citizens' ability to practice their religion; in such cases, the offending laws didn't coerce the respective believers to take actions repugnant to their beliefs, the standard adopted by Taylor. In *Kunz v. New York*,[49] for example, the Supreme Court reversed a conviction for violating a New York City ordinance that prohibited public worship meetings in the street without first obtaining a permit from the police commissioner. Kunz, a Baptist minister, was convicted for holding a meeting without the requisite permit. The Court, in striking the ordinance, found that it gave an administrative official, the police commissioner, offensive discretionary power to control in advance the right of citizens to speak on religious matters on the streets of New York. As such, the ordinance was ruled invalid not because it coerced any activity on Kunz or others like him, but because it acted as a prior restraint on the exercise of his First Amendment rights.

Similarly, in *Cantwell v. Connecticut*[50] the Supreme Court overturned the conviction of a Jehovah's Witness arrested under a general law against inciting a breach of the peace. As in *Kunz*, the offensive statute didn't coerce any actions that were contrary to Cantwell's religious belief. What was problematic was a law so general and indefinite that it permitted too wide a discretion in its application. The Court found that Cantwell had not engaged in assault or threats of bodily harm, intentional discourtesy, or personal abuse. "On the contrary we find only an effort to persuade a willing listener to buy a book or to contribute money in the interest of what Cantwell, however misguided others may think him, conceived to be true religion. . . . [T]he petitioner's communication, considered in the light of the constitutional guarantees, raised no such clear and present menace to public peace and order as to render him liable to conviction of the common law offense in question."[51]

Thus, Judge Taylor's reading that the Free Exercise Clause can be invoked only when there is some governmental coercion on a plaintiff's religious beliefs or practices is a delimitation of constitutional protection of religion not supported by precedent. All that is required in Free Exercise cases is a showing that a governmental action has an effect that results in the restriction of religious exercise. Governmental restriction will be invalid whether it results from a requirement that is repugnant to a citizen's religious practice or the action is such that it prevents religious practices. Clearly, the destructive disappearance of the river valley would fit the latter description of an invalid governmental restriction of Cherokee religion. Taylor's insensitivity to the Cherokee belief in the sacred reality of the river valley itself, the heart of their claim, is betrayed by his terse one-sentence conclusion that the Cherokees would suffer no special harm since "[t]he flooding of the Little Tennessee [river] will prevent everyone, not just plaintiffs, from having access to the land in question."[52] But the line exposes more than judicial ignorance of the tribal issue and a paucity of constitutional analysis. It obliquely suggests the perspective that ultimately controlled the disposition of the case.

Judge Taylor's view reflected the commonly held paradigm of land as property with the uncomplicated proposition that ownership entitled access to the property for oneself and the denial of all others from it. For Taylor, the principle was both absolute and fundamental, excluding, as a matter of law, all other claims, even those of First Amendment significance. Instead of properly acknowledging the protection accorded to Cherokee religious belief by the Constitution and then submitting the TVA Tellico dam project to the test of whether it constituted a compelling state interest of sufficient magnitude to outweigh tribal religious freedom, Taylor assumed the primacy of governmental property interests over the Cherokee valuation of the land as a sacred reality. A First Amendment freedom pertaining to the nature of land was automatically subjugated to the government's ownership rights in the land as property. In fact, Taylor's minimal reference to the Free Exercise Clause effectively reduced it to a mere question of access rights. He never addressed freedom of religion as an independent value; it was subsumed and controlled as a category of property interests. This bent accounted for Taylor's startling refusal even to acknowledge the religious nature of the Cherokee claim; he refused to even recognize that their claim to preserve the river valley was an authentic First Amendment religious issue. Characterizing the Cherokee suit solely through the lens of property as an attempt to retrieve access to land now owned by the government, he abruptly dismissed their complaint under the First Amendment as constitutionally void. He dispatched Cherokee belief in the sacred character of their ancestral land in two brief sentences: "The free exercise clause is not a license in itself to enter property, government-owned or otherwise, to which religious practitioners have no other legal right of access. Since plaintiffs claim no other legal property interest in the land in question . . . a free exercise claim is not stated here."[53]

The Cherokees appealed Taylor's decision to the United States Court of Appeals for the Sixth Circuit. Because the TVA responded quickly to take advantage of the judge's decision and had begun the final stages for the damming of the river, the Cherokees filed a motion for an injunction during the pendency of their appeal. Fearful that the TVA would flood the river valley basin before the appeals court could review Judge Taylor's dismissal, thus rendering their Free Exercise claim moot, the Cherokees sought temporary judicial relief from the dam's irreparable harm. Despite the recommendation of its own staff attorney, who advised the appellate court that "the case is unique, and its outcome may affect the very survival of the American Indian and his culture. At the very least, the case appears to be of sufficient importance to warrant a temporary injunction,"[54] the request was denied without explanation. By the time the court of appeals finally issued its opinion, the river valley, without the temporary protection of an injunction, had disappeared under the impounded waters from a completed and operational Tellico dam.

But even though the appellate court refused them the injunction they sought, the Cherokees argued for declaratory relief, a judicial determination that their First Amendment rights had been violated and that the district court had erred in its summary dismissal of their complaint. In their appeal, the Cherokees criticized the TVA's bald assertions and the district court's unquestioning acceptance that governmental property interests presumptively prevail without any need for balancing the Cherokees' constitutionally protected religious belief in the sacred character of the contested land. The tribe argued that such judicial presumption and the court's uncritical literal reading of the Tellico amendment to the Energy and Water Development Appropriations Act of 1980 effectively placed the TVA and its nonessential, destructive project beyond the law. The Tellico project had been repeatedly rejected by the appropriate congressional committees as not exempt from the Endangered Species Act. It had been subsequently discredited on economic as well as environmental grounds by a cabinet-level review board. It managed to survive congressional and executive repudiation only by legislative subterfuge that conspired to place it above the restrictions of the Endangered Species Act and "any other law." That the district court turned a blind eye to the threat that such expansive language posed to the constitutional safeguards of the First Amendment's religious freedom was to collaborate in the very legislative abuse that the original amendments were designed to thwart.

Additionally, the Cherokees scored the district court's dismissal of their complaint because they lacked any property interests in the Tellico region. The tribe clarified that it had never disputed the government's ownership of the land, but completely rejected the district court's unsupported position that without a property interest in the river valley, the Cherokees were absolutely barred from asserting a constitutional right to the free exercise of their religion toward the land now held by a governmental corporation, the TVA. The Cherokees correctly pointed out that the different parties who had previously brought suits challenging the Tellico project, first under the National Environmental Policy Act and later under the Endangered Species Act, had no property interests in the Tellico lands, yet the courts had required the TVA to comply with the provisions of those statutes. In effect, the district court in Tennessee had erected a more stringent requirement for a constitutional claim than had been required for the previous statutory claims. To impose the barrier of owning property to plead the violation of a First Amendment religious freedom would have imposed a standard that would deny anyone, not just the Cherokees, the possibility of ever exercising First Amendment religious rights on government-owned property. The Cherokees urged the Sixth Circuit to rebuff the TVA and the district court's virtual rewriting of the First Amendment to read: "Congress shall make no law respecting an establishment of religion, or prohibiting the free exercise thereof, *except on government owned property*."[55]

In opposing the Cherokee appeal, the TVA nevertheless reiterated that "plaintiffs have no property interest in the land involved, and neither they nor their ancestors have had any property interest in it or right of access to it for 140 years."[56] Pursuing its myopic focus on land as property, the TVA cited *Kleppe v. New Mexico*,[57] in which the Supreme Court had recently construed the Property Clause of the Constitution, which reads simply that "Congress shall have power to dispose of and make all needful rules and regulations respecting the Territory or other Property belonging to the United States."[58] In *Kleppe*, the Court addressed the issue of federal versus state power on public lands; specifically, did Congress have the authority to make regulations regarding wild free-roaming horses and burros on public lands within the state of New Mexico? In holding that Congress possessed the requisite authority under the Property Clause, the Supreme Court observed that the clause granted expansive powers to Congress over all public lands including "to control their occupancy and use, to protect them from trespass and injury, and to prescribe the conditions upon which others may obtain rights in them."[59] But the Court's remarks and discussion that "the power over the public land thus entrusted to Congress [through the Property Clause] is without limitations"[60] was altogether qualified by the context of New Mexico's challenge not to heed a congressional statute, but instead to exercise its own sovereignty over horses and burros roaming on public lands within the state. The case was entirely one of jurisdiction where the Supreme Court ruled that when Congress enacts legislation for public lands pursuant to the Property Clause, it necessarily overrides any conflicting state laws. "A different rule would place the public domain of the United States completely at the mercy of state legislation."[61] Nowhere does *Kleppe* raise or discuss the question, presented by the Cherokees, of governmental responsibility to hear and appropriately resolve claims of religious belief and practice with respect to land. The TVA simply arrogated *Kleppe*'s language about congressional authority over public lands, impermissibly generalizing a principle of Congressional preeminence over state authority in rule making about such lands into an absolute dominion over them beyond constitutional constraint.

Although not as misleading as the distortion of *Kleppe*, the TVA's similar reliance on a second Supreme Court decision, *Adderley v. Florida*,[62] was equally inapposite. The issue in *Adderley* was whether a county sheriff could rightly arrest demonstrators who were protesting Southern segregation policies for trespassing on the premises of the county jail as contrary to Florida law. In holding that the sheriff acted appropriately and did not violate the demonstrators' First Amendment freedoms of speech and assembly, the Court condemned "the assumption that people who want to propagandize protests or views have a constitutional right to do so whenever and however and wherever they please."[63] But to apply a Supreme Court ruling on the general legitimacy of trespass statutes and the limited right of civil rights demonstrators to stage protests in only certain specified public spaces to the Cherokee claim was another indication of the TVA's refusal to countenance the sacred character of the land.

The Cherokees' was not an issue of free speech or expression as in *Adderley*, but one of belief: that the land held by the TVA was holy, and that before the government could destroy it by flood and deprive them of its religious significance, it had to demonstrate a compelling state interest for doing so. Revealingly, the TVA admitted the necessity of that standard compelling-interest test because "where there is a direct clash between rights possessed both by individual plaintiffs and the Government, a balancing is of course required."[64] But since the TVA was insensitive to the notion of land as anything other than property, the whole question turned on who held legal title to the Tellico property, the Cherokees or the government. The government had the exclusive right to use its property, which the Cherokees, lacking any proprietary interest, had no basis to contest. Ignoring the heart of the Cherokee claim that the land itself was a sacred reality and fundamental to their belief, the TVA refused to recognize the tribe's status as religious claimants, seeing them only as potential trespassers to whom the government owed no special duty, since its property would be used without discrimination: the dam and its consequent flood would exclude the public at large, not just the Cherokees, from the river valley. According to the TVA, no compelling-interest test was needed where land as property controlled the issue and defined the parties as those with full and exclusive ownership rights for the use of the property and those who had none. On such terms, the determination of the tribal complaint warranted the simple dismissal ordered by the district court, which the TVA urged the court of appeals to affirm.

On grounds wholly unanticipated from the issues raised at the district court level and in the parties' appellate briefs, the Sixth Circuit, sitting as a panel of three judges, affirmed the dismissal of the Cherokee complaint. The panel rejected the district court's ultimate determination of the case based on the government's position as owner of the Tellico lands and the corresponding lack of any property interest in the same lands by the Cherokees. Although a factor for consideration, the absence of Cherokee ownership was not held by the panel to be conclusive "in view of the history of the Cherokee expulsion from Southern Appalachia followed by the 'Trail of Tears' to Oklahoma and the unique nature of the plaintiffs' religion."[65]

This initially sympathetic judicial notice of the coercive removal of the Cherokees and their forced exile from the lands they now sought to protect next moved the court of appeals to engage the two-step analysis for deciding a Free Exercise claim under the First Amendment. As identified by the Supreme Court, a determination first had to be made as to whether the governmental action complained of did in fact create a burden on the exercise of the plaintiffs' religion. In the current case, would the government's dam at Tellico and the consequent flooding of the river valley basin interfere with Cherokee religious belief and practice? If it did so, then the second step would be to balance Cherokee religion against the government's interest, with the government having to submit to the test of showing an overriding or compelling reason for its action.

As already noted, the Cherokee complaint, with its accompanying affidavits from tribal members and anthropologists, simply indicated the traditional tribal belief in the Little Tennessee River valley as a sacred reality, and the "immense and immeasurable" harm believers would suffer from its destructive inundation by the impounded waters from the Tellico dam. For the Cherokees, their claim had correctly satisfied the first step in the required analysis, and much of their argument was directed at the second step, convincingly exposing the government's inability to demonstrate any state interest sufficiently compelling to warrant the destructive flooding of the Cherokee's sacred land. Although the TVA had made disparaging remarks about the size of the plaintiff bands of Cherokees (some 15,000) in comparison with the larger Cherokee Nation (some 50,000), which had settled in Oklahoma, and although the TVA claimed that the Cherokees were guilty of laches in raising their First Amendment claim too late in an action that they had protested as early as 1966, the TVA never explicitly attacked the constitutional insufficiency of the tribal allegations. It had been accepted by both the TVA and the district court that the Cherokees had raised a constitutionally cognizable claim based on an infringement of the Free Exercise Clause of the First Amendment.

Therefore, it was profoundly shocking when the Sixth Circuit ruled to affirm the lower court's dismissal, not because the Cherokees owned no property interest in the river valley, but because the appellate court had imposed a novel standard to test the constitutional validity of a claim based on the Free Exercise Clause of the First Amendment. According to the Sixth Circuit's novel and much stricter criteria, the Cherokees "have not alleged infringement of a constitutionally cognizable First Amendment right. In the absence of such an infringement, there is no need to balance the opposing interest of the parties or to determine whether the government's interest in proceeding with its plans for the Tellico Dam is 'compelling.' "[66] In one and a quarter pages of the federal reporter, the Sixth Circuit reviewed three cases, only one of which was decided by the Supreme Court, and from them cobbled together a standard that the panel then imposed on the Cherokees and ruled that the tribal claim was unable to satisfy. The three cases included: *Wisconsin v. Yoder*,[67] in which the Amish were granted a religious exemption from sending their children to public school beyond the eighth grade; *Frank v. Alaska*,[68] in which an Athabascan Indian was exonerated for killing a moose in violation of game laws, because the moose was a centerpiece in an Athabascan ritual; and *People v. Woody*,[69] in which peyote was ruled to play a central role in the ritual of the Native American Church, an organization of American Indians. From these three, the Sixth Circuit crafted "a centrality or indispensability" standard and concluded that "examination of the plaintiffs' affidavits discloses no such claim of centrality or indispensability of the Little Tennessee Valley to Cherokee religious observances. . . . [The Cherokees] have fallen short of demonstrating that worship at the particular geographic location in question is inseparable from the way of life (*Yoder*), the cornerstone of their religious observance (*Frank*), or plays the central role in their religious ceremonies and practices (*Woody*)."[70]

In adopting the standard as it did, the Sixth Circuit so diluted the meaning of the Free Exercise Clause as to render it a virtual nullity. Under that standard, only those religious beliefs or practices that play a central role in religious ceremonies, or are the cornerstone of religious observance, or are inseparable from one's way of life, qualify as claims that can be based on the Free Exercise Clause of the First Amendment. Lesser religious beliefs or practices could not, under the Sixth Circuit's standard, form the basis for cognizable First Amendment claims, and other currently protected religious practices would now be subject to governmental infringement, including the sale of religious literature in public places, the refusal to salute the flag, opposition to Sabbath work, proselytizing on federal property, tax exemptions for sales of religious literature, and refusals by non-believing officeholders to take religious oaths. Within every tradition it would be easy to imagine significant devotional practices and ceremonies that would fall outside of the protection of the Free Exercise Clause using the Sixth Circuit's "central," "inseparable," or "cornerstone" standard. But more importantly, the Supreme Court has repeatedly avoided drawing theological distinctions between central and non-central religious beliefs and has forewarned courts against the interpretation of particular church doctrines and the relative importance of those doctrines to religion.

In its assertion that only those religious beliefs and practices that are "inseparably" and "intimately" related to an organized group's style of daily living will merit Free Exercise protection, the Sixth Circuit misinterpreted the Supreme Court's *Yoder* decision. In that case, involving the singular and ostensibly isolated community of the Amish, there existed an unmistakable interdependency of religious conviction and communal lifestyle. The question for the Supreme Court was the extent to which that lifestyle would be permitted to interfere with reasonable governmental concerns to educate children until they reach the age of sixteen. The critical question was the rationale behind the Amish refusal to send their children for formal education beyond the eighth grade.

If the Amish decision had been based solely on "their subjective evaluation and rejection of the contemporary secular values accepted by the majority,"[71] the Court would have found that to be a "philosophical and personal rather than religious"[72] belief and not accorded it protection under the First Amendment. The issue turned not on the Amish way of life in general, but on the Court's determination that their specific rejection of mandatory education beyond the eighth grade was religiously motivated. In so deciding, the Court took notice of the many evident signs of how religious belief penetrated all aspects of Amish life, including education. But the comprehensive and striking inseparability of Amish faith and daily culture was only evidence that the Court weighed to answer the narrower question of whether their non-compliance with Wisconsin's compulsory school attendance law was constitutionally protected.

The Sixth Circuit incorrectly expanded the Supreme Court's evidentiary description of Amish lifestyle into a legal standard to determine whether a court would even acknowledge from the start that a claim under the Free Exercise Clause had been made. In doing so, the court of appeals announced a standard for First Amendment protection much stricter than that sanctioned by the Supreme Court. In *Yoder* the high court ruled that a claim would be recognized as valid under the Religion Clauses if there was a showing that it was "rooted in religious belief" beyond mere subjective evaluation or personal philosophy. Beyond that, any further indications that the claimed belief or practice is "intimately related to the daily life" of the plaintiff should be weighed as evidence when the court later considers whether the government has a more compelling state interest that will prevail over the religious liberty.

Yet even if it had not erred in its formulation of its "centrality or indispensability" standard, the Sixth Circuit incorrectly construed it as applied to the Cherokee claim. In doing so, the court of appeals betrayed its misunderstanding of the basic notion that informed the tribal complaint: the land of the Little Tennessee River Valley was itself the sacred reality that would be destroyed by the floodwaters from the Tellico dam, a wasteful government project devoid of any state interest beyond the local pork-barrel political scheme that manipulated its congressional passage. Without the land, there was no Cherokee religion; to destroy the land was to destroy the critical religious experience of being connected to a holy, ultimate reality. Rescuing the river valley from inundation was preserving the entity without which traditional Cherokee religion was a groundless abstraction. The equivalence between land and religion could be no more direct. The failure of the court of appeals to recognize that inherent connection and to insist that the Cherokees had insufficiently alleged an infringement against their religious liberty reflected the court's severely impoverished and reductive understanding of both religion and land.

For the court, religion was circumscribed to a particular set of human actions and behavior, shorn of psychic depth. Because of a narrow and rigid assumption that religion is a matter of practices and observances, the court dismissed as superfluous what was, in fact, the very substance of the Cherokee attempt to save the river valley: their experience of a vital relationship to its land as a primordial sacred reality. Remarkably, the court acknowledged that this was the testimony of the Cherokee affidavits, but proceeded to rule them insufficient. "[T]he affidavits . . . at most . . . established a feeling by the individual affiants that the general location of the dam and impoundment has a religious significance which will be destroyed by the flooding."[73] That acknowledgment should have constituted judicial recognition that the Cherokees had properly alleged a constitutionally valid claim based on the Free Exercise Clause. But because the court of appeals had improperly departed from the Supreme Court's standard in *Yoder*, and because religion, for the court, was centered in human behavior rather than in the land, the court demanded further demonstrations of "the centrality" of the Little Tennessee River Valley to Cherokee religion. Persistently referring to Cherokee religion in terms of Cherokee activities—"observance," "worship," "ceremonies," or "practices"—the court had no sense of the primacy of the land that inspired, evoked, and gave meaning to those activities. In the remarks of the court, the river valley recedes to but the function, rather than the heart of Cherokee religion; it exists as the site or place, very much "the back-ground," where Cherokees "perform" their religion.

But in fact, the Cherokee affidavits disclose comparatively little information about the specifics of their religious practices. Instead, they witness to the very being of the land as that from which they came as a people; that which has sustained them and given them self-definition throughout their history; from which they were wrongfully uprooted and forcefully exiled by the expansionist aggression of the United States government; that which yet shelters the community of their deceased ancestors; that whose very existence embodied sacred power. Any reference to practices of gathering medicinal plants, ritual immersions in the river, pilgrimages, or any other ceremonial activities were just so many traditional Cherokee responses to the primary reality of the land as a living, holy presence. Without the river valley, Cherokee religion as denominated by the court of appeals would have had no meaning. By the logic of its own standard, the court's refusal to find a necessary "centrality" or "indispensability" between the river valley and Cherokee religion was without justification.

But the court's further unwillingness to follow the recommendation of Judge Gilbert S. Merritt, who dissented from the opinion of Judges Pierce Lively and Damon J. Keith, was unnecessarily harsh to the Cherokees, depriving them of a final chance to offer further proof that their claim did in fact meet the novel standard now being imposed by the court of appeals. Judge Merritt correctly noted that it was within the appellate court's discretion to remand the case to the district court, where the Cherokees could more precisely allege their claim in the language of "centrality" and "inseparability" demanded by the court of appeals. A basic fairness justified such a discretion, since the Cherokees could not have anticipated the new standard at the time they filed their original complaint and affidavits. Perhaps, had they been allowed such liberality, the Cherokees might have amended their complaint to include among their earlier testimonies one made against the Tellico dam at a congressional hearing in 1978 by the Cherokee Jimmie Durham. In noting the meaning of the Cherokee word *Eloheh*, he succinctly illustrated the linguistic inseparability between religion and land, even as he spoke of the difference between land as property and land as sacred reality:

> Is there a human being who does not revere his homeland, even though he may not return? . . . In our own history, we teach that we were created there, which is truer than anthropological truth because it was there that we were given our vision as the Cherokee people . . . In the language of my people . . . there is a word for land: Eloheh. This same word also means history, culture and religion. We cannot separate our place on earth from our lives on the earth nor from our vision nor our meaning as a people. We are taught from childhood that the animals and even the trees and plants that we share a place with are our brothers and sisters. So when we speak of land, we are not speaking of property, territory, or even a piece of ground upon which our houses sit and our crops are grown, we are speaking of something truly sacred.[74]

The Sixth Circuit's dismissal of the Cherokee claim and its refusal to grant a remand to the district court where the Cherokees would undoubtedly have been able to conform their pleadings to the requisite language exemplifies on the judicial level the kind of "insensitive and inflexible enforcement of Federal policies and regulations" that the American Indian Religious Freedom Act had identified as a source of the infringements suffered by tribal religious traditions. In fact, the Sixth Circuit utterly failed to engage the act and made no reference to it or its values as they may have applied to the Cherokee claim. But although extreme in its complete disregard of that recently enacted legislative concern for Native American religions, the Sixth Circuit foreshadowed in the cases to follow a consistent judicial failure to find anything more substantial in the act than hollow congressional sentiment.

2

Badoni v. Higginson:
Navajo Religion, National Monuments, and the Colorado River

Some six months after the United States Court of Appeals for the Sixth Circuit refused to grant constitutional protection to the sacred land of the Cherokees, permitting the impounded waters from the Tellico Dam to flood their ancestral homeland in the Little Tennessee River Valley basin, the United States Court of Appeals for the Tenth Circuit in Denver, Colorado, dismissed the appeal of Navajo Indians similarly confronted with the disappearance of sacred land under invasive waters impounded from yet another government-sponsored dam.

In this case the river was the Colorado, which rises in the high Rocky Mountains of north central Colorado, cutting a winding path for 1,440 miles southward to the Gulf of California. Its drainage basin covers 244,000 square miles and includes parts of seven states—Wyoming, Colorado, Utah, New Mexico, Nevada, Arizona, and California. For seventeen miles it forms the international boundary between Arizona and Mexico before flowing eighty miles through Mexico to the gulf. Draining the largest, most arid sector of the North American continent, the Colorado River continues to be a critical source of water for the states through which it flows. In 1922 the Colorado River compact was signed, dividing the entire river basin into two parts, the Lower Basin, consisting of Arizona, Nevada, and California, and the Upper Basin of Wyoming, Utah, Colorado, and New Mexico. According to the compact, the river's water was apportioned at 7,500,000 acre feet per annum to each basin, with recognition given to a portion to be released to Mexico. In 1948 the Upper Basin states entered into another compact, to further divide the Upper Basin waters among them. Then in 1956 Congress passed the comprehensive Colorado River Storage Act, which planned the future development of the Colorado River, regulating its flow and storing water, making it possible for the states of the Upper Basin to utilize, consistently with the provisions of the 1922 compact and the 1948 compact, the apportionments made to and among them. To that end, the congressional act authorized the construction and operation of a series of four dams, one of which was the Glen Canyon Dam. The storage reservoirs created by each of these dams enabled the Upper Basin states to meet their obligations to the Lower Basin states. If sufficient, the storage would then permit the Upper Basin states to utilize the water allocated under their compacts, and to use the revenues to develop participating projects for irrigation.

The reservoir that formed behind Glen Canyon Dam after its completion in 1963 was Lake Powell, which, when activated to its capacity, could contain some 25,000,000 acre feet of water storage. And in fact, Glen Canyon Dam itself was equipped with power-generating facilities so that the waters discharged from Lake Powell could supply large amounts of electricity capable of providing additional power to the Southwest and the Pacific coast. The reservoirs behind the other three dams when combined contained only 6,400,000 acre feet of water. Thus, Glen Canyon Dam and its reservoir, Lake Powell, were crucial links in the Colorado River water and power development scheme. The other dams and subsequent projects that had been built as part of the Colorado River Storage Act were essentially dependent on Lake Powell to provide the basic storage necessary to fulfill the delivery requirements to the downstream states of the Lower Basin and Mexico. So long as the water stored in Lake Powell could meet those requirements, the Upper Basin states could develop the water allocated to them for irrigation, hydroelectric generation, and other water-related projects. If the water level in Lake Powell were limited, some Upper Basin projects could be impaired.

Glen Canyon Dam sits on the Colorado River in Arizona near the Utah boundary. After its completion in 1963, Lake Powell began to form, backing up and filling the canyons adjacent to and behind the dam, until by 1970 it had traveled back some fifty-eight miles to enter an area in Utah whose isolated and remote canyons contained one of the most remarkable sandstone formations found on the planet. Believed to be the world's largest natural bridge, Rainbow Bridge arches 309 feet high with a span of 278 feet. Within a year of having been sighted by the first party of white men, the quarter section of land of some 160 acres surrounding the bridge was declared a national monument by President William Taft on May 30, 1910. But the extensive region surrounding and including Rainbow Bridge had long before been frequented by Navajos who sought refuge in the tortuous and forbidding terrain during the campaigns carried out against them by the U.S. Cavalry in the mid-1800s. The tract of land that created the first Navajo reservation in 1868 did not at first include the vicinity of Rainbow Bridge, but was confined to areas in Arizona. But in 1884 the area in Utah adjacent to the reservation known as Pauite Strip, which did contain Rainbow Bridge, was added. Thus, at the time it was designated a national monument, Rainbow Bridge was completely surrounded by, but removed through executive order, from the Navajo reservation. The monument was placed under the jurisdiction of the National Park Service.

In recognition of the wondrous beauty of Rainbow Bridge, Congress provided in its passage of the Colorado River Storage Project Act that adequate protective measures should be taken in the operation of Glen Canyon Dam to preclude impairment of the national monument. Congress also stipulated that no dam or reservoir authorized under the act should be within the confines of any national park or monument. So in 1971, when it was clear that the waters of Lake Powell had begun to seep into the confines of the Rainbow Bridge monument, the environmental organization Friends of the Earth sued the secretary of the interior to take preventive action to halt the lake's flow from further spreading and engulfing the monument area. Although the United States District Court for the District of Utah upheld the complaint and ordered actions to be taken to prevent Lake Powell's entry and future encroachment into the boundaries of the Rainbow Bridge monument, the United States Court of Appeals for the Tenth Circuit reversed the decision.

Studying the congressional record concerning Rainbow Bridge subsequent to the passage in 1956 of the Colorado River Storage Project Act, the appellate court held that on some twelve separate occasions Congress chose not to incur the expenditures necessary to protect Rainbow Bridge and its surroundings from the advancing waters of Lake Powell. The court ruled that the specific language of the original 1956 act to protect Rainbow Bridge from the dams and reservoirs of the Colorado River storage system had been reversed through subsequent congressional denial of budget requests for the structures necessary to protect the monument and explicit congressional prohibition against the use of money for such purpose. The court found no congressional impropriety in such a reversal, since the action was straightforward, direct, and came after hearings on the subject had apparently led members of Congress to conclude that the protective works would have been more detrimental than the presence of water in and around Rainbow Bridge. The court of appeals rejected the alternative remedy that had been sought by Friends of the Earth as too severe a threat to the viability of the entire Colorado River storage system.

Instead of the unsightly and expensive protective dams, pumps, and tunnels that would have to be constructed around the Rainbow Bridge National Monument, Friends of the Earth had argued that Glen Canyon Dam and Lake Powell should be operated at a reduced level, cutting the water storage to about half of the design capacity. Although that would have reduced the expansion of Lake Powell into the Rainbow Bridge area, the court found such a reduction to be contrary to the effectiveness of the whole water storage system as envisioned by Congress in the 1956 storage act. The reduction of water stored in Lake Powell as the principal regulating reservoir would have, in the court's view, substantially reduced the amount of water available to each of the Upper Basin states and would have impaired the operation of many facilities that had already been constructed and others authorized but not yet built; to lower the water storage level in Lake Powell would have threatened the ability to meet downriver water obligations and interfered with the generation of electrical power and the capacity of irrigation projects at sites throughout the river storage system.

With its decision, the court of appeals ratified what Congress itself had never made explicit. Congress never amended or repealed the specific language in the Colorado River Storage Project Act of 1956 that Rainbow Bridge National Monument should be protected from the operational consequences of Glen Canyon Dam and that no dam or reservoir from the storage project should be within any national park or monument area. Instead, while ostensibly subscribing to the values of preserving sites of remarkable natural beauty and contour, Congress consistently rejected the funds necessary to protect the pristine integrity of Rainbow Bridge. Having chosen to exploit the Colorado River for its maximum potential irrigation and industrial uses, Congress repeatedly ignored its own stated commitment, refusing to incur the costs for the national monument's protection from an expansive Lake Powell. For the Tenth Circuit Court of Appeals, the case represented "a collision" between congressional concern for national parks and monuments on the one hand and the maximum development of the Colorado River on the other. The court refused to challenge the legitimacy of Congress's subsequent priority given to the water storage and use system and its consequent systematic refusal of funds to halt the rising seepage of Lake Powell at the base of Rainbow Bridge. In the view of both Congress and the court, assured by geological studies that had been conducted, the massive sandstone arches of the bridge would be safe from any structural damage and suffer no harm. Indeed, it was anticipated that the spread of Lake Powell into the confines of the monument area would provide an easy water access for tourists into the remote and isolated terrain that had concealed Rainbow Bridge within its canyons. For among the multiple uses to which Lake Powell and the adjacent lands would be applied was a national recreation area whose several marinas would provide the boats that would soon be on the lake's waters, including those at the very base of Rainbow Bridge.

But if Congress no longer saw the waters of Lake Powell as a threat, but as an enhancement that would facilitate tourist enjoyment of the national monument, a very different view was held by Navajo ancestral inhabitants of the reservation, which, for a brief period at the end of the nineteenth century, had included the 160-acre tract that later was taken as the Rainbow Bridge National Monument. For them, Rainbow Bridge recalled that primordial time when the Holy People or gods, having lived among human ancestors and all kinds of animal peoples, finally left to live more to themselves. Yet, some of these Holy People chose to remain within the canyon where they had been living and became permanently fixed there as Stone People. There they have stayed, seeing all and hearing all, bestowing their protective powers and blessings on all who acknowledge their presence with offerings of precious stones, pollen, prayers, and songs. Standing alone or in groups, these Holy People reveal themselves within the contours of their canyon sanctuary as cave sites, secluded pools of spring water, or striking outcroppings from the canyon floor or walls. The most remarkable of these sacred Stone People are the two Rainbows, male and female, arching together in perfect marital union, whose soaring creativity has given birth over the ages to countless numbers of clouds, rains, and young rainbows. Sending their offspring to bless the Navajo lands with vitalizing moisture, the sandstone Rainbow Couple have been the most revered of the Holy People inhabiting the canyon for generations of Navajo pilgrims and priestly singers. But the once protective canyon, concealing many of the Navajos from the U.S. Cavalry in the 1860s and continuing to bless Navajo populations with the sustaining rain children sent by the Rainbow Couple, now was threatened by the artificial waters of Lake Powell. When its seepage had backed into the canyon, submerging several of the Holy People and advancing upon the sacred Rainbow Couple, the Navajos sought protection from the United States Constitution.

RESPONSE OF THE DISTRICT COURT

Chief Judge Aldon J. Anderson, who heard the Navajo complaint, admitted that their First Amendment claims presented a unique challenge not only to the officials of the Interior Department named as defendants, but to the court itself. The Cherokee suit against the Tennessee Valley Authority would not be filed for another two years, so no precedent could be looked to for guidance. As it turned out, the grounds on which Judge Anderson dismissed the Navajo claim would themselves become the arguments to throw out the Cherokees.

Judge Anderson noted that the "severe emotional and spiritual distress"[1] of the Navajo plaintiffs stemmed from Lake Powell's submersion of the base of Rainbow Bridge and the inundation of holy sites and springs in its vicinity and the Navajos' consequent inability to perform religious ceremonies. Likewise, the behavior of tourists at times interfered with prayers and ceremonies, at times disturbed the offerings left by the Navajos at their prayer sites, and at times defaced Rainbow Bridge itself or otherwise desecrated its holy precincts under the influence of alcohol with litter and noise. But the characterization of the religious harm suffered by the Navajo that was most strikingly included in Anderson's opinion was the Navajos' claim that the waters of Lake Powell, flooding the canyon to a depth of some twenty feet directly under the arch of Rainbow Bridge, covering its base and completely immersing other formations at which prayers had customarily been offered, had in effect "drown[ed] entities recognized as gods by the plaintiffs."[2] Anderson was aware that Rainbow Bridge and "certain geological formations in the . . . area have held positions of central importance in the religion of the Navajo people of the Navajo Mountain area for at least 100 years. These shrines, which are regarded as the actual incarnate forms of Navajo gods have performed protective and rain-giving functions for generations of Navajo singers."[3]

The equivalence between religion and land could not have been stated any more directly than in the Navajo allegation. Clearly, they were not raising a claim insisting on any native, aboriginal rights to Rainbow Bridge and its surrounding canyon. Nor were they contesting the series of actions taken by the United States government exercising its sovereignty over Navajo lands, beginning with the Treaty of 1868, which created the original Navajo reservation from land in Arizona. Then, in 1884 an area in Utah, adjacent to the reservation known as the Paiute Strip, that included Rainbow Bridge and its canyon, was added to the reservation. When it was believed that the Paiute Strip had mineral potential, it was taken back by executive order in 1892, only to be returned again in 1933, except for the

160 acres that had been taken in 1910 as the Rainbow Bridge National Monument. Finally, in 1958 the government acquired those Navajo lands necessary for the Glen Canyon Dam and its reservoir, Lake Powell. The Navajo complaint brought to Judge Anderson challenged none of these actions in which the government exercised its proprietary interests over Navajo-related lands. Theirs was not a challenge to the possessory status of Rainbow Bridge as a government-owned national monument. It was rather an assertion of belief in the nature of the canyon and its formation as embodying living, sacred beings to whom the Navajos prayed for well-being and rain.

To the Navajo medicine men and the adult members of the Shonto chapter, the Navajo Mountain chapter, and the Inscription House chapter of the Navajo Nation who brought the claim, the invasive waters of Lake Powell were not merely changing the scenery of the canyon floor, but were threatening the integrity and existence of their living, spiritual sandstone guardians. The influx of tourists boating through the canyon floor, generally unaware or boisterously indifferent to the sacred presences past and above which they heedlessly floated, contributed to the desecration of the Navajos' living landscape. The Navajo claim, then, was rooted in a religious conception of land and grounded in the Free Exercise Clause of the First Amendment, asking the court "to order [the government] defendants to take appropriate steps to operate Glen Canyon Dam and Reservoir in such a manner that the important religious and cultural interests of plaintiffs will not be harmed or degraded, and to issue rules and regulations to prevent further destruction and desecration of the Rainbow Bridge area by tourists."[4]

Disturbingly, Judge Anderson was unable to differentiate a claim alleging the religious valuation of land and the government's responsibility in its management to traditional tribal beliefs from a challenge for ownership rights in the land. Confronted by a perceived threat to the object of their religious belief, the Navajo plaintiffs raised the issue of the government's duty to protect and preserve the land from the asserted harm; to what extent did the First Amendment reach land held and managed by the federal government? That was plainly the substance of the case. Yet Anderson peremptorily refused to acknowledge the issue. Citing no precedent or legal authority, he simply ruled that without a property interest in the Rainbow Bridge National Monument, the Navajos would not be heard on their religious argument. The limit of Anderson's perception was the construct of land as property; beyond that, he would recognize no other value upon which a complaint could be brought. Since the monument land belonged to the government and not the Navajos, he would entertain no further conception of land as sacred, upon which the Navajos had advanced their constitutional plea. Though Rainbow Bridge might in fact be the living, sacred being that the Navajos claimed, Anderson would not countenance the Navajo charge that the government was transgressing their religious belief and practice, in the absence of any tribal ownership rights to the bridge and its canyon. Dismissing them, he wrote: "Thus, even assuming that all of the assertions as to the actuality and sincerity of plaintiffs' beliefs are true, the court finds that the assertions do not give rise to a cognizable First Amendment claim under the circumstances of the instant case."[5]

Judge Anderson's rationale for restricting his judicial regard only to a consideration of property interests was an injudicious concern for government control of its lands. To accord religious significance to land was to grant constitutional stature to claims capable of disrupting governmental possession. Relying on a scenario conjured by the government defendants, he betrayed his ignorance of the historical context and the relief that the Navajos were seeking. His analogy was as follows: "A person might sincerely believe that he or a predecessor encountered a profound religious experience in the environs of what is now the Lincoln Memorial in Washington, D.C., and that experience might cause him to believe that the Lincoln Memorial is therefore a sacred religious shrine to him. That person, however, could hardly expect to call upon the courts to enjoin all other visitors from entering the Lincoln Memorial in order to protect his constitutional right to religious freedom. The weakness in plaintiffs' claims is apparent."[6] The weakness however, lay in the judge's reliance on an analogy that completely ignored the fact that Rainbow Bridge, before ever becoming a national monument in 1910 and before ever attracting the crowds of tourists arriving on the spreading waters of Lake Powell, existed as the protective, sustaining, sacred being to whom generations of Navajos directed their prayer. Unlike the Lincoln Memorial, built to honor the memory of a deceased president, the arches of Rainbow Bridge had vaulted the sky from time immemorial in the natural movements of earth, wind, and water and stood as a living, holy presence to the Navajos. Nor was it accurate to suggest that the Navajos sought the total exclusion of all others; they had asked only that the government recognize their religious understanding of Rainbow Bridge and that its management of tourists reflect that awareness in regulations protecting the area from destruction or degradation. In its use of the analogy, the government defendants exposed a fear that religious valuations of land would lead to dispossession of governmental property. With his reliance on the analogy, Judge Anderson adopted the government's position, improperly attempting to thwart such claims by denying them a hearing. By suppressing as a matter of principle claims of religious belief and practice concerning land and subordinating them to property interests, he made an injudicious policy determination and abdicated his responsibility to allow competing constitutional values to be expressed, weighed, and resolved under the specific circumstances from which they emerged.

Having denied the Navajos his judicial cognizance of their First Amendment claim, Anderson nevertheless proceeded to fault their position by invoking an erroneous interpretation of *Wisconsin v. Yoder*. As had the Sixth Circuit Court of Appeals in *Sequoyah v. TVA*, Anderson incorrectly identified what was only a description of the Amish lifestyle noted by the Supreme Court in *Yoder* and made that into the standard under which courts should determine what constitutes a bona fide and sincere religious claim protected by the First Amendment. The Supreme Court spoke of the traditional life of the Amish as "one of deep religious conviction, shared by an organized group and intimately related to daily living."[7] As if to justify his original denial of a hearing absent a property interest in Rainbow Bridge, Judge Anderson applied this description of the Amish as the norm against which he measured and found inadequate Navajo religious belief and practice. Specifically, he faulted the training and status of the medicine men among the plaintiffs and the number of visits to, and ceremonies attended by, the plaintiffs at Rainbow Bridge. He concluded that "there is nothing to indicate that at the present time the Rainbow Bridge National Monument and its environs has anything approaching deep, religious significance to any organized group, or has in recent decades been intimately related to the daily living of any group or individual. . . . Plaintiffs fail . . . to demonstrate . . . a vital relationship of the [ceremonial] practices in question with the Navajo way of life or a 'history of consistency' which would support their allegation of religious use of Rainbow Bridge in recent times."[8]

The judge's conclusion, however, is flawed on several counts. Fundamentally, it derives from an incorrect reading of *Yoder*. In that case, as already discussed in the previous chapter, the Supreme Court had held that a claim would be recognized as valid under the religion clauses of the First Amendment if there was a showing that it was "rooted in religious belief" beyond mere subjective valuation or personal philosophy. Beyond that, any further indications that the claimed belief or practice is "shared by an organized group, and intimately related to daily living" should be weighed as evidence when the court later considers whether the government has a more compelling state interest that will prevail over the religious liberty. Reference to beliefs and practices shared by an organized group and intimately connected to daily life were not meant to be universally prescriptive conditions for granting recognition of a valid First Amendment claim; such language was peculiar to the specific lifestyle and circumstances of the Amish and central to their argument about the threat of secular values from exposure to public school education beyond the eighth grade. By imposing phrases characterizing Amish life as the rubric that the Navajos had to satisfy, Judge Anderson misinterpreted the Supreme Court's decision in *Yoder* and distorted his evaluation of Navajo religious tradition.

Having seized upon the necessity that the beliefs of the Navajo plaintiffs be "shared by an organized group," Judge Anderson misrepresented the fact that the training of the Navajo medicine men among the plaintiffs had not been "tribally organized or carried out."[9] Implying an absence of some official recognition of their status "by the Navajo Nation as such,"[10] the judge ignored evidence of the individual, decentralized, and private nature of the training of Navajo medicine men and suggested that the political entity of the Navajo Nation somehow had to give its approbation in some official way. Looking for standardized procedures and approval by the tribal government for the training of Navajo "clergy" and finding none, he questioned the authenticity and sincerity of the religious beliefs of the Navajo plaintiffs as insufficiently "shared by an organized group."

Similar inappropriate conclusions were drawn by the judge regarding the relative infrequency of the plaintiffs' visits to, and ceremonies conducted at, Rainbow Bridge or in its vicinity. Considering the responses to interrogatories by only four of the medicine men among the Navajo plaintiffs, Judge Anderson tallied their visits and ceremonial celebrations and found their quantity lacking. Impermissively, the judge had ignored responses filed on behalf of two of the Navajo chapters or local organizations of Navajo adults who were also plaintiffs and interviews conducted by an expert witness on Navajo religion whose testimony had been admitted as "established and true." These supported a view of more consistent and frequent visits and ceremonialism than reckoned by Judge Anderson, whose selective scrutiny placed the burden of embodying the entire Navajo religious belief and practice toward Rainbow Bridge and its canyon on a few of the individual named plaintiffs who were not intended to exhaust the experience of a broader class.

Under the aegis of an incorrectly interpreted standard from the *Yoder* case, Anderson unfairly took a numerical count of Navajo presence at and around Rainbow Bridge based on the testimony of a few plaintiffs whose status as representative of a larger group of believers and practitioners was not evaluated. Finding their presence weak, he repudiated their testimony and discredited their entire complaint by determining that Rainbow Bridge did not have "anything approaching deep, religious significance [or] . . . been intimately related to the daily living of any group or individual." Responding to land primarily as property and interpreting religion primarily through ceremonial behavior, Anderson never addressed the belief that was central to the Navajo complaint: more than terrain owned by someone, Rainbow Bridge was a living, sacred being, the object of faith and prayer for the Navajos who sought to protect it from a perceived harm and degradation consequent to government actions at Glen Canyon Dam and its reservoir. Judge Anderson's judicial responsibility to determine whether the Navajo belief qualified for protection under the First Amendment was obstructed by his own refusal to see land as anything beyond its property interest, letting its holder exclusively define its nature and use, barring all others. But even if he had allowed the Navajos without a property interest to register a cognizable claim as to the religious significance of Rainbow Bridge, his perception of religion was so skewed by quantifiable ceremonial practices that, absent a certain quota of those ceremonies, he completely disregarded the sincerity and authenticity of the primary belief that gave meaning and justification to whatever ceremonial practices were observed. Although they were only derivative expressions of and responses to the central Navajo belief in Rainbow Bridge as an embodied spiritual presence, Judge Anderson took the number of ceremonial visits to and observances at Rainbow Bridge as definitive. Determining that these secondary expressions of religious belief did not conform to some unspecified norm, he dismissed the belief itself as unworthy of constitutional protection.

Having denied the Navajos his judicial recognition of their claim, first on grounds that they lacked a property interest in the Rainbow Bridge National Monument and then on the assertion that they lacked even sufficient religious interest in it, Anderson concluded that the government interests in Glen Canyon Dam regarding water storage, power generation, and water distribution agreements among states and with the Mexican government outweighed any consideration the Navajo claim might otherwise have been given. Judge Anderson also denied the Navajo claim that Glen Canyon Dam and Lake Powell had to be subjected to an environmental impact statement and denied a Navajo request that the court halt operation of the dam and its reservoir pending the completion of such a statement. Essentially, Anderson ruled that since the Department of the Interior was still considering and formulating its position regarding the applicability of the National Environment Policy Act to, and the necessity of an environmental impact statement for, Glen Canyon Dam, the issue was not presented properly before the court because the department had not taken a position of sufficient clarity and finality to allow meaningful judicial review.

RESPONSE OF THE TENTH CIRCUIT COURT OF APPEALS

The Navajos appealed Judge Anderson's dismissal of their suit and his grant of summary judgment to the defendant federal officials. The appeal was heard by Judges Robert McWilliams, Jean Breitenstein and James Logan sitting as a panel for the full United States Court of Appeals for the Tenth Circuit. The major issue for review was Anderson's disposition of the First Amendment claim under the Free Exercise Clause. The first element the panel addressed was to reject Judge Anderson's dictate that property rights in Rainbow Bridge National Monument precluded the Navajos from any claim that the government was infringing on their practice of religion by its operation of Glen Canyon Dam and the consequent formation of Lake Powell. Without any detailed analysis, the panel simply noted that in the management of its property, the government could "not offend the Constitution." In principle, the Free Exercise Clause of the First Amendment extended to government activity on government-held lands; whether, in fact, it dictated changes in government policy with regard to those lands would depend upon further analysis of the specific claim. Government title to the land would be a factor to be weighed, but not an automatic shield to deny allegations of constitutional significance from being heard.

The court of appeals panel next corrected Judge Anderson's misinterpretation of the *Yoder* decision on what constitutes a bona fide religious claim qualifying for protection under the Free Exercise Clause of the First Amendment. The court avoided the error of adopting the language descriptive of the Amish lifestyle as a universal standard, and instead correctly delineated the simple rule that the practice allegedly infringed upon had to be based on a belief that was religious (rather than purely idiosyncratic or philosophical) and was to be sincerely held by the person asserting the infringement. Having been satisfied that the claim is a religious one, a court must then engage in a two-step process, which the court of appeals properly identified. "We first determine whether government action creates a burden on the exercise of plaintiffs' religion. . . . If such a burden is found, the action is violative of the Free Exercise Clause, unless the government establishes an interest of sufficient magnitude to override the interest claiming protection under the Free Exercise Clause. . . . Only those interests of the highest order and those not otherwise served can overbalance legitimate claims to the free exercise of religion.'"[11]

But abruptly, the court of appeals ignored the very process it had just agreed was the correct procedural analysis to follow. More specifically, it reversed the Supreme Court's two-step process and incorrectly concluded at the outset that since it found compelling government interest for building and maintaining the Glen Canyon Dam and Lake Powell as its reservoir, it would not even address the question of whether this involved an infringement on Navajo religious freedom. The court of appeals should have first decided whether the government dam and the subsequent expansion of Lake Powell constituted a burden to the Navajos' free exercise of religion. Only upon explicit determination that a burden existed should the court have proceeded to the second step and evaluated whether the nature of the governmental interest in operating and maintaining the dam was of sufficient magnitude to override the Navajos' claim for protection under the Constitution's Free Exercise Clause.

It may be argued that had the court of appeals followed the correct procedure it had stipulated, it would ultimately have concluded that the government's interests were, in fact, of such a magnitude that they would necessarily stand despite the harm inflicted upon the religious belief and practices of the Navajos. But the procedural irregularity was egregious, since it effectively repeated Judge Anderson's refusal to grant formal judicial recognition that the Navajos had suffered religious harm in the flooding of Rainbow Bridge and the surrounding land. This denial of recognition exemplifies the convergence of claims for the free exercise of religion on the one hand and the conception of land as sacred reality on the other. The court of appeals' inclination to entertain first and only the status of land and water as property used and managed for governmental purposes, and the court's consequent unwillingness to weigh an alternative valuation of the same land as a religious entity, deprived the Navajo plaintiffs of a comprehensive consideration of their complaint. The court's readiness to embrace the government's use of the land, and its insensitivity to the Navajos' perception of land as sacred (through its irresponsible reversal of the correct procedural analysis) accounts for the court's glib dismissal of government wrongdoing. The court generalized that most free-exercise claims challenged government dictates compelling citizens to violate the tenets of their religion or conditioning a benefit or right on the renunciation of a religious practice. Concluding that government prohibition or coercion was a necessary element to constitute a violation of religious freedom, the court found that the Navajos had suffered no harm. Since they were as free as anyone else to enter the national monument grounds, and since the government had not explicitly prohibited them from their religious exercises in the area of Rainbow Bridge, the government had inflicted no penalty upon Navajo belief or practice.

Even though the court of appeals had rejected the notion that without a property interest in the Rainbow Bridge area the Navajos were precluded from even making an allegation of religious infringement, the court's conclusion that they suffered no religious harm betrayed its allegiance to a property conception of land. From such a perspective, the government held and managed Rainbow Bridge as a national monument, and any responsibility it may have had to the Navajos had been met by affording them access to the area like any other members of the general public. Fairness was exclusively an issue of access, because the court's frame of reference was entirely that of the rights and privileges attaching to property, which was incapable of comprehending the heart of the Navajo claim. For the Navajos, the flooding of Rainbow Bridge and its vicinity was not merely a question of inhibiting access, but of altering, indeed of "drowning" the sacred presence that they revered and prayed to in the land itself. Unable to move beyond land as property, the appellate court's analysis not only failed to adjudicate the Navajo belief in the land's subjectivity as a living, holy reality; it failed utterly to grasp the nature of the religious harm against which the Navajos sought constitutional protection.

The court's denial of infringement against Navajo belief and practice remained evident in its response to the Navajos' request that if they could have no relief from the submersion of their sacred sites, they could yet receive "some measured accommodation to their religious interest"[12] in the form of non-Navajo tourists' behavior. Referring to Rainbow Bridge National Monument, the court noted with approval the government's "unquestionably ... strong interest in assuring public access to the natural wonder"[13] and asserted that the Navajos enjoyed the access they did only through the National Park Service's acquiescence. The court's remark was without any trace of the obvious irony that the Navajos and their ancestors had a position of priority on the land in question long before the creation of any federal park agency, and that it was precisely their desire to preserve the reverent wonder they had for Rainbow Bridge's land and water that led them to file their complaint in the face of potential tourist desecration and destruction.

Among the measures the Navajos sought from the court to mitigate noisy tourist intrusion during ceremonies or tourist disturbance of prayer offerings left at particular sites, or the defacement of canyon walls and even Rainbow Bridge itself, were prohibitions against beer drinking at the monument and closing it on reasonable notice when ceremonies were to be held. The court of appeals, however, denied any additional government policing restrictions or extraordinary permits for Navajo temporary privacy on the principle that such accommodation to Navajo belief and practice would turn the monument area into "a government-managed religious shrine,"[14] which would amount to a violation of the First Amendment's religious establishment clause. The court took no judicial notice that the land had existed as a Navajo "shrine" prior to its appropriation by the government, and the court's claim that accommodating the requests to control tourist presence and behavior would violate the Establishment Clause was without merit.

It is well-accepted constitutional jurisprudence that the government may act to accommodate religious beliefs, and the court of appeals should have been directed by several Supreme Court rulings that sanctioned that principle. In *West Virginia State Board of Education v. Barnette*[15] the Court held invalid a public school regulation mandating compulsory salute and pledge of allegiance to the American flag that did not allow for an accommodation to the religious sensibilities of Jehovah's Witnesses, who view such a practice as idolatrous. Although *Barnette* stands for broad protection of individual freedom against government attempts to prescribe political and ideological orthodoxy and coercion of citizens to conform to it, its decision more narrowly supports judicial willingness to accommodate the objections of a religious minority without fostering "an establishment" of their belief.

Likewise, *Sherbert v. Verner* substantiates the notion that not every concession to religious belief or practice amounts to a degree of government sponsorship that would trespass against the separation between religion and the state that the Establishment Clause requires. In *Sherbert*, the Supreme Court ruled that if an employer refuses to accommodate the religious needs of an employee and the employee is subsequently dismissed, the state cannot deny unemployment compensation. The court struck down a South Carolina law that effectively disqualified a member of the Seventh-day Adventist Church from receiving unemployment benefits because she had refused work on Saturday, the Sabbath day of her faith. Without providing such a believer with an exemption permitting her to refuse jobs that required her to work on Saturday and thus avoid the classification that disqualified her from unemployment payments, South Carolina impermissibly penalized her religious belief and its practice regarding its Sabbath. By so finding, the court did not establish the Seventh-day Adventist religion in South Carolina, any more than it later did for the Old Order Amish religion in *Wisconsin v. Yoder*, which permitted its adherents an exemption to that state's education law, allowing them, on religious grounds, to stop sending their children to school after the eighth grade.

Just as the plaintiffs in *Barnette, Sherbert,* and *Yoder* did not seek to have their religions favored by government action, but sought only relief from the harsh impact of government regulation as it affected their beliefs and practice, so too did the Navajos in *Badoni* seek only "some measured accommodation" that would mitigate the harm and destruction to their holy site from government-sponsored flooding and tourism. But the court of appeals panel was not guided by the Supreme Court on permissible accommodation. Instead, it characterized the Navajo petition as one seeking "affirmative action by the government," which the panel implied was an unconstitutional "advancement" of religion. Making no attempt at a comprehensive and interpretive analysis, the panel merely provided a partial statement of a three-part test that had evolved to evaluate whether particular governmental actions would violate the Establishment Clause of the First Amendment. A full articulation of the test had been stated by the Supreme Court in *Committee for Public Education and Religious Liberty v. Nyquist*,[16] in which it ruled that governmental action will survive an Establishment Clause challenge if it can be shown that the action is motivated by a secular legislative purpose, that its primary effect neither advances nor inhibits religion, and that it does not require excessive government entanglement with religious institutions and practices.

A thorough application of the test to the relief sought by the Navajos would have assured the court of appeals that the ameliorative steps they petitioned would have trespassed none of the three requirements. The National Park Service had already issued regulations for the conservation and protection of the monument area against disorderly conduct, intoxication, and possession of alcoholic beverages by minors, defacement, littering, and tampering with personal property. Except for their suggestion of a total ban on beer drinking, and the possibility of temporary closings of the monument grounds to conduct certain ceremonies, the Navajo request for controlling the impact of tourist behavior coincided completely with steps already adopted by the government as a secular legislative purpose to conserve and protect the monument grounds. If anything, the Navajos sought a more effective enforcement of these otherwise secular measures.

It was the second prong of the test that was seriously misinterpreted by the court of appeals as applied to the Navajos. The court implied that making the accommodation for better control of tourist behavior would have the primary effect of advancing Navajo religion and was thus prohibited. But the court's assumption was severely flawed by inadequate analysis. The full test was to assure that the primary effect of the contemplated government action neither advanced nor inhibited religion. The appellate court should have pursued an inquiry into the inhibition of

Navajo belief and practice that had already been suffered with the flooding of Rainbow Bridge and the submersion of other sacred sites within the canyon. The government's refusal to take more effective measures to prevent the influx of unregulated tourist activity from degrading the area and interfering with the remaining possibilities for Navajo ceremonialism and prayer would be nothing less than increased inhibition of Navajo religion. The court should have therefore concluded that failure to respond to the Navajos' request, doing nothing to modify the impact of its dam and reservoir, implicated the government in an impermissible diminishment of tribal religion. Any steps taken to avoid that inhibition would clearly not have transgressed the Establishment Clause.

Finally, the court should have completed its review by noting that no "excessive government entanglement" with Navajo religion would result from acceding to the measures they had requested. Having initially entangled itself with the religious sensibility of the Navajos by submerging the lands of Rainbow Bridge, the government further implicated itself by facilitating the tourist industry's pleasure-boating entertainments within the sacred precincts. Given its initial construction of the dam and subsequent development of the area as a tourist attraction, it would have been facetious for the government to argue that any attempts to ameliorate tourist intrusion on Navajo religious ceremonies and prayer would have been an "entanglement" prohibited by the Establishment Clause.

The appellate court's correct and comprehensive application and analysis of the three-part test would have shown, then, that the relief sought by the Navajos would not have transgressed the Establishment Clause. Rather than demonstrating an illicit support or sponsorship for Navajo religion, steps taken by the government to provide more effective control of tourist behavior were appropriate accommodations to Navajo belief and practice without which the government would compound the harm already inflicted by its flooding and subsequent tourist development of the Navajo sacred site. The appellate court's failure to pursue a complete judicial review of the Establishment Clause issue was matched by its serious misapplication of a familiar line of freedom of assembly and freedom of expression cases.

The court had already erred by its irregular determination that the government had a compelling state interest in the construction and maintenance of Glen Canyon Dam and its reservoir, which precluded the court from addressing in its primary, proper order the fact that the government was burdening the free exercise of Navajo religion with its project. Having earlier betrayed its inclination to entertain first and only the status of land and water as property used and managed for governmental purposes, the court again displayed that tendency by finding a right of tourists to the recreational use of the Rainbow Bridge Monument superior to, and incompatible with, the religious interests the Navajos sought to preserve. Since the court provided no justification for that conclusion, no guidance for weighing and judging the competing values of recreational tourist access on the one hand and customary religious belief and practice on the other, its position was merely consistent with its bent toward exclusive government usage and development of its property interest in the land. Favoring the original government interest for constructing Glen Canyon Dam as compelling, the court of appeals extended its approval to the subsequent development of Lake Powell and Rainbow Bridge National Monument as tourist attractions with similar elevated significance. Implying that tourist access could not be qualified by government regulation to minimize interference with the practice of Navajo religion, the court simply cited, without explanation or application, several Supreme Court cases that the appellate court uniformly construed to support a broad one-sentence generality that the "exercise of First Amendment freedoms may not be asserted to deprive the public of its normal use of an area."[17] In fact, the cases more precisely illustrate the willingness of the Supreme Court to protect freedom of expression and assembly from governmental attempts to censor or otherwise suppress such freedom through overly broad statutes against disturbing the peace or through excessive discretion given to officials granting or withholding permits for use of a public forum.

Thus, in *Shuttlesworth v. City of Birmingham*[18] the Court held unconstitutional a city parade ordinance that directed a city commission to issue a permit "unless in its judgment the public welfare, peace, safety, health, decency, good order, morals, or convenience require that it be refused." The Court struck the ordinance because it gave unbridled and virtually absolute power to the municipal agency controlling who enjoyed public expression through parades. Similarly, in *Cox v. Louisiana*[19] the Court found that a Louisiana breach of the peace statute was unconstitutional in its overly broad scope, allowing people to be punished merely for peacefully expressing unpopular views. The Court also ruled against a Baton Rouge parade ordinance that prohibited all street assemblies and parades, but that was selectively enforced by the authorities at their total discretion, allowing some to march and others not. Condemning such a practice, the Court declared that "it is clearly unconstitutional to enable a public official to determine which expressions of view will be permitted and which will not or to engage in invidious discrimination among persons or groups either by use of a statute providing a system of broad discretionary licensing power or, as in this case, the equivalent of such a system by selective enforcement of an extremely broad prohibitory statute."[20] Previously, the Court in *Niemotko v. Maryland*[21] reversed the conviction of Jehovah's Witnesses for holding a meeting without a permit on the ground that the denial of the permit had rested not on fear of disorder, but rather on official dislike of the Witnesses and their views. Finally, the city ordinance involved in the case of *Hague v. CIO*[22] required a permit for meetings on public ground, the permit to be refused by the licensing official only for the purpose of preventing riots, disturbances, or disorderly assemblies. But the facts left no doubt in the Court's mind that the licensing power had become an instrument for the arbitrary suppression of the free expression of views on national affairs and politics. The Court held again that such arbitrary suppression could not be given to licensing officials, no matter what cover of law they claimed to act under.

Although ostensibly recognizing the importance of streets and parks as critical, appropriate places for the public expression and communication of ideas, the cases cited by the court of appeals do not identify an unfettered right of recreational access to public lands, exclusive of other First Amendment freedoms. Much more directly, they condemn government power when it is used selectively to curtail or inhibit the exercise of constitutional freedoms as equally possessed and enjoyed by all. Applied to the Navajo plaintiffs, the cases do not support government refusal to protect them in the exercise of their religion. The government, having failed to prevent the inundation of their sacred sites, altering their physical state and rendering them partially inaccessible, compounded the harm by facilitating and encouraging the presence of tourists whose behavior, at times, further interfered with Navajo ceremony and prayer. Rejecting the Navajos' request for a more effective enforcement of the park service's own regulations, in the name of not disturbing a tourist right of recreational access to the area, was, however, an inconsistency that perpetuated religious harm and was a clear abuse of governmental power, condemned by the very cases that the court of appeals cited. To claim that steps taken to mitigate tourist interference with Navajo religion would violate an overriding tourist right of access was to selectively disregard the rules already enacted to constrain certain tourist activities within the monument grounds. If prohibitions against possession of alcohol by minors, defacement, littering, and tampering with property did not offend tourist access, the Navajo request for their enforcement was no more intrusive.

Failing to note the basic compatibility between current park service regulations and the kinds of relief the Navajos requested, the court of appeals wrongly implied that the Navajos sought the complete exclusion of tourists altogether. Although they had suggested that the monument grounds be temporarily closed to the public on infrequent occasions to ensure privacy for their prayers and ceremonies, the Navajos plainly stated that they sought "only some measured accommodation to their religious interest, not a wholesale bar to use of Rainbow Bridge by all others."[23] It was a serious failure by the appellate panel to correctly hear the Navajos' request for temporary closure of the monument grounds as only one of several possible options (the others being chiefly the enforcement of park service regulations) for the government to provide some accommodation to their religious interests. The panel suggested that the Navajos' exclusion of all others for indefinite periods would jeopardize the monument as a public forum for the exchange of ideas. But the panel's lofty characterization of the monument as such, through the borrowed phraseology from an unrelated Supreme Court decision from 1939, was disingenuous. The reality of Lake Powell and Rainbow Bridge National Monument as a national recreational area, sustaining a significant volume of boating and other outdoor activity entertainments for an increased tourist population, had little in common with the kinds of political activities referred to in *Hague v. CIO*, despite the appellate panel's pretensions. The excerpted passage read that "[w]herever the title of streets and parks may rest, they have immemorially been held in trust for the use of the public and, time out of mind, have been used for purposes of assembly, communicating thoughts between citizens, and discussing public questions. ... [T]he privilege of a citizen of the United States to use the streets and parks for communication of views on national questions may be regulated in the interest of all . . . but it must not, in the guise of regulation, be abridged or denied."[24] To imply, as the appellate panel did, that the Navajo request for some accommodation to their religious privacy would threaten the status of Rainbow Bridge National Monument as an important forum for civic discourse was to distort on the one hand the nature of the relief sought by the Navajos, and to ignore on the other the apolitical recreational character of Lake Powell and the monument area. The possibility of an infrequent delayed opening or an early closing of the monument grounds to allow for Navajo prayer and ritual might temporarily alter one's hiking path or navigational course without ever infringing on the communication of thoughts and the discussion of public questions insinuated by the court of appeals.

Despite its initial rebuke of the district court's ruling that the Navajos could not even make a claim based on the Free Exercise Clause of the First Amendment without a property interest in Rainbow Bridge, the court of appeals panel soon exposed its own incapacity to entertain a notion of land and water other than as a property conception. The court correctly stated the two-step process for resolution of free-exercise claims beginning with the determination of whether government action creates a burden for the exercise of religion. If such a burden exists, only then does the court consider whether the government might have such a compelling state interest in the offending activity that it will override the religious interest seeking protection. Impermissibly, the court reversed the procedure, asserting that the government interest in maintaining a multi-state water storage, irrigation, and power-generation project was so compelling that the court wouldn't even address the question of whether the project infringed on Navajo religious freedom.

Taken by the status of land and water as property used and managed for governmental purposes, the court of appeals refused any further consideration of the Navajos' understanding of Rainbow Bridge as a living, sacred reality. Although the court properly reiterated the Navajo belief in the bridge and other canyon formations as protective, life-sustaining beings, responsive to prayers and ceremonial offerings, it refused to make a formal determination that in the light of such a belief, the government-sponsored dam, reservoir, and tourist population infringed on the free exercise of Navajo religion. With its procedural reversal, the court, in effect, denied full judicial recognition of the religious harm suffered by the Navajos. It duly registered their complaint, arising from their belief in the religious significance of Rainbow Bridge and its canyon, only to dismiss its gravity as unworthy of a sustained evaluation against the competing property interests of the government to use and develop the land and reservoir waters as it chose. Preemptively deciding the government interest to be compelling, and thus overriding the Navajo interest, a measure of the court's failure to adequately comprehend the nature of the religious claim was its trivial contention that since the Navajos were as free to enter the monument grounds as everyone else and were free to engage in ceremonies in the area, there was no religious deprivation. From within the confines of its perspective of government land use and development as compelling, no judicial consideration was reserved for the submerged and muted beings under the waters of Lake Powell, the sacred presences manifesting to Navajo faith their healing, protective, rain-bestowing power through the sandstone contours of Rainbow Bridge and other canyon formations. Navajo access to the monument and the ability to engage in religious exercises were hollow freedoms and the mere peripherals of Navajo religion, which was evoked and animated by the experience of life-sustaining sacred power from within the earth of Rainbow Bridge and its canyon. Ironically, the court of appeals itself acknowledged the evocative nature of "this natural wonder"[25] without permitting itself to further conclude that its wondrous being was the heart of Navajo belief that the Navajos sought to protect from the threatening waters of Lake Powell and the subsequent improprieties of an uninformed, recreation-minded public.

The court's unwillingness to engage in a more comprehensive and profound disclosure of Navajo religion was a function of its premature decision that whatever the Navajo belief, the government interest to use and develop the land was paramount. The court's orientation remained as such throughout its strained and meager attempt to raise the Establishment Clause as an absolute barrier against any accommodation to Navajo religious interests seeking some measured relief from the interference, and even degradation, from certain tourist behavior. Finally, the court's fixation with the government's property interest in land as its sole frame of reference led it to brusquely disregard the guidance it might have taken from the American Indian Religious Freedom Act. Like the court in *Sequoyah v. Tennessee Valley Authority*, the Court of Appeals for the Tenth Circuit merely alluded to the act's name, making no attempt to inform its decision through an engaged discussion with its policy concerns. Together, *Sequoyah* and *Badoni* became the disturbing precedents upon which a federal court in the District of Columbia would next place its reliance.

3

Wilson v. Block: *Skiing the Slopes of a Sacred Mountain*

If the *Sequoyah* and *Badoni* cases witnessed the sacrifice of sacred land to the thrall of government-sponsored water projects, the San Francisco Peaks of northeastern Arizona, one of the most revered mountains in the religious landscape of both the Hopi and Navajo Tribes, succumbed to a government-subsidized, privately operated recreational resort.

Since the boundaries of the Navajo reservation extend through northeastern New Mexico, northeastern Arizona and southeastern Utah, Rainbow Bridge stands in one of its more remote reaches. The San Francisco Peaks, on the other hand, rising some 12,633 feet above the surrounding Colorado Plateau and just north of Flagstaff, is the dominant geological formation visible to the majority of Navajo reservation dwellers living in northeastern Arizona and can be seen from all Hopi villages, whose entire reservation lies within the same general area of Arizona. Each tribe has its distinct understanding of the Peaks, which is a single mountain where ancient volcanic activity, followed by periods of glaciation and steady erosion, carved several different summits or peaks, giving rise to the mountain's common designation as the San Francisco Peaks.

To the Hopi, the Peaks are the home of the Kachinas, spiritual beings who assist the Creator as his emissaries to humanity. For some six months of the year, the Kachinas travel to the Hopi villages and participate with the tribe in the various religious ceremonies and rituals referred to as the Kachina Cycle. Then, beginning in late July or early August and extending through mid-winter, the Kachinas return to the Peaks for the next six months and take up residence. The Hopi people believe that the Kachinas' activities on the Peaks give rise to the rain and snow storms that nurture the villages with life-sustaining water and food and thus, their happiness, health and well-being. No other place is more sacred than the Kachina Peaks, which is the object of annual pilgrimages by Hopi elders and other tribal members who deposit prayer offerings of eagle feathers, turquoise, and other ritual objects at innumerable sites. Moreover, eagle feathers and fir boughs are prayerfully gathered each year from the Peaks for their extensive liturgical use during the elaborate ceremonialism that defines the six-month-long Kachina Cycle.

To the Navajos, the San Francisco Peaks is one of four sacred mountains marking the boundaries of their ancestral homeland; together, the four mountains form a traditional "hogan" or house, protecting and sheltering the entire Navajo nation. But the San Francisco Peaks are especially revered as the physical embodiment of one of the Holy Ones or Navajo gods, with various parts forming the head, shoulders, and knees of a body reclining and facing to the east, and the trees, plants, rocks, and earth making up the skin. The Navajos pray directly to the Peaks as a living, sacred being to whom they are intimately related. In the words of Faye Tso, a Navajo medicine woman, "[The Peaks] are spiritually connected to every living Navajo. From our feet, to our legs, to our shoulders, to our head, we are connected to the peaks."[1] That vital continuity between the Peaks and the Navajo people is symbolically attested to in the custom of medicine men and women placing soil from the Peaks in the medicine pouches they carry. In the microcosm of the soil and the stones and plants that may likewise be gathered from the Peaks and placed in the pouch, the sacred power and energy of the Peaks is made present for the healing prayers and ceremonies that are central concerns of Navajo religious experience. Some eighty different plants that grow on the Peaks are known to be gathered for such ritual use[2] and are often later placed back on the Peaks in the form of offerings at the conclusion of the healing ceremonies. The Peaks are endowed with life and are called upon not only for the blessings of material and physical well-being, but for the restoration of psychic harmony and rejuvenation for those suffering mental and "inner pain."[3] But the sanctity of the Peaks and the healing energy they bestow does not immunize them from harm. Precisely because they are a living, organic entity, the Peaks can suffer a loss of vitality from damage to their integrity.

Thus, the threat of a privately operated ski resort of 777 acres on the high elevation lands of the San Francisco Peaks would have been a significant expansion over the modest facility that had insinuated itself from its initial presence during the middle 1930s when a small ski club from Flagstaff began using an old cabin as a base camp on a lower prairie of the

Peaks. Then, in 1937 a new base camp was built higher up on the mountain and was used until it was destroyed by fire in 1956. At that time it was restored as a modest lodge. Until 1958, when a Poma lift was installed, a rope tow was the only mechanism for moving skiers up the slope. A single chairlift was installed in 1962. But in April 1977, Northland Recreation, Inc., which had obtained permits from the U.S. Forest Service, proposed a substantial alteration, affecting the western shoulder of the Peaks. Pursuant to the plan, the one chairlift would be increased to five, raising the lift-carrying capacity by 441 percent. In addition to the clear-cutting of trees necessary to construct the lifts themselves, many new acres of slopes were to be cleared and recontoured, increasing the slope carrying capacity to 233 percent of its previous level. A new lodge facility would be constructed to accommodate the wining and dining of more than 900 people at one time. The dirt road that had previously been used for access to the skiing area would now be a widened paved one, and there would be an eight-acre parking area. To the Navajos, the physical changes wrought to the structure of the Peaks themselves by such an expansive development was likened to a painful incision to the human body or more frequently, to a cancer growing within the Peaks' body.[4] Such analogies expressed the organic integrity of the Peaks as a living, sacred being, whose reconfiguration to accommodate the envisioned ski resort would distort its essential identity as a protective, healing presence bestowing life and energy on the people who for generations had sung and prayed to its inner reality.

For the Hopi, the ski development represented an insulting commercialization and trivialization of the home of the Kachinas, which threatened to be overwhelmed by people whose recreational pursuits would so secularize the Peaks that, in time, Hopi society would no longer be able to sustain its immemorial belief that the Peaks were in fact their "single most important shrine and sacred place."[5] What had been throughout their history a place of prayer and pilgrimage would, for future generations of Hopi, be incapable of projecting its sacred identity among the skiing throngs and would ultimately become not merely a victim of desecration, but an object of fantasy. To preserve the holiness of the San Francisco Peaks was for the Hopi simultaneously an act of religious devotion toward the Kachinas and the instinct for cultural survival: the coherence between the Peaks as home of the Kachinas and the self-identity of the Hopi as a distinct people was exact. It was that congruency between the religious significance of the Peaks and Hopi self-understanding that animated the concern of Abbott Sekaquaptewa, the chairman of the Hopi Indian Tribe, in his remarks opposing Northland's proposal:

It is my opinion that in the long run if the [ski] expansion is permitted, we will not be able successfully to teach our people that this is a sacred place. If the [present] ski resort remains or is expanded, our people will not accept the view that this is the sacred home of the Kachinas. The basis of our existence as a society will become a mere fairy tale to our people. If our people no longer possess this long-held belief and way of life, which will inevitably occur with the continued presence of the ski resort, then it follows they will also no longer possess the entire Kachina belief. This will have a direct and negative impact upon our religious practices. The destruction of these practices will also destroy our present way of life and culture.[6]

In their separate suits filed on March 2, 1981, the Hopi Indian Tribe and the Navajo Medicinemen's Association, representing the combined religious interests of some 170,000 Hopi and Navajo tribal members, sought to protect the intrinsic sanctity of the San Francisco Peaks in its integrity. Whether the mountain was hallowed by the presence of the Kachinas in the experience of the Hopis, or was itself the earthen body of a divine being as understood by the Navajo tradition, the tribes sued to protect the object of their religious belief in its entirety and wholeness. Their prayers and rituals were directed to the Peaks as a sacred entity in its full 75,000 acres. To them, the notion of segregating a discrete 777-acre parcel as the reserve of a private corporation that would commercially develop the area as a recreational playground was as foreign as it was repugnant. The organic conception that informed their religious understanding perceived the Peaks in the totality of its land mass as one indivisible reality—thus, the earlier noted allusions to the ski resort as a wound inflicted upon, or a cancerous growth within, the holy body or sacred residence of the mountain. Central to the Hopi and Navajo complaints was their common intuition that the impact of Northland's expanded development proposal would not be circumscribed to the physical dimensions of the allotted acreage, but would desecrate the fundamental integrity of the entire San Francisco Peaks venerated in the ancient mythologies and contemporary practices of the two tribal religions. In addition, they protested the actual ways in which their religious practices had suffered from the increased use of the ski facility over the years and throughout the seasons not only by ski enthusiasts, but also from those who, during summer months, used the facility's access road and lift for hiking on the mountain.

The tribes specified the disturbance they suffered in making their pilgrimages to the Peaks and their prayer upon them in requisite silence and solitude. In addition, they said, the increased recreational use of the mountain interfered with the ritualized gathering of herbs, eagle feathers, tree boughs, stones, soil, rain, spring water, dew, and flower pollen that was used for prayer offerings and for healing and other liturgical celebrations.

It was not only that the ceremonial context for gathering such materials from the Peaks was jeopardized by the casual presence of those seeking leisure rather than religion from the slopes of the mountain. Their increasing numbers threatened the viability of the Peaks as the habitat of certain fauna and flora and thus their very availability for Hopi and Navajo ritual use. Then, too, there was the serious problem of harm done to the Hopi prayer shrines set up at innumerable sites on the mountain. However discreet their placement, they were often disturbed by the unwitting curiosity of recreationists attracted by the bundled offerings of eagle feathers, turquoise, and other Indian artifacts. Additionally, outright looting of shrines was not unusual and was admitted to be a major problem by one of the government's own expert witnesses. Although confined to his observations about the plight of the Hopi mountain shrines, his remarks indicate that transgressions against Navajo as well as Hopi religious practices that had been alleged in their complaints would be exacerbated by the influx of people expected from the proposed expanded ski resort.

> A major cause for concern is that any increase of traffic on the mountain will lead to more desecration of the shrines than heretofore. The concern is a real one. White people seem to be especially attracted to Hopi shrines and loot them with no compunction. I have been present when prayer wands, stolen from the ice cave shrine by a Forest Service employee, were accepted and catalogued by the Museum of Northern Arizona. . . . The Hopis fear that increased use of the area will put the shrines at greater risk and that they cannot trust those whose job it is to protect them. . . . These shrines *cannot* be identified and fenced. To do so would attract looters as a red cape before a bull. Instead, use of the whole inner basin [of the Peaks] must be severely restricted and carefully monitored.[7]

The Hopi and Navajo complaints named as defendants John R. Block, secretary of agriculture; R. Max Peterson, chief forester of the Unites States Forest Service; the United States Forest Service; and the United States of America. Filed in the Federal District Court for the District of Columbia, the cases were assigned to Judge Charles R. Richey, who consolidated both cases with a third filed by Richard F. Wilson and Jean Wilson, owners of a private ranch on the western slopes of the San Francisco Peaks who likewise opposed the further commercial expansion on the mountain. But Judge Richey permitted the Wilsons, who were non-Indians, to enter arguments in support of the Hopi and Navajo religious claims only in a capacity of *amicus curiae*. He held that there was no compelling reason to allow them to litigate the constitutional rights of the tribes, who were in the best position to assert their own case before the court. Shortly after the initiation of the suit, Northland Recreation, Inc. was granted permission to intervene as a defendant.

But if Northland had designed and was prepared to invest in its "master plan" for the Snow Bowl ski resort, it was the U.S. Forest Service and the Department of Agriculture that, by granting permission to the corporation, implicated the stricture of the First Amendment under whose Free Exercise Clause the Hopis and Navajos sought to protect their sacred mountain and their religious practices addressed to and performed on it. In 1898, by executive authority, the area of the Peaks had been designated as the San Francisco Mountain Forest Reserve, and in 1907 it was incorporated into the Coconino National Forest, currently consisting of some 1,835,767 acres in Arizona. Both tribes contended, however, that prior to such designations, the United States government was on notice that the Peaks had religious significance to both Hopis and Navajos, who had revered the Peaks for centuries prior to their incorporation into the national forest system. It was their contention that had the United States been faithful to its duty as guardian and trustee of the Indians, had it protected their religions and educated them in their rights, the Snow Bowl ski facility would never have been built in the first place. In the early 1930s when recreational skiing first began on the Peaks, it was still the policy of the Bureau of Indian Affairs to prohibit Indian religious ceremonies as criminal offenses, and it was not until a decade after the Forest Service constructed the first road and ski lodge on the Peaks that Indians were accorded the right to vote. So to suggest, as Northland later did in the litigation, that the Hopis and Navajos were delinquent in initially resisting skiing activities on the mountain reflected a callous ignorance or disregard for the historical disabilities that hampered any formal legal actions they might have taken to prevent the profanation of their holy Peaks.

In fact, at the time Northland submitted its plan for the expanded resort, Congress had not yet passed the American Indian Religious Freedom Act, which, however lame its protection later proved, did acknowledge that Native American religious experience was often intimately related to sacred sites and had suffered infringement from, among other things, government policies and actions with regard to such sites. Yet even before such legislation, the Hopis and Navajos protested in the late 1960s and early 1970s the proposal by Summit Properties, Inc., who then held the permit to operate the ski facilities, to build a lift on the Peaks and condominiums nearby. Joining with others, their opposition was sufficiently intense to halt the necessary zoning approval, at which point Summit divested itself of the permit which was then acquired by Northland Recreation in April 1977. Despite the obvious religious objections that the Hopis and Navajos registered in response to Summit's designs, Northland submitted to the Forest Service in July 1977 its "master concept plan" that envisioned the expansion of the road bringing skiers to the Peaks' slopes, a multi-acre parking area; a ski lodge whose restaurant would accommodate 900 patrons, more ski lifts, and widened ski slopes.

Pursuant to the National Environmental Policy Act, the Forest Service conducted a public hearing and comment period, soliciting alternatives to Northland's plan. Following that process, which included the responses of various Indian tribes, groups, and individuals, the Forest Service assessment team identified six proposed alternatives ranging from the one favored by the Hopis and Navajos for the complete elimination of all artificial structures from the Peaks, including all skiing facilities, to the full development scheme as proposed by Northland Recreation. The additional four alternatives provided for various degrees of increased development and expansion of the current ski facilities, roads, ski lifts, and ski trails.

On June 23, 1978, the Forest Service filed a draft Environmental Impact Statement evaluating the six alternatives and until the end of September solicited public response to it. The forest supervisor of the Coconino National Forest issued his decision on February 27, 1979, adopting a "Preferred Alternative" plan different from any of the six that had been set forth originally, but it nevertheless allowed for extensive development and exploitation of the Peaks, substantially altering the western shoulder of the mountain. It authorized the cutting of fifty acres of forest for new ski runs, the construction of a whole new ski lodge, reconstruction of the existing chairlift with the addition of three new ones, improved restroom facilities, the pavement and widening of the previously dirt access road; and the approval of the eight-acre parking lot.

When the Navajo Medicinemen's Association and other groups filed an appeal on March 27, 1979, with the regional forester in protest, he reversed the decision of the forest supervisor and ordered that development plans be halted. He determined that the maintenance of essentially a status quo situation, allowing only for repair and replacement of existing facilities as required by obsolescence, public safety, and deterioration, would best balance the competing needs of the Native American religions and recreational interests of the public. He also concluded that the Snow Bowl, although one of the few ski areas in Arizona, was not and could never be made into an outstanding sporting area, and therefore declined to expand it further. But Northland appealed to R. Max Peterson, chief forester of the Forest Service who, on December 31, 1980, reinstated the decision of the forest supervisor to allow development according to the "Preferred Alternative." When, in a letter of January 9, 1981, John R. Block, secretary of agriculture, declined to exercise his discretion to review the matter, the Hopis and Navajos had exhausted their administrative remedies and filed their complaint with the district court.

Since Congress had passed the American Indian Religious Freedom Act during the time in which they were administratively contesting Northland's and then the forest supervisor's development plans, the Hopis and Navajos formally charged that the government, through the agency of the Forest Service, by allowing the expanded ski resort to be constructed on the Peaks, had violated their First Amendment right to the free exercise of their religion, as well as the recently enacted legislation on their behalf. In addition, they alleged that the government's approbation of recreational development on their sacred mountain violated the fiduciary duties owed to Indians by the United States; that it violated the Endangered Species Act by threatening the existence of *Senecio franciscanus*—a yellow-flowered plant growing at the top of the Peaks; that it violated the National Historic Preservation Act regarding the effects that the expanded ski resort would have on two National Register historic sites within the mountain's vicinity; that it violated the National Wilderness Act by preventing the area's future discretionary classification as "wilderness"; that it violated the Multiple-Use Sustained-Yield Act by arbitrarily favoring the local economy and recreational desires of nearby Flagstaff, Arizona, when considering the uses of the Peaks over its religious significance to the tribes; that it violated the National Environmental Policy Act because the final Environmental Impact Statement failed to adequately address the environmental consequences of the proposed expansion with respect to threatened plant species, Native American religion and culture, the economy, and certain historic and cultural sites. Finally, the tribes charged that the decision of the Forest Service transgressed the Administrative Procedure Act in that it revealed governmental bias and prejudice in favor of further commercialization of the Peaks.

RESPONSE OF THE DISTRICT COURT

Relying on the *Sequoyah* and *Badoni* decisions, Judge Richey dismissed the fundamental issue of the Hopi and Navajo claim that the government's sponsorship of a privately developed and commercially operated ski resort on the San Francisco Peaks infringed on their constitutionally protected freedom of religion. He concluded that notwithstanding the sincerity of the Hopi belief in the Peaks as the home of the Kachinas and the Navajo belief that they were the very body of a divine being, the recreational development would not unconstitutionally burden their exercise of religion. Despite both Hopi and Navajo testimonies to the contrary, Judge

Richey denied that any judicially recognizable harm was inflicted on the two tribal traditions by the Northland project. In his opinion, the judge relied exclusively on the statements of two non-Indian anthropologists who testified as experts on Hopi and Navajo culture for the government. From their affidavits he concluded "that as long as the Indians have continued access to the Peaks, the Snow Bowl [ski resort] will not impinge upon the continuation of all essential ritual practices."[8] Although this was flatly contradicted by specific testimony in Hopi and Navajo affidavits and ignored by him, Richey's reductive delimitation of religion to "ritual practices" was the more egregious and consequential error.

The tribes did, of course, seek to protect their ability to collect soil, plants, eagle feathers, fir boughs, and other liturgical elements from the Peaks, as well as to preserve the shrines and pilgrimage routes on the mountain and the ability to pray and conduct ceremonies on its slopes. But their primary concern was to preserve the integral holiness of the Peaks as the sacred residence of the Hopi Kachinas and the living, terrestrial body of a Navajo deity. Whatever practices were conducted on the mountain by the two tribes were evoked by their joint recognition of its fundamental spiritual nature. To protect tribal religion was to prevent harm to the presence residing within or embodied by the mountain, without which the variety of Hopi and Navajo prayers and ceremonial activities would be meaningless. According to their testimony, that living presence could be driven from its sanctuary, as would be the case with the Kachinas, or its dynamism and healing vitality could itself be diminished and weakened, according to Navajo belief. Both threats were posed by the government-approved commercial development that would promote and exploit the mountain as a recreational resource, altering its character and populating its slopes not with reverence and devotion, but the thrill of the down slope run. Although the Peaks had long accommodated opportunities for public hiking, camping, horseback riding, and climbing (which the tribes made no attempt to terminate), the expanded ski resort and its facilities would bear such defining impact upon the mountain as a center for recreational sport and its attendant leisures of eating and drinking that it would distort all semblance of its original spiritual identity that had elicited generations of Hopi and Navajo prayers, pilgrimages, and rituals. The latter were tribal responses to the holy presence abiding within or manifesting as the mountain that the Hopis and Navajos sought to protect from becoming a state-sponsored, for-profit, sport and recreation playground. It was their argument that the Free Exercise Clause of the First Amendment prohibited the government from so altering the character of the San Francisco Peaks as to render absurd any religious practices directed toward them. No compelling state interest could justify trivializing the holiness of the mountain for the entertainment pursuits of those who could afford the resort's facilities.

But Judge Richey's understanding of religion as protected by the First Amendment was severely limited. It utterly failed to comprehend the numinous dimension of the Peaks as the fundamental religious experience of the Hopis and Navajos, which in turn evoked and gave definition to the multiple prayer and ritual behaviors conducted on or in relation to the sacred mountain. Richey artificially sundered that range of Hopi and Navajo ceremonial response from the spiritual reality that their shared belief perceived as the inherent identity of the mountain. It was that religious identity of the Peaks that the two tribes sought to preserve inviolate from government-sanctioned secularization. Their prayers, pilgrimages, shrines, and rituals made no sense apart from the integrity of the Peaks as a sacred reality: to distort the latter was to render the former meaningless. Yet because Judge Richey was incapable of valuating the status of the Peaks as anything other than governmental property, he in effect severed the vital connection between the Peaks as the primary religious entity and the various tribal practices directed toward and intrinsically related to it. With the Peaks reduced to the category of mere property, he was free to dispatch the Hopi and Navajo claim that the government was unconstitutionally harming the free exercise of their religion by its promotion of the ski resort development.

Seizing on the recent precedents of the *Badoni* and *Sequoyah* decisions, the judge quickly concluded that the government had imposed no burden on tribal religion because the operation of the resort had "no coercive effect . . . against the practice of their religion."[9] Since he had stripped the Peaks of their religious significance to their sole condition as government property, what remained of tribal religion were the variety of Hopi and Navajo "practices" which, because they were not prohibited by the government, were not violated. So long as the government had made no explicit prohibitions against any of the Indian activities in or around the San Francisco Peaks, no infringement on their religious exercise had been suffered. Outrageously, the judge even insinuated, based on a government allegation of a single incident that was repudiated by the Navajo plaintiffs, that the Indians as a whole had actually benefited by using the ski lift to gain easier access to higher elevations of the Peaks to conduct their prayer.[10] With equal impropriety, he implied that the tribes' apparent willingness to tolerate skiing activity for almost fifty years, as well as the placement of natural gas, telephone, electric transmission lines, water tanks for stocks, along with cinder extraction and mining that had been conducted for almost thirty years on the Peaks, suggested no harm to their religious beliefs and practices, but instead, a capacity to coexist along with the development of the mountain. Callously ignoring the historical realities that had hampered their legal recourse in the past, as already noted above, the judge apparently ignored the face of the tribal complaints, which stated their religious objections not only to an expanded ski resort, but even to the one already there.

Falling comfortably back on *Sequoyah v. TVA*, the judge noted that there, the Sixth Circuit ruled that the complete submersion of the Little Tennessee Valley basin, claimed to be sacred to the Cherokees, did not unconstitutionally infringe on their religious exercise, since an insufficient showing had been made of the valley's "centrality or indispensability" to Cherokee religious observances. Revealing how thoroughly inadequate was his understanding of land as sacred, Judge Richey, relying on the Sixth Circuit in its *Sequoyah* decision, asserted that the Hopis and Navajos had insufficiently shown that the 777-acre site of the expanded ski resort was "central or indispensable to their religion."[11] Like the Sixth Circuit, Judge Richey's perception of Indian land was focused through the sole lens of government property. Any notion of the land itself as a numinous, sacred reality went unrecognized through the controlling, monolithic paradigm of property. Thus, claims about the religious character of land were interpreted as questions about human religious behavior (ceremonies, rituals, prayers, pilgrimages) conducted on, or in relation to, government-owned property and the limits to which the government could interfere with those religious behaviors by restricting access to or otherwise disposing of the property in question.

Since the integrity of the San Francisco Peaks as a sacred reality did not figure in his primary conception of it, Richey looked to whether the religious activities of either the Hopis or Navajos would be infringed upon by the proposed ski resort development. Because the Forest Service, in its modified acceptance of Northland Recreation's plan, had not prohibited the tribes from the Peaks; had not prevented them from collecting soil, tree boughs, stones, or any other objects from the Peaks; and had not prevented them from making pilgrimages to and praying upon the Peaks, the Forest Service had not violated the Free Exercise Clause of the First Amendment with respect to Hopi and Navajo religion. Since their religions could be practiced on any other area of the Peaks, Judge Richey deemed that the 777-acre section for the Snow Bowl ski resort was not sufficiently "central or indispensable" to their religion. He opined that compared with the Cherokees in the *Sequoyah* case who suffered the complete inundation of their sacred land and thus, all accessibility to it, the Hopis and Navajos would suffer minimal loss. The notion that they were enduring "mental and emotional anguish"[12] at having to watch the progressive development and commercialization of their most sacred mountain, impacting the very heart of their religious experience, was lost on Judge Richey. His primary understanding of the San Francisco Peaks as property cast the tribal attempt to prevent their further desecration as an impermissible threat under the guise of the First Amendment to deprive the government of its full possessory interest to dispose of the locale as it chose. Seriously mischaracterizing the tribal complaint against government subsidization for a privately operated, commercially run ski resort as a demand to restrict all public access to the Peaks, the judge exposed his allegiance to protecting the government's proprietary interest in the mountain. Referring to the Indian plaintiffs, he wrote: "They are essentially claiming that anyone asserting a religious interest in government property, albeit a sincere one, has a constitutional right to demand that the government grant them access to it, yet restrict the rights of the public to, and any development of, this property in order to facilitate the exercise of their religious beliefs. This court will not extend the First Amendment to such limits."[13]

That same commitment to government property as the fundamental legal status of the Peaks, raised by Judge Richey against the Free Exercise Clause that had been invoked by the tribes to protect them from commercial development, permitted him to summon the Establishment Clause as further rationale to dismiss their suit. Belonging to the government, which had annexed and incorporated them into the Coconino National Forest in 1907, the San Francisco Peaks had been shorn of their preeminent religious identity bestowed upon them from within the ancient beliefs and customs of the Hopi and Navajo traditions. Granting judicial recognition only to their comparatively recent status as federally held land, Richey, invoking the *Badoni* decision, charged that the Indians sought to turn government property into a restricted tribal religious shrine. Just as the *Badoni* court had done with Rainbow Bridge, Richey ignored the testimony of an ancient history that had long defined the San Francisco Peaks as the sacred residence of Hopi Kachinas and the very body of a Navajo deity; the Peaks were active tribal shrines both long before and at the time of their enclosure by the federal government. Richey asserted that if the government refrained from subsidizing the further secularization of the Peaks by denying Northland's development permit, it would be tantamount to affirmative action on behalf of Native American religions, and thus, prohibited by the Establishment Clause of the First Amendment. Such an interpretation reflected the thrall with which the notion of federal property exercised its myopic control over judicial judgment. Incapable of validating the Peaks' religious identity, long predating their 1907 redefinition as national forest land, Judge Richey interpreted the Hopi and Navajo request as a demand to create a religious shrine on government property; instead, their claim was to prevent the government from destroying an already existing, long-venerated shrine within the tribes' religious landscape. Far from seeking any affirmative action or special benefit from the federal government, the Hopis and Navajos simply sought the freedom to worship their sacred mountain as they had done before it had ever been acquired by the government, or before the territory of Arizona had ever come under the jurisdiction of the United States, or even before the founding of its government. That historical perspective was lost on Richey, however, since his fundamental orientation toward the Peaks was determined by their status as federal property.

Having dispatched their constitutional claims, the judge next responded to the tribal argument that the Forest Service had violated the American Indian Religious Freedom Act (AIRFA) in authorizing the expansion of the skiing facilities on the San Francisco Peaks. Although the Cherokees in the *Sequoyah* case and the Navajos in the *Badoni* litigation had each relied on AIRFA, neither of the courts in those cases offered any analysis of that legislation. In *Sequoyah* the court merely noted that the appropriation bill that had authorized the building of the Tellico Dam comprehensively preempted all other legislation, including AIRFA, from preventing its construction. In *Badoni* the court of appeals simply declined any consideration of AIRFA's constitutionality or its possible application to the Navajo claim concerning Rainbow Bridge. Thus, Judge Richey's interpretation was significant as the first judicial response to the act. His reading of it, though brief, was sufficient to expose its scant capacity to require anything more than bureaucratic consideration of native religions by agencies of the federal government before they could proceed with actions having consequences on tribal belief and practice. It became clear, with Richey's remarks, that although AIRFA might mandate a certain administrative regard for indigenous religions, its actual protections for them were negligible.

Having quoted AIRFA's broad policy intention "to protect and preserve for American Indians their inherent right of freedom to believe, express and exercise (their) traditional religions . . . including, but not limited to, access to sites, use and possession of sacred objects, and the freedom to worship through ceremonies and traditional rites,"[14] Judge Richey agreed with the government defendants that the act created three specific duties, all of which had been fulfilled by the Forest Service. Federal agencies were to evaluate their policies and procedures with the aim of protecting Indian religious freedom, they were to consult Indian groups in light of any proposed agency actions, and they were to refrain from prohibiting access, possession, and use of religious objects and the performance of ceremonies. Richey accepted the administrative record that the Forest Service had had meetings with groups of Hopis and Navajos both on and off the reservations and held public hearings where their representatives had testified against the proposed ski expansion; such meetings and hearings complied with the first two duties required by AIRFA. In his analysis of the Free Exercise claim, Judge Richey had already stressed the continued access of the tribes to the Peaks and their apparent freedom to still make pilgrimages, conduct ceremonies on, and gather liturgical objects from the mountain without any explicit prohibitions from the Forest Service. Unresponsive to the harm they suffered from progressive government secularization of the Peaks, Richey held that the Forest Service had complied with the third duty imposed on it by AIRFA. In reaching his conclusion on that issue, the judge cited the legislative history that led to the passage of AIRFA, which stated that the act's purpose was to "insure that the policies and procedures of various federal agencies as they might impact upon the exercise of traditional Indian religious practices, are brought into compliance with the constitutional injunction that Congress shall make no laws abridging the free exercise of religion."[15]

Focused as it was upon the exercise of "Indian religious practices," AIRFA was unable to protect, with any directness, the fundamental holiness of land, the experience of which was primary and gave rise to the broad range of ritual and ceremonial responses that defined "Indian religious practices." So then, without the primordial sense of the San Francisco Peaks as an integral, sacred reality, the variety of Hopi and Navajo religious exercises, their pilgrimages, offerings, healing chants, and other prayers conducted on and directed toward the Peaks would be groundless. The profound psychic trauma that anguished tribal sensibilities in the face of government-condoned commercialization, trivializing their sanctuary as an amusement park,[16] was not alleviated by the fact that the Forest Service didn't prevent them from walking, gathering, making offerings, or praying on the Peaks. Thus, as Judge Richey's reading of it revealed, a literal satisfaction of the duties mandated for federal agencies by AIRFA did not prevent those agencies from so altering or otherwise disposing of government-held lands as to radically distort the numinous character that defined those lands as sacred realities in the faith perception of generations of Native American tribes. Just as it was unable to restrain the submersion of the Little Tennessee River valley venerated by Cherokee faith, or the flooding of Rainbow Bridge and its canyon considered holy to Navajo belief, so AIRFA was impotent to prevent the profanation of the San Francisco Peaks revered by both Hopi and Navajo religion.

Judge Richey granted summary judgment to the government defendants on the remaining counts in the Hopi and Navajo complaints with one exception. The allegation that the ski resort violated the National Environmental Policy Act because of the inadequacy of the Final Environmental Statement did not convince the judge that the Forest Service had failed to consider environmental consequences of the proposed expansion. Nor did he uphold the claim that development of the Snow Bowl project would transgress the Endangered Species Act by threatening the continued existence on the Peaks of the alpine plant *Senecio Franciscanus*, also known as the San Francisco Peaks groundsel. Although evidence suggested that the greatly increased numbers of hikers who would use the resort's facilities throughout the summer months would imperil the small population of the yellow plant, the court would not afford it protection because it had not been officially listed by the secretary of the interior as "endangered" or "threatened"; nor was the court convinced of an unreasonable delay in the process of the requisite listing as to merit judicial intervention. Similarly, Judge Richey agreed with the government defendants that the National Wilderness Preservation System Act did not apply to the land on the San Francisco Peaks which had not been previously classified as "primitive," nor had the area of the ski resort and its facilities been designated "predominantly of wilderness value," formalities that were necessary to activate the protections of the act. A further tribal claim was that the Forest Service had abused its discretion under the Multiple-Use Sustained-Yield Act, which regulated the administration of national forests. But Richey saw no evidence of an arbitrary or capricious decision to favor the economy and recreational interests of nearby Flagstaff over the religious significance of the Peaks. Accordingly, he refused to question the Forest Service's determination that the religious practices of the Hopis and Navajos were compatible with the other multiple uses of the Peaks, which as part of the national forest system could be "administered for outdoor recreation, range, timber, watershed, and wildlife and fish purposes."[17] Closely related to that decision was the judge's dismissal of the tribal allegation that the Forest Service violated the Administrative Procedure Act through bias and prejudice in favor of further commercialization of the San Francisco Peaks; he ruled an insufficiency of evidence to support the claim.

The only count to survive summary judgment for the government was that brought under the National Historic Preservation Act. Judge Richey found that the Forest Service had not, as required, examined the proposed ski resort site to identify properties eligible for inclusion in the National

Register of Historic Places, nor consulted with the Arizona State Historic Preservation Officer about the effect the development would have on two National Register properties near the resort area, or about the possible eligibility of the San Francisco Peaks themselves as qualifying for inclusion in the National Register. He remanded all three issues to the Forest Service, which determined after several months that the proposed ski development site contained no properties either listed or eligible for listing on the National Register; that it would not affect the historic qualities of the Merriam Base Camp or the Fern Mountain Ranch, which were already on the National Register and near the ski area; and that finally, the San Francisco Peaks themselves were not eligible for listing. Accordingly, on May 14, 1982, Richey granted the government final judgment on all counts and lifted the temporary stay he had imposed against development.

ON APPEAL TO THE U.S. COURT OF APPEALS FOR THE DISTRICT OF COLUMBIA CIRCUIT

The Hopi and Navajo appeal, consolidated with that of the Wilsons, was heard by a panel of Judges Edward Allen Tamm, Ruth Bader Ginsburg, and J. Edward Lumbard. In their criticism of the district court, the tribal appellants scored the lower court's grant of summary judgment for the government on the constitutional issues. A determination of summary judgment is appropriate only when there exists no material issues of fact between the parties and the court can make its decision merely by applying relevant law. The effect of summary judgment is severe, since it deprives the losing party of its opportunity to go forward and fully try its case, developing its claim by the testimony of witnesses at a trial. Before granting summary judgment, a court must be certain that there are no disputed facts between the parties and must give the benefit of all favorable inferences that can reasonably be drawn from the submitted evidence in favor of the party against whom summary judgment will be applied.

In their appeal, the tribes argued that there clearly existed conflicting factual matters between them and the government defendants. Basing itself only on the evidence of two government expert witnesses, the district court had wrongly concluded that the expansion of the ski resort would have little if any impact upon the practice of Hopi and Navajo religion. Thus, the court had stated "that the Snow Bowl (ski resort) will not impinge upon the continuation of all essential ritual practices."[18] The court supported that conclusion by repeating from the same government witnesses that the soil and ritual elements used in tribal ceremonies did not actually have to come from the Peaks; that the ski resort area was not used by the Hopi in their pilgrimages on the Peaks; and that in fact, the tribes were not alleging that the government with its endorsement for the resort was directly interfering with or impeding their religious ceremonies.[19]

The tribes reviewed the submitted affidavits of nineteen experts in Navajo and Hopi religion, the overwhelming majority of whom were practitioners, each describing the various ways in which Indian religious practices and beliefs were infringed upon by the skiing facilities, thus directly contradicting as matters of fact the assertions made by the district court based on the government witnesses. In addition, the tribal affidavits described other practices that had been disrupted by the ski resort's facilities. Neither those practices nor their disruption had been denied by the government's two witnesses, yet the district court ignored them in its decision. So, for example, there were affidavits testifying to the inability of Navajos to pray in the area of the Snow Bowl ski facility because of the disturbance and distractions; the inability to use a customary sweat lodge that had once existed in the proposed development area for lack of privacy and quiet; the anticipated difficulties with an expanded ski resort of finding fir boughs and eaglets for Hopi ceremonialism; and the claim that Hopi pilgrimages do in fact pass through the resort area and have been disrupted because of a lost sense of the locale's spirituality. There were Navajo affidavits testifying to the necessity that feathers, tree boughs, stones, soil, rainwater and flower pollen all be gathered from the Peaks; several affidavits specified how the ski facilities interfered with or prevented the collection of sacred herbs. The tribal appellants thus argued that the "facts" relied on by the district court were at best controverted and, in some ways, unsupported even by the two non-Indian anthropologists whose testimony had been submitted by the government. Under such circumstances, there was no justifiable basis for the court's grant of summary judgment to the government defendants, and it was erroneous for the court to ignore the tribal allegations of how their religious exercise was harmed when those allegations were uncontroverted and unimpeached by testimony entered for the government defendants. Even if the district court chose not to go forward with a plenary trial, it could have indicated that it had weighed the competing affidavits and had rejected the Indian affidavits for some valid reason. Given that the court did not do so, and apparently ignored the Indian affidavits completely, granting summary judgment for the government was erroneous. In their appeal, the tribal parties sought the court of appeals to remand the case for plenary trial.

From their procedural critique, the Hopi and Navajo parties next moved to a consideration of their substantive constitutional and statutory argument in defense of their religious freedom. The district court had correctly stated the two-step process for the analysis of free-exercise claims: to first determine whether government action does, in fact, create a burden on the exercise of the particular religion, and if such a burden is found, then to insist as the second step that the government demonstrate a compelling interest of the highest magnitude, sufficient to override the religious interest claiming protection under the Free Exercise Clause. In holding that the government permission for the commercial expansion and operation of the ski resort did not amount to an impermissible burden of Hopi and Navajo religion, the district court generalized that free-exercise claims challenged either government dictates that compelled citizens to violate the tenets of their religion, or government actions that conditioned a benefit or right or reward on a citizen's rejection of a religious practice. The court concluded: "The government here has not forced the (Hopi and Navajo) plaintiffs to embrace any religious belief or to say or believe anything in conflict with their religious tenets; nor have they forced plaintiffs to choose between their religious beliefs and some public benefit. Therefore the Court must look to whether there is a 'coercive effect' in that the defendants have prohibited the plaintiffs' practice of their religion. We find there is no such prohibition and, therefore, no such coercive effect which violates the Free Exercise Clause."[20] As already noted, the district court had adopted an artificial and rigid delineation between the San Francisco Peaks as government property on the one hand, and as a religious reality on the other. In the court's conception, the legal status of the Peaks as property was comprehensive and excluded their valuation as a religious entity. For the court, tribal religion was relegated wholly to the realm of Hopi and Navajo practices, with the Peaks as only the mountain locale in reference to or upon which those varied religious practices were performed. That same judicial mind-set, neatly segregating the Peaks as government property from tribal religion, permitted the district court to ignore the clearly stated tribal complaints about the expanding secularization of their sacred mountain and to flatly insist that they suffered no religious harm. So long as the tribes enjoyed access to the mountain and had not been prohibited from conducting whatever ceremonies they chose upon it, their religion had endured no unconstitutional coercion by the government's permission to significantly increase the recreational potential of the Peaks.

In their appeal the Hopis and Navajos faulted the reasoning of the district court which, by the same rationale, would find no wrong with a prison warden insisting on organizing recreational activities in an area set aside for religious services during the very time those services were being conducted. Defending the aptness of their analogy, the tribes depicted themselves as religious prisoners of the government, which may not have denied them freedom of movement, but exercised absolute control over their sacred mountain whose recreational exploitation deeply violated their religious sensibilities and promised to further obstruct their religious practices, which were already curtailed by the skiing facilities and its users.[21]

In exposing the legal inadequacy of the district court's assertion that violations against the Free Exercise Clause of the First Amendment were confined to outright government prohibition or coercion, the tribal appeal relied on the rulings of the Supreme Court in the cases of *Sherbert v. Verner* of 1963[22] and the then recent *Thomas v. Review Board of the Indiana Employment Security Division* of 1981.[23] Both cases had been cited briefly by the district court, but merely as fact situations involving unconstitutional government action that conditioned a benefit or right on one's rejection of a religious practice. The tribal appeal argued that the two cases also supported the principle that the Free Exercise Clause of the First Amendment would condemn governmental actions that placed substantial, though indirect, pressure on religious practitioners to modify their beliefs.

It may be recalled from the first chapter's discussion that in *Sherbert*, the plaintiff was a Seventh-day Adventist who was discharged by her employer because she refused to work on Saturday, the Sabbath day of her faith. Finding that her religious convictions did not constitute "good cause" for refusing available work, the South Carolina Employment Security Commission refused her application for unemployment benefits. But when the South Carolina Supreme Court upheld the commission's determination, the United States Supreme Court reversed. It ruled that the woman's disqualification to receive unemployment benefits was not a form of direct state coercion of the woman's religious principles and practices. It nevertheless violated the freedom of her religious exercise and was an unconstitutional offense. South Carolina's welfare regulations in effect presented the woman with a choice between following the precepts of her religion and thus forfeiting unemployment benefits, or alternatively, abandoning her religion's precepts to accept work on the Sabbath. The Supreme Court held that the consequence of such a policy amounted to the imposition of a fine upon the woman's adherence to her religion; however indirect, such government action was an impermissible burden upon religious liberty and could not stand.

In the more recent *Thomas* case, the Supreme Court had further defined unconstitutional violations against the exercise of religion absent any explicit state coercion. It involved the similar circumstance of unemployment benefits denial. Here the plaintiff was a Jehovah's Witness who had quit his job at a factory when he was transferred to a department making turrets for military tanks. Since that position and any available alternatives were directly engaged in the production of weapons, the plaintiff left, asserting that he could not do such work without violating his religious beliefs. He was denied unemployment compensation under an Indiana law barring benefits to one who quit his job "without good cause in connection with the work." The Indiana Supreme Court ruled that a termination motivated by religion did not constitute "good cause" and upheld the denial of benefits. In reversing that decision, the U.S. Supreme Court, relying on *Sherbert*, held that the government burdens free exercise when it forces an individual to choose between a government benefit and fidelity to religious belief. Finding the coercive impact on religion to be indistinguishable from that in *Sherbert*, the Court stated: "Where the state conditions receipt of an important benefit upon conduct proscribed by a religious faith, or where it denies such a benefit because of conduct mandated by religious belief, thereby putting substantial pressure on an adherent to modify his behavior and to violate his beliefs, a burden upon religion exists. While the compulsion may be indirect, the infringement upon free exercise is nonetheless substantial."[24]

Reading *Sherbert* and *Thomas* together, the Hopis and Navajos asserted the district court's error for its insistence that violations of the Free Exercise Clause required, if not some government action forcing a choice between religious belief and a government benefit, then an actual prohibition or direct coercion of religious exercise. The tribal appeals argued that both cases do not support so narrow a reading of illicit government interference with religion. Although they both arose in the context of governmental denial of unemployment benefits, bearing minimal factual resemblance to the tribal attempts to protect the San Francisco Peaks, *Sherbert* and *Thomas* stand for the untenability of government actions whose consequences, however indirect and benignly intentioned, burden religious belief by placing pressure on the adherent to modify his behavior and violate his beliefs. Such a burden can be justified only by a showing of compelling state interest of the highest order that cannot be satisfied by less restrictive means.

The tribal appeals contended that the decision of the Forest Service to approve the commercial expansion and operation of the ski resort on the Peaks fit the government action proscribed under *Sherbert* and *Thomas*. The pressures placed upon the Indian plaintiffs as a result of the development project had forced them to alter their ceremonial use of the area, forgo collection of needed plants, and restrict the making of pilgrimages and leaving offerings. More invasively, the Snow Bowl ski resort development threatened to desecrate the identity of the Peaks as the mountain held sacred by both Hopi and Navajo peoples.

The chairman of the Hopi Indian tribe had already testified to the difficulty of sustaining the ancestral belief that the Peaks were the venerated home of the Kachinas once the ski resort expansion had been completed. He spoke to the erosion of faith in the holiness of a mountain increasingly populated by government-induced throngs of recreationists. What had been a basis of their self-identity as a culture over the generations would be increasingly difficult for younger Hopis to appreciate, as the impact of the ski resort would progressively redefine the mountain's identity, casting their ancient belief to the quaintness of an outgrown fairy tale. The tribal appeals then stressed, that as a consequence of government action, they would be compelled either to abandon their most sacred place because it had lost its religious significance or to fundamentally modify their religious doctrine to conform to the changed circumstances wrought by the Forest Service. The compulsion they suffered was real and substantial, a greater infringement than that suffered by the plaintiffs in the *Sherbert* and *Thomas* cases, who were faced only with the loss of a secular benefit—unemployment benefits—without any actual interference with their religious practices. At worst, they had to make a choice whether or not to forgo their religious beliefs. The Hopi and Navajo appeal argued that they, by contrast, had no choice; as long as the Snow Bowl ski resort continued to operate, the tribes could do nothing that would permit them to carry on those religious practices that would be hampered by the resort and its activities. Even more, the tribes could do nothing to alter the desecration of their holy mountain in its integral entirety. If the Supreme Court had found that the plaintiffs in *Sherbert* and *Thomas* had been unconstitutionally burdened by having to choose between their religious belief and government benefits, how much more intolerable was the burden imposed on tribal belief and practice that enjoyed no choice but to be passively endured?

Pressing their analysis, the tribes restated the legal principle that once a government action has been found to burden religion, the government must clearly show that the burden is justified by a compelling state interest of such a nature "that only those interests of the highest order and those not otherwise served can overbalance legitimate claims to the free exercise of religion."[25] Recalling the circumstances in the *Yoder* case, the tribes pointed to the weighty state interest that Wisconsin had in maintaining a well-educated citizenry such as to compel mandatory school attendance until the age of sixteen. The Supreme Court had nevertheless ruled that such lofty state interest was of insufficient magnitude to override the religious interests of those Old Order Amish families who viewed the compulsory education requirement as a threat to their religious belief and practice. Similarly, in both the *Sherbert* and *Thomas* cases, South Carolina and Indiana respectively had advanced significant state interests of protecting public funds from depletion by potentially deceitful or malingering claimants seeking unemployment compensation. But the Supreme Court had ruled that such threats to state resources, although possible, did not constitute the kind of "gravest abuse, endangering paramount interests" that alone could warrant the kind of infringement on religious belief that the states had imposed by disqualifying the benefit claims of the Seventh-day Adventist in *Sherbert* and the Jehovah's Witness in *Thomas*.

In their appeal, the Hopis and Navajos charged that any interest the Forest Service may have had in fostering the commercial development of the San Francisco Peaks for skiing and other recreational pursuits was marginal compared with the public education concerns in *Yoder* and the protection and sound administration of state welfare disbursements in *Sherbert* and *Thomas*. If the interests of Wisconsin, South Carolina, and Indiana were deemed to lack the requisite magnitude to justify the harms to religious belief, the recreational interest of the Forest Service in a ski resort development for the Peaks could hardly qualify as compelling. The ancestral interests of Hopi and Navajo religious cultures could not be infringed upon by mere assertions from the Forest Service of government managerial discretion over the Peaks granted by virtue of the Multiple-Use Sustained-Yield Act or the National Forest Management Act. Such legislation did not elevate a public interest in sports and recreational leisure to the level of the requisite compelling state interest that alone could abrogate the protections guaranteed to the tribal traditions under the Free Exercise Clause of the First Amendment.

Once it has been shown that no compelling state interest exists, the analysis needs to proceed no further; the Forest Service decision to permit Northland Recreation's ski resort expansion should have been rescinded. But to clarify a mischaracterization of their demand and to ensure a thorough response in the eventuality that skiing and recreational activities were wrongly determined to pass as compelling government interests, the tribal appeal noted the final prong in free-exercise claims. Even if the particular government interest is found to be of sufficient significance as to be judged "compelling," it must yet be shown that the specific means by which the government intends to pursue its purpose is "the least restrictive" means of furthering its interest. The government must demonstrate that no alternative means exists to achieve its objective without infringing on First Amendment religious rights. If it is available, the less harmful alternative must be followed. In their appeal, the Hopis and Navajos identified just such an alternative in the regional forester's decision of February 1979 to prevent any expansion development on the Peaks. He had determined that the maintenance of essentially a status quo situation, allowing only for repair and replacement of the existing facilities as required by obsolescence, public safety, and deterioration, would best balance the competing needs of the tribal religions and the recreational interests of the public. The Hopis and Navajos reiterated that they were not seeking to ban all public access to the Peaks. Their objection was not to the host of activities that might be enjoyed on the Peaks by anyone choosing to hike, camp, horseback ride, mountain climb, picnic, cross country ski, or otherwise appreciate the mountain. They sought only to prevent the government, which had been aware of the religious significance of the San Francisco Peaks when it designated them a mountain forest reserve in 1898, from encouraging and sponsoring the conversion of their sacred mountain into an expanded, commercially operated resort area. Not attempting to coerce the public to accept the religious significance for which their traditions venerated the Peaks, nor seeking to expel non-tribal members from its slopes, the Hopis and Navajos nevertheless objected to government inducements designed to attract and accommodate such numbers of those seeking recreational entertainment as to substantially alter the character and profane the holy presence that had evoked Hopi and Navajo prayers from generations of their ancestral pasts. It would have been most satisfying to the religious sensibilities of the tribes to have the complete removal of even the old skiing facility, which since the late 1950s had interfered with tribal religious practices and offended the reverent propriety that the sacred mountain elicited from them. But its continuance was less objectionable and intrusive than Northland Recreation's proposed resort development of a new and bigger ski lodge, more chairlifts, widened slopes, paved access road, and multi-acre parking site. If the government were to insist that commercial recreational skiing on the San Francisco Peaks constituted a "compelling state interest," the Northland resort was clearly not "the least restrictive means" of furthering that governmental intent without further harm to Hopi and Navajo religion. Only a halt to further development and the maintenance of the status quo would properly qualify as the alternative, recommended by the regional forester, that would continue to afford the skiing opportunity demanded by the government without further exacerbating the already burdened beliefs and practices of the Hopi and Navajo religious traditions.

Finally, the Hopi and Navajo appeal responded to the district court's claim that if the government denied Northland Recreation, Inc. the permission to develop its ski resort complex on the San Francisco Peaks to protect the free exercise of the tribal religions, such action would constitute a violation of the Establishment Clause. Asserting that such protection for Indian beliefs amounted to impermissive affirmative action, the court revealed its limited grasp of the relationship between the Free Exercise Clause and the Establishment Clause of the First Amendment. It essentially took the position that any acts of the government to protect the free exercise of a particular religion were forms of governmental support favoring that religion, which would violate the prohibition of the Establishment Clause. Such an invidious reading of the two clauses dooms any attempts to grant relief to religions from burdensome government restrictions and renders the protections of the Free Exercise Clause hostage to a rigidly absolute negation through the Establishment Clause. In so holding, the district court ignored the testimony of the same Supreme Court decisions that offered corrections to its wrongly held insistence that claims based on the Free Exercise Clause require direct government prohibition or coercion of religion.

Taken together, *Yoder v. Wisconsin*, *Sherbert v. Verner*, and *Thomas v. Review Board* represent an important category of cases dealing with the application of the Establishment Clause. Many establishment cases revolve around the issue of whether a religiously affiliated group should be permitted to derive benefits from the secular government that it would not otherwise enjoy. Such cases have often involved disputes over financial and other government aid to religious schools or the place of prayer and other religiously related activities in public schools. *Yoder*, *Sherbert*, and *Thomas*, however, raise the question of whether a religious group should be relieved of a burden created by the operation of the secular government. Significantly, the Supreme Court ruled in all three cases that such relief did not violate the Establishment Clause. In *Sherbert* and *Thomas*, the Court struck down the unemployment schemes that placed a state-created burden on Seventh-day Adventists and Jehovah's Witnesses respectively: regulations effectively forced them to make a choice between their eligibility to receive unemployment benefits and their religiously held beliefs about work on their Sabbath as in *Sherbert* or about participating in the manufacture of armaments as in *Thomas*. Similarly, in *Yoder* the Court ordered the Amish to be exempt from the state's compulsory school attendance law, which threatened to undermine fundamental beliefs and values of Amish religion. As in *Sherbert* and *Thomas*, the Court specifically held that such accommodation of religion did not offend the Establishment Clause since it didn't represent the kind of involvement between religious and secular governmental institutions that the Establishment

Clause sought to prevent. Specifically, the Court wrote that: "Accommodating the religious beliefs of the Amish can hardly be characterized as sponsorship or active involvement. The purpose and effect of such an exemption are not to support, favor, advance, or assist the Amish, but to allow their centuries-old religious society, here long before the advent of any compulsory education, to survive free from the heavy impediment compliance with the Wisconsin compulsory education law would improve."[26]

In their appeal, the Hopis and Navajos identified their plight with that of the Amish, insisting that they sought no support or advantage from the government, but merely the right to continue as they had for generations, revering the holy presence of the San Francisco Peaks free from the structural distortion and active interference that the ski resort and its attendant population of users would inflict. Refuting the district court's claim that the tribes sought to turn the Peaks into "a government-managed religious shrine," the Hopis and Navajos insisted that the Peaks had been a government-managed shrine from the very moment the federal government annexed and incorporated them into the Coconino National Forest. In so doing, the United States had assumed a definite control over Hopi and Navajo religious traditions, which the government was responsible for protecting. It would be an inexcusable violation of that duty for the government to later argue that the Establishment Clause barred steps it might take to preserve the conditions appropriate to the sanctity of the Peaks and the religious sensibility of the Indian tribes praying and conducting ceremonies on it. The district court failed to correct this serious distortion of the Establishment Clause because it had itself failed to be instructed by the *Yoder*, *Sherbert*, and *Thomas* decisions in the important balance between the two religion clauses of the First Amendment. The court should have been informed by the testimony of those three cases that the obligation of the government to refrain from interfering with religion may very well oblige it to take such steps to accommodate the free exercise of a particular religion that will not offend the Establishment Clause if by so doing the government does not actively promote, financially support, or otherwise insinuate itself into that religion's affairs. No such sponsorship, funding, or involvement was threatened if the government were merely to forgo its tenuous interest in a commercial ski resort and thereby preserve the religious character of the San Francisco Peaks, in turn allowing the Hopi and Navajo traditions to worship as they had for untold generations.

The *Yoder*, *Sherbert*, and *Thomas* cases were directly relevant to the kind of issue raised by the Hopi and Navajo claim regarding the permissibility of granting relief to a religious group from a burden created by the operation of the government. But instead of heeding the Supreme Court's guidance in those cases and finding that the Establishment Clause didn't prevent the government from protecting Indian belief, the district court had invoked a three-part test that was more appropriate for use in very different circumstances. To determine whether a religious group could enjoy government-derived benefits without violating the Establishment Clause, the Supreme Court in the 1971 case of *Lemon v. Kurtzman*[27] identified three conditions that had to be met if particular government action was to avoid the censure of the Establishment Clause. The government act or law had to reflect a secular purpose, its primary effect could neither advance nor inhibit religion, and it could not foster an excessive government entanglement with religion. Without any analysis, the district court in one sentence summarily declared that if the government were to rescind the Forest Service decision to permit commercial development of the San Francisco Peaks, it would be motivated by a religious, rather than secular purpose, and its primary effect would be to advance Indian religion; it therefore was found to violate the Establishment Clause test.

In their appeal, the Hopis and Navajos criticized the district court's reliance on the *Lemon* test as more appropriate to cases weighing the legitimacy of state aid to religiously affiliated groups. While the tribes demonstrated the correct analysis through the precedents established in the *Yoder, Sherbert,* and *Thomas* cases, they nevertheless argued that even under the three-pronged *Lemon* test no violation of the Establishment Clause prevented the government from renouncing its support for the ski resort. If one of the primary "secular" functions of government was the protection of religious freedom, halting the commercial development of the San Francisco Peaks fulfilled that government obligation by preventing harm to Hopi and Navajo belief and practice at their ancestral sacred site. Similarly, the American Indian Religious Freedom Act expressed a congressional resolve to protect tribal religious practices, recognizing the important cultural contribution of Indian traditions to American life. Thus, there would be no violation of the Establishment Clause if the government's decision to protect the Peaks were based on the secular purpose of protecting Hopi and Navajo cultures as important contributions to the national heritage.

Concerning the second condition, the Hopis and Navajos contended that religion is not "advanced" by protecting it from influences or action which, if not checked, would further inhibit or burden it. There was no more neutral a posture the government could take than to preserve the status quo on the San Francisco Peaks. The religious interests of the tribes would be neither further burdened nor advanced by preservation of the status quo, yet skiers and other members of the public would continue to have access to and use of the mountain and the existing facilities.

As to the third and last condition, it scarcely needed comment. The government had already "entangled" itself in Hopi and Navajo belief when it incorporated their holy mountain into the national forest system. By allowing the construction of the first ski lodge and the growing population of its users, the government insinuated itself all the more into the tribal religions, whose practitioners were forced to passively endure the desecration of their holy reality and the increasing interference with their pilgrimages, prayers, and ceremonial rites. The expansive resort project envisioned by Northland Recreation, further altering the structure of the Peaks and significantly compounding the numbers of recreationists and the stream of cars that would be accommodated by paved roads and a multi-acre parking area would only increase the government's impact and burden on Hopi and Navajo religion. If the government were to recognize that tribal belief and practice had a far more substantial and compelling interest in the San Francisco Peaks than its own claim to fostering a commercial skiing venture there, its decision to refrain from proceeding with that development could hardly be criticized as an "entanglement" with Hopi and Navajo religion. Just the opposite would be true: the government would move to extricate itself from further burdening the exercise of those religious traditions.

DECISION OF THE COURT OF APPEALS

The Hopi and Navajo appeal exposed the district court's faulty application of the *Lemon* test and at the same time demonstrated nevertheless that the relief the tribes sought satisfied all three conditions of the test, proving no violation of the Establishment Clause. Their effort, however, was unavailing. The Court of Appeals for the District of Columbia Circuit never bothered to address the merits of their argument on that issue once it ruled that the Indians would not prevail in their free-exercise claim. In upholding Judge Richey's conclusion that the tribes had not shown an impermissible government burden on their religions, the appeals court separately considered the effects of the ski resort development upon Hopi and Navajo religious beliefs and upon their practices. Exonerating the government of any direct burden on Indian beliefs, the court considered the argument that an indirect burden had nevertheless been imposed. The tribal appeal had contended that both the Sherbert and Thomas cases stood for the untenability of government actions whose consequences, however indirect and benignly intentioned, burden religious belief by placing pressure on the adherent to modify his behavior and violate his beliefs. Specifically, the tribes argued that the grant by the Forest Service to Northland Recreation, Inc. to develop the San Francisco Peaks would so desecrate and destroy the spiritual character of their sacred mountain as to force them "to fundamentally modify their religious doctrine to conform to the changed circumstance"[28] that altered their holy site from one of veneration to one of government-sponsored commercial sport and amusement.

The court of appeals refused, however, to abide an expansion of the *Sherbert* and *Thomas* decisions beyond the factual circumstances common to both cases: the denial of public welfare benefits by a state government to adherents of a religious belief that would not permit them to accept a condition of work deemed requisite for the reception of such benefits. The court insisted that "*Sherbert* and *Thomas* considered only whether the government may legally condition benefits on a decision to forego or to adhere to religious belief or practice. Those cases did not purport to create a benchmark against which to test all indirect burden claims."[29] Applying its restrictive reading, the court noted that the Hopis and Navajos had suffered no deprivation of government benefits by the decision of the Forest Service to allow a ski resort on the San Francisco Peaks. From that, it summarily concluded that the development project, although "inconsistent" with tribal beliefs and the cause of their "spiritual disquiet," nevertheless did not burden their freedom to believe in the holiness of the Peaks. Ignoring the affidavits submitted by the Hopi and Navajo plaintiffs, which testified to an intense "mental and emotional anguish" as they witnessed the progressive secularization of their sacred mountain[30] the court of appeals injudiciously mischaracterized the religious harm experienced by the tribes with its cavalier designation as mere "spiritual disquiet." Such callous insensitivity, matched by the court's refusal to acknowledge the destructive nature of the Forest Service's decision on tribal religion, betrayed the court's fundamental inclination to view the tribal complaint as a threat to the government's property interest in the San Francisco Peaks. Whereas the Hopis and Navajos sought constitutional protection against the alteration and destruction of a sacred being and the dwelling place of other sacred beings, the Court of Appeals for the District of Columbia Circuit heard a claim "to restrict the government's use of its own land."[31]

The tendency of the court of appeals to view land primarily in terms of property and to evaluate claims of its status as a sacred reality from within that context was exacerbated by its reliance on the earlier case of *Sequoyah v. TVA*. In *Sequoyah*, the Sixth Circuit Court of Appeals had failed to understand the basic notion that had informed the complaint brought by the Cherokees: the land of the Little Tennessee River Valley was itself the sacred reality that would be destroyed by the floodwaters from the Tellico dam. Without the land, there was no Cherokee religion; to destroy the land was to destroy the critical religious experience of being connected to a holy, ultimate reality. Rescuing the river valley from inundation was preserving the entity without which traditional Cherokee religion was a groundless abstraction. But the Sixth Circuit failed to comprehend that inherent connection between religion and land. For the court, religion was circumscribed to a particular set of human actions and behavior, a matter of "observances," "practices," and "ceremonies." The court had no sense of the primacy of the land as the sacred reality that inspired, evoked, and gave meaning to those activities. The Little Tennessee River Valley, in the view of the court, existed not at the heart of Cherokee religion, but as merely the site or place where the Cherokees "performed" their religion.

The Court of Appeals for the District of Columbia Circuit in *Wilson v. Block* adopted the legacy of *Sequoyah v. TVA* with its notion that religious activities were discrete and transferable from one place to another and that land remained only the context and not the end itself of religious belief and practice. The District of Columbia Circuit revealed the operative paradigm of land as secondary and incidental to religious belief and practice with its own admission that "development of the Peaks would severely impair the practice of [Navajo and Hopi] religions if it destroyed the natural conditions necessary for the performance of ceremonies and the collection of religious objects."[32] The court was unable to correctly identify the Peaks in their integrity as the primordial sacred reality without which the derivative tribal practices were meaningless. In the court's understanding, the land remains but the ancillary condition, the background entity for the ritual and customary activity of the two tribes. So long as the government's land use would not prevent those activities from being performed at some other site, the court would not recognize any harm to the religious freedom of the Hopis and Navajos. Pointing out that the commercial development would affect only 777 acres of the 75,000 acres of the entire Peaks region, the court ruled that the tribes could not prove "the indispensability of the small portion of the Peaks encompassed by the Snow Bowl permit area."[33] With its ruling, the court confirmed its inclination to view land primarily in terms of property. It had initially characterized the tribal claim to protect the integrity of their holy mountain as a challenge to the proprietary interests of the government. Here, the court's insinuation of the numerically insignificant acreage reserved for the commercial development of the Peaks and its assertion of tribal failure to prove the religious necessity of that portion reflects the court's assessment of the mountain land as essentially inert, quantifiable, and fungible as just so many interchangeable locales and settings for the allocation of tribal religious behavior on the one hand and commercial recreational interests on the other.

Such a conception of land led the court of appeals, following the court in *Sequoyah*, to insist that the various tribes "at a minimum demonstrate that the government's proposed land use would impair a religious practice that could not be performed at any other site."[34] According to the courts' logic, if the same religious behavior could be carried out on an adjacent parcel of land, then the parcel to be used for governmental purposes was not indispensable to tribal religion, and no subsequent use of it, whether it be as the floodplain in *Sequoyah* or as the ski resort in *Wilson*, would be recognized as a transgression against tribal religious freedom. In such a perspective, religion is confined to human activity, and the land where the observances are performed or observed has been shorn of its sacred character. In the view of the court, it exists primarily not as a holy reality, but as property held and managed by the federal government. As such property, the land can be divided into any number of discretely segregated tracts of various sizes where tribal religious practices may be tolerated, but never permitted to restrict governmental usage without the burden of proving the indispensable nature of the particular area to tribal religion. But as long as the *Sequoyah* and *Wilson* decisions are followed, the burden will be an impossible one to sustain.

So long as there is the segregation of religion and land, where the land in question is viewed by the courts through the prism of federal property, and religion is defined as action done on, but not derived from the land, the partition of sacred land sites to accommodate government action on such sites will invariably be held not to violate the free exercise of tribal religion. The analysis of the courts will not be grounded on the primacy of the ancestral tribal experience of the particular site as holy, but on its character as land belonging to and managed by the federal government. The judicial orientation will thus interpret the particular tribal claim to protect and preserve the sacred reality of the land in question primarily as an attempt to restrict the government's use of its own land. Under the *Sequoyah* and *Wilson* rulings, before the court even needs to ask whether or not the government action for the particular site is of a sufficiently compelling nature, it may simply refuse to acknowledge that any harm of constitutional significance will be inflicted on the tribal religious tradition by that action and may dismiss the tribal complaint. No matter how destructive or structurally disturbing the government disposition of the land will prove, no matter how traumatic or offensive that will be to the tribal sense of sacred presence manifesting in and through the land, there will be no judicial recognition of religious harm if tribal religious ceremonies, prayers, and other ritual observances can still be conducted somewhere on the site; tribal religion will be deemed protected even as the land, the primordial holy reality that evoked and gave meaning to the variety of liturgical expressions conducted on and addressed to it, suffers so fundamental a change in its physical identity as to jeopardize the recognition of its sacred character.

Having upheld Judge Richey's dismissal of the Hopi and Navajo claims under the Free Exercise Clause, the Court of Appeals for the District of Columbia Circuit sustained his judgments against the tribes on all remaining counts, including the American Indian Religious Freedom Act, the Endangered Species Act, the Wilderness Act, and the National Historic Preservation Act.

4

∾

Frank Fools Crow et al. v. Tony Gullet et al.:
State Tourism on Sacred Land

If the *Badoni* and *Wilson* cases witnessed the growing incursions of government-sponsored commercial and recreational tourist development on land long held sacred in the ancestral traditions of Native American religions, the efforts of South Dakota to appropriate and market Bear Butte as a tourist attraction precisely in its identity as the holiest mountain and most active site of worship for the Lakota and Tsistsistas Indian Nations represented a new level of crass insensitivity to and exploitation of tribal religious freedom.

Bear Butte, which sits in striking solitude on the plains of South Dakota just outside the northeastern periphery of the Black Hills, is an exposed remnant of an obtrusive mass of igneous material known as a laccolith. Although South Dakota insinuated, without legal or historical citation, that the Lakota were not present in the area of the Black Hills or the Butte until sometime in the early eighteenth century, uncontested evidence submitted by the Lakota themselves suggested their presence as early as 901 A.D.[1] The Lakota Nation, commonly but incorrectly referred to as Sioux, is an original nation of the northern plains, a social and political union of seven peoples, (the Oglala, Brule, Hunkpapa, Minneconjou, Oohenunpa, Sihasapa, and Itazipo) speaking one language and practicing one religion. At the time of their suit against South Dakota, they resided chiefly on the Pine Ridge, Rosebud, Lower Brule, Cheyenne River, and Standing Rock Indian reservations and numbered more than thirty thousand.

The Tsistsistas Nation, commonly but incorrectly referred to as Cheyenne, are an original nation and people of the northern plains, allied for centuries with the Lakota Nation. Although speaking an unrelated language, they practice a similar religion of equally ancient origins. At the time of their suit against South Dakota, Tsistsistas people resided on the Cheyenne-Arapaho and Northern Cheyenne Indian Reservation and numbered more than five thousand.

It is commonly held by both the Lakota and Tsistsistas traditions that the Black Hills are the place of origin where both peoples first came into the world. In their joint experience, Bear Butte was the place of their first instructions and has remained throughout their histories as the central and most powerful ceremonial site, where they come in intimate contact with the Creator. In both traditions, Bear Butte is most particularly a place of visions and dreams, where holy men and women, priests, and tribal members of both the Lakota and Tsistsistas traditions have gone for more than a thousand years to seek guidance, knowledge, and physical and spiritual renewal.

It is understood in the Tsistsistas tradition that the Creator and Mother Earth joined at Bear Butte to form the world's axis, where the sacred four directions meet. The sacred mountain, then, is the pillar that supports the firmament above and forms the highest point on earth. Bear Butte connects the spirits above the earth to those below. Eternal in time, the Butte stands as a monument to and a remnant of the primordial creation. In the Tsistsistas tongue, Bear Butte is known as the Learning Hill. For in a cave deep within the mountain, the prophets Sweet Medicine and Erect Horns were given the sacramental Medicine Arrows (still kept at Watonga, Oklahoma) and Buffalo Hat to guarantee the survival of the Tsistsistas Nation. But the masculine sanctity of the Arrows and the feminine power of the Buffalo Hat are exhaustible and must be periodically regenerated in the Sun Dance and Arrow Renewal ceremonies, which were taught to the people at Bear Butte for the reenactment and renewal of the covenant.

As important as those and other ceremonies are in Tsistsistas liturgical life, however, it is the vision quest, as the core religious experience, that brings the practitioner to stand alone on Bear Butte, itself the most sacred altar, where he will pray and fast and wait in solitude for the experience of sacred power to manifest and bless him with the resolution of the spiritual, emotional, or physical crisis that has beset him. Here, Lakota religion, with its own unique elaboration of seven ceremonial rituals, most closely approximates the Tsistsistas vision quest conducted on Bear Butte. While Hanblechayapi or "Crying for a Vision" may be celebrated on any appropriately isolated mountain, to hold the sacred pipe and to experience oneself at the center of the universe, calling on the Great Spirit in the company of all things who are one's relatives, is perhaps most efficacious at the center of the world, Bear Butte. Whether the vision seeker be of the Tsistsistas or Lakota Nations, he is usually accompanied to the base of Bear Butte by his spiritual mentor, his family, medicine men and women, and other supporters who are purified along with him in a sweat lodge ceremony and remain in prayer with him at the base as he ascends to remain alone on the Butte for an average of four days of intensive prayer and fasting. During that time he may well receive some extraordinary visionary experience imparting wisdom, insight, or healing power for the welfare of others. Yet others may return with a simpler, yet deeper self-understanding and sensitivity to the presence of the Great Mystery and a more profound awareness of and sense of inclusion within the cosmic community where all beings have their own knowledge and power to impart to those who are attentive and receptive.

Whatever the result of one's quest, one's time on Bear Butte is a turning from the noises and distractions of ordinary daily living, a reconfirmation, through solitude and self-denial, of one's dependency upon the Creator as the source and center of one's being. To be on Bear Butte is to temporarily sever all that binds and restricts one to a world of purely material and secular significance, shedding all semblance of pretense and self-sufficiency, ascending the mountain-altar in radical loneliness, purified through the prayers of the sweat lodge ritual at the base, to stand in the utter immediacy of the divine, creative Presence. Although traditional tribal prayers may be helpful resources to orient one's attention, the individual may choose to remain in silent meditative attentiveness, fully confident in the divine wisdom to discern the deepest commitments of mind and heart that mere words often elude. Before returning to the base of the Butte to be reunited in further prayer and final purification with those who have kept vigil with them in ritualized drumming and song, solitary seekers may leave behind as gestures of their faith and commitment offerings of sacred objects such as pipes, feathers, shells, quilts, pemmican, and tobacco.

For some one thousand years, then, Bear Butte has continued to be the mountain whose base witnesses to the strong social solidarity of Lakota and Tsistsistas faith, where members of the respective nations join in supportive prayer and purification rituals to strengthen the commitments of those who ascend the Butte to express the complementary richness of the two religions. On the higher slopes and top of the Butte they have stood in the most intense and private self-surrender to the immediacy of the divine that their faith, unencumbered of all distractions, sees, hears, and discerns in the stark loneliness and encompassing beauty of the mountain-altar. As it has been in the Middle and Southeast with the Cherokees, in the Southwest with the Navajos and Hopis, so, too, here in the northern plains of the Midwest, Lakota and Tsistsistas peoples were engaged in the exercise of religion long before the passage of the First Amendment to the United States Constitution made religious freedom a protected right. But as with the Cherokees, Navajos, and Hopis, the Lakota and Tsistsistas Nations soon learned that their religious faith, grounded in and addressed to the numinous reality of land, received scant protection from a majoritarian religious and legal culture for whom the sacred nature of the earth was scarcely conceivable from under the dominant categorization of property.

So it was that in the last thirty-five years of the nineteenth century, as white settlers continued to invade Lakota lands west of the Missouri river and others carved out great trails headed for Oregon's Willamette Valley and the western gold fields, the tribes and their buffalo herds were subject to constant harassment. But in a treaty of September 15, 1851 (11 Stat. 749),[2] and another of April 29, 1868 (15 Stat. 635),[3] the United States government did recognize and confirm that the tribes enjoyed immemorial occupancy and possession of Bear Butte. In the treaty of 1868, the government acknowledged the Great Sioux Nation, which covered approximately the western half of present-day South Dakota. Nevertheless, the voracious demand for Indian lands continued to grow, and on March 2, 1889, Congress enacted legislation carving seven individual reservations from what its own treaty of a mere twenty-one years previously had designated the Great Sioux Nation (25 Stat. 888).[4]

According to Section 21 of that legislation it was decreed:

> That all of the lands in the Great Sioux Reservation outside of the separate reservations herein described are hereby restored to public domain, except American Island, Farm Island, and Niabrara Island, and shall be disposed of by the United States to actual settlers, only, under the provisions of the Homestead law.[5]

With extraordinary insensitivity, Bear Butte, which had been recognized by former treaties as immemorially occupied and possessed by the Lakota and Tsistsistas Nations, was not incorporated into any one of the seven reservations nor included as one of the three named exceptions, and subsequently passed into private ownership until 1962, when it was purchased for $50,000 by the state of South Dakota from one Harold Bovee. Subsequently, it was designated and established as a state park in perpetuity by the South Dakota Legislature, which delegated its management to the State Department of Game, Fish, and Parks.

At the time of its purchase, South Dakota acknowledged that Bear Butte had remained over the years an important religious site for the Lakota and Tsistsistas Nations, neither of which had ever relinquished their rights to continue to use the Black Hills or Bear Butte for religious and ceremonial purposes as they had done since time immemorial. Indeed, South Dakota had an undisguised interest in preserving Indian religious practice at Bear Butte as a unique inducement to a state tourist industry that already enjoyed forty-five state parks for public-access recreational use with a total of more than 90,000 acres. Additionally, the United States government itself operated and managed two national parks and a national monument in the Black Hills area totaling some 272,000 acres, and national forest systems of nearly two million acres. Thus, the state of South Dakota enjoyed more than ample alternatives to promote recreational hiking, camping, and sightseeing. What was unique about Bear Butte and a specific reason for which South Dakota had commissioned it as a state park was precisely its status as "a traditional, significant religious site for the Lakota and Tsistsistas people."[6] But even though the state claimed to maintain the park in part to serve and assist Indian worshipers, its clear mandate was to manage "Bear Butte State Park for the benefit of the general public [that it might] discover the importance of the Butte to the original development of the Black Hills, as well as the geological and Indian religious values of the Butte."[7] Not only did South Dakota take possession of Bear Butte with full knowledge if its central importance to Lakota and Tsistsistas religious belief and practice, but it did so with the conscious purpose of making Bear Butte accessible to the general public as a cultural and historical site, uniquely illustrating the survival and contemporary observance of the tribal religions. South Dakota neither consulted with nor sought the consent of the Indian nations whose most private religious quests it sought to display.

Instead, beginning in 1967, it constructed a visitor's center on the south slope of the Butte along with a main access road. In addition, the state constructed a residence and maintenance shop a little south of the visitor's center, and two parking lots, one of which serviced the center. On the Butte itself, hiking trails were designated, and wooden platforms were set up at periodic sites along the trails ostensibly for scenic overlooks, but from which tourists could view Lakota and Tsistsistas vision quest seekers in any number of their chosen prayer spots all over Bear Butte. The natural tribal inhibition toward the presence of such invasive spectators was often exacerbated by tourist behavior untutored and insensitive to the common courtesy, let alone respectful propriety, which the very nature of Bear Butte as a sacred site and the religious observances being conducted there demanded. Requisite silence and prayerful reflection were not the instinctive habit of the ordinary tourist, to say nothing of those who hiked the Butte drinking beer and other alcoholic beverages. Noise from radios, car horns, motorcycles, and groups of tourists hollering on the Butte or calling to others below deeply disturbed the sense of harmony and intensified concentration of the tribal vision seekers.[8] Although state park officials informed tourists not to stray from the established hiking trails or from the viewing platforms, their very existence facilitated the distracting appearances of tourists attempting to photograph, record, or otherwise observe whatever native ceremonialism they happened upon, heedless of the psychic interruption they might be causing or the ritual prohibition they might be transgressing. This last might include bringing food and water onto the Butte while a quest was in process, symbolically breaking the absolute fast by which all seekers signified their sincerity; disturbing or even removing religious offerings left by the visionary seekers; or violating a customary norm of purification with the presence of women during their menstrual period.[9]

By 1982, Bear Butte State Park had increased its tourist population to more than 10,000 visitors a year. But the very attraction that drew such numbers was itself the most seriously threatened by them. The physical isolation and solitude that created the context and defined the ambience essential to the prayerfulness of the vision quest was increasingly jeopardized by the tourist culture that South Dakota unilaterally invited onto Bear Butte. It had become more apparent to the Lakota and Tsistsistas people that South Dakota, with its designation of Bear Butte as a state park, was progressively changing the very character of their most sacred mountain, and in the process, was directly interfering with their religious belief as well as their practice. In their eyes, the structures that the state had constructed on and in the immediate environs of the Butte—the main access road, visitor's center, parking lots, maintenance shop, and wooden viewing platforms—were not merely the offensive means by which the state facilitated the arrival and stay of an invasive tourist population. As artificial structures and changes in the natural topography, they desecrated the sanctity of Bear Butte, whose holiness as the center of the world and the place of the most immediate contact with the Creator demanded its preservation, unencumbered by mere human edifice or alteration.

So it was as a significant threat that the Lakota and Tsistsistas responded to the unanticipated announcement in the spring of 1982 that the Department of Game, Fish, and Parks planned a series of construction projects at Bear Butte State Park. By letter to several of their leaders, Tony Gullet, manager of the park, informed them that on April 1, the department would initiate work relocating the park shop and building an access road to its new location, repair and blacktop the main access road into the state park, and build a new access road and parking lot for "ceremonial worshipers" adjacent to the area traditionally used as a campsite by those tribal members who kept ritual vigil at the base of the Butte with the solitary vision seekers above. The letter directed that until the work was completed, the traditional campsite would be closed. The Tribes were subsequently informed that all worshipers would be restricted to a campsite at Bear Butte Lake, some two miles away, which was used by non-Indian tourist campers. At that site, however, the tribal members would not be able to hold the prescribed sweat lodge ceremony, essential for the ritual purification of all those participating in the vision quest, nor would they be able to engage in the traditional drumming and singing ceremonies conducted during the nights they were in vigil. Additionally, they would be forced to camp among non-Indian tourists who would have little understanding of the vision quest ceremonialism and would not have participated in the purification ceremonies required for all those at a traditional vigil campsite. Once again, the Indians would be confronted by unwanted exposure to groups of spectators who, with or without an appropriate respect, were simply not prepared to enter as invited participants into one of the most sacred of tribal religious ceremonies.[10] Although it was later waived by the park manager, the tribal worshipers were initially required to pay a nightly fee for every tent they would raise during their time of vigil.[11]

Gullet's letter concluded that after the construction projects were completed, further restrictions would be permanently enforced with regard to the access and use of the traditional ceremonial campsite.

> Due to increased use of the [traditional religious] group area, the limited space available, the lack of facilities and the detrimental impact to area resources, changes have been made in our management policy for the group area. First, after the area is opened for use, people here for religious purposes will be issued a permit that will authorize them to use the area for five (5) days. The option of up to five additional days, if necessary to complete religious activity, will be available. The permit will require the name and address of each vehicle operator, the vehicle license number and the number of people per vehicle. The permit will provide permission for collecting grasses and herbs for religious purposes. The permits authorizing group use will be issued only between May 1 through September 30. Second, vehicle parking will be permitted only in the new parking lot and when the lot at the group area is filled to capacity, no additional users will be given permits.[12]

To the Lakota and Tsistsistas Nations, Gullet's letter signified more than a continued disregard on the part of South Dakota of their religious beliefs and practices as they were centered on Bear Butte. It represented a new and disturbing level of state infringement upon their constitutionally protected religious freedom. On the one hand, it was clear that the state had no intention of removing the offending viewing platforms, visitor's center, maintenance shop, roads, parking lots, and any other alterations it had made to the Butte's natural features. Instead, the letter gave an unambiguous signal that South Dakota would in fact replace worn structures and add new ones. Then again, no relief could be expected from a tourist population whose very numbers and presence, apart from any inappropriate or disrespectful behavior they might exhibit, intruded upon the solitude, silence, and ritual purification crucial to the vision quest and its attendant ceremonialism. Without even the pretense of any assurance that attempts would be made to better address the interference to their religious practice from the tourism the state had cultivated, Gullet's letter instead announced regulations temporarily prohibiting the Lakota and Tsistsistas from their traditional campsite, permanently subjecting them to registration procedures, permanently confining them to a new parking area whose space would determine the number of worshipers permitted to enter the park, and permanently curtailing their stay at the Butte to an initial five-day period with the possibility of an additional five days, only at the discretion of park officials. Not content to have claimed possession of their sacred mountain, to have exploited without permission the most private religious experience on it for the enjoyment of non-Indian campers, hikers, and other recreational tourists, South Dakota made clear its intentions to further control Lakota and Tsistsistas religion by imposing a licensing scheme to monitor their presence, length of stay, and the numbers permitted at the Butte. To guard their ancestral place of prayer from the renewed desecration of the construction projects, which would themselves induce and accommodate the arrival and stay of even more non-religious spectators, and to liberate themselves from the intolerable interference of the state's administrative constraints, the two nations sought constitutional protection.

ANALYSIS AND DECISIONS OF
THE FEDERAL DISTRICT COURT

Frank Fools Crow, traditional head chief and spiritual leader of the Oglala Lakota people, Pete Catches, and Grover Horned Antelope, respected Lakota medicine men, and Arvol Looking Horse, the nineteenth generation Keeper of the Sacred Pipe, were joined as named plaintiffs by Larry Red Shirt, Selo Black Crow, and Francine Nelson as practitioners of traditional Lakota religion. They were joined by Bill Red Hat Jr. and Terry

Wilson, Arrow Priests of the Tsistsistas religion, Laird Cometsevah, a traditional chief of the Tsistsistas Nation, and Walter Hamilton, Arrow Priest and president of the Southern Cheyenne Research and Human Development Association. The plaintiffs brought suit on behalf of themselves as individuals and on behalf of the entire Lakota and Tsistsistas Nations. Proceeding as a certified class action, the nations brought their complaint against Tony Gullet, the manager of Bear Butte State Park, the South Dakota State Department of Game, Fish, and Parks, and the state of South Dakota. Filed at the United States District Court for the District of South Dakota, Western Division, the case was heard and decided by Chief Judge Andrew W. Bogue.

As their first claim for relief, the nations alleged that South Dakota, through its officers and agencies, by restricting and regulating access to Bear Butte had violated the free exercise of tribal religion. By limiting the frequency and duration of the Lakota and Tsistsistas presence on the Butte, the state had significantly interfered with their capacity to conduct ceremonies and to seek visions and dreams in the appropriate manner and at the appropriate time of the year. The state's closure of the traditional ceremonial campsite on April 1 extending indefinitely "until the contractor has completed work"[13] threatened to intrude on the period of the summer solstice, which is the climax of the annual ritual cycle for both of the tribal traditions and thus, the most significant time to be on the Butte. The nations alleged that they were "entitled under the Free Exercise Clause to continue without alteration or interruption those ceremonies and forms of worship which they have conducted on Bear Butte for thousands of years, and which are essential to, and intimately related to their daily lives."[14]

The same allegation was the basis for the tribes' second claim under the American Indian Religious Freedom Act, offered as an independent ground for granting them relief against the state's actions and also as a guide for interpreting the Free Exercise Clause as it related especially to protecting Indian access to sacred sites.[15] The tribal nations also argued that the state's interference with their religious freedom violated Article 18 of the Universal Declaration of Human Rights and Article 18 of the International Covenant on Civil and Political Rights, "which guarantee every person's 'freedom . . . to manifest his religion or belief in teaching, practice, worship and observance' subject only to necessities of public health or safety."[16] Claiming that both articles represented the law of nations, and as such had been incorporated into the law of the United States, the Indian plaintiffs sought a third basis of relief under them.

The common ground for the fourth, fifth, and sixth claims for relief was the state's construction of roads, bridges, parking lots, and other public-access facilities on Bear Butte which, as alterations of its natural features, were desecrations that would "interfere with the power and spiritual unit of the site, and increase traffic, tourism and noise, distracting and disrupting ceremonial activities, and preventing plaintiffs from conducting ceremonies and from seeking visions and dreams in the proper manner and without interruption."[17] Since the natural topographic integrity and isolation of Bear Butte was "essential to the continued value and effectiveness of religious practices conducted there,"[18] the construction projects were alleged to be disruptive intrusions upon the free exercise of Lakota and Tsistsistas religion, and thus violations of their constitutional rights. The projects were likewise alleged to violate the American Indian Religious Freedom Act, whose policy of protecting access to sacred sites "cannot be enjoyed if essential ceremonial lands and natural features are altered, defaced or destroyed, or if traffic and tourism in and on ceremonial shrines and lands is encouraged and increased. Freedom to have and use a church necessarily entails freedom from destruction or desecration of that church, and from uninvited intrusion by non-members."[19] On the same grounds, Article 18 of the Universal Declaration of Human Rights and Article 18 of the International Covenant on Civil and Political Rights were likewise invoked to condemn the construction project. Both of those instruments of international law reinforced the tribal contention that since freedom to practice, worship, and observe one's religion, "necessarily entails the free and unhindered use of ceremonial objects, relics and places, and reasonable privacy from uninvited intrusion and interruption."[20]

While the two Indian nations were deeply distressed and outraged by South Dakota's efforts "to make a zoo out of [their] people's church [i.e., Bear Butte], especially knowing that privacy is central to the successful completion of ceremonies,"[21] they did not seek exclusive rights to Bear Butte or the removal of all tourists from the area. They merely sought relief from those efforts by the state to attract the tourists to the Butte and, once there, to bring them into closer and more frequent contact with Indian worshipers. Their complaint asked the court to declare their right to full, unrestricted, and uninterrupted religious use and enjoyment of Bear Butte without alteration, defacement, or desecration of its natural features by the state; a permanent injunction against the state from restricting or otherwise regulating their access to and use of Bear Butte for religious purposes and from in any way altering, defacing, or desecrating the natural features of the Butte; and an order directing the state to remove such public-access facilities as parking lots and all structures from the Butte and permanently enjoining the state from any and all future construction of such facilities.

Ultimately, Judge Bogue dismissed the Lakota and Tsistsistas complaint on all claims and granted summary judgment for the government defendants. In reaching his decision, however, the judge utterly failed to address the tribal contention that the very alteration of the natural features of Bear Butte diminished the sacred power of the ceremonial ground and constituted a violation of the tribal religions. The judge made no response to the central issue of the complaint: the notion of land as religious entity. Instead, he conformed to the traditional pattern of viewing land as property, and religion as a set of human practices or behavior, beginning his analysis with the assertion that "[i]t is clear to this Court that plaintiffs have no property interest in Bear Butte or in the State Park."[22] He proceeded to ignore the submitted testimony of Indian affidavits and the explicit language of the complaint itself, with his suggestion that during the twenty-year period that South Dakota had owned and managed Bear Butte as a state park, "it appears that plaintiffs' religious practices managed to coexist with the diverse developments that occurred there."[23] The implication of such an injudicious disregard of the record was that if Indians hadn't complained beforehand, their current accusation lacked a sufficient gravity; if they had tolerated the initial building and construction projects when the state took possession of Bear Butte as a state park, how offensive could they be? The insinuation was followed up by yet another judicial irregularity when the judge relied on the purely hearsay testimony of Tony Gullet, the manager of Bear Butte State Park, that Indian religious campers had requested that the state provide safer and better access to the ceremonial grounds. Given that the government defendants had admitted they had never consulted with any Lakota or Tsistsistas medicine men nor held any public hearings before commencing their projects, and since Gullet could neither identify by name the people who "appeared to me to be American Indian people" nor could the government produce any Lakota or Tsistsistas person to corroborate the alleged requests that the state build the road, parking lot, and other structures, Gullet's statement should have been completely disregarded. Because it had been offered as testimony to prove the truth of alleged utterances by unidentified people, it was objectionable hearsay and should never have been relied upon by Judge Bogue.[24]

In his decision, Bogue made no reference to the intrusive nature of the platforms that had been erected on the Butte, from which tourists could view not only scenic vistas from the mountain, but also gain closer access to vision seekers engaged in their prayerful quests. Ignoring the Indian complaints that such structures were both desecration to the natural features of the Butte and sources of distraction and disruptive invasions upon the privacy that would normally be accorded to any other denominational religious ritual, the judge accepted the state's testimony that the platforms had been built "as a means of minimizing the contacts of tourists with worshipers . . . [and] that there are places on the Butte to which worshipers may go out of the sight of the general public. Although worshipers may still hear other hikers and campers . . . many of the sources of noise at the Butte are outside defendants' control."[25] Clearly swayed by South Dakota's exclusive property interest in Bear Butte, Judge Bogue was unwilling to probe beyond the claimed good intentions of the state to ameliorate the impact of the tourist presence that it had promoted, to recognize the substantive infringement on Indian belief and practice that those supposed ameliorations were themselves inflicting. He invoked that part of Judge Richey's district court decision in *Wilson v. Block* that refused to extend First Amendment Free Exercise protections to religious claims against the government's interests in its property.[26] Although as a principle of law that was later repudiated by the court of appeals for the District of Columbia,[27] its instruction was unavailing for Judge Bogue, who followed the judicial tradition of the *Sequoyah, Badoni,* and *Wilson* cases by failing to engage the proposition that grounded all other allegations of the tribal complaint: Bear Butte was itself the sacred reality whose holy presence was to be revered in its natural integrity and that continued to manifest its power of purification and communion to the indigenous peoples of the plains. Instead, Bogue joined those judicial precedents by granting no recognition to the Butte as a religious entity, but fixing it solely in its category as government property, managed and developed as a state park, and segregating religion to those practices that the Lakota and Tsistsistas happened to conduct on state land. Bear Butte thus became mere locale, given over to "competing recreational and religious uses" that the government claimed to administer "through the creation of distinct 'activity sites'."[28]

With the Butte reduced to property, and religion confined to Indian behavior, Judge Bogue next reviewed specific actions of tourists from which the tribes sought particular relief. Making no allusion to the burden sustained by Lakota and Tsistsistas privacy by the very presence of increased numbers of spectators on the mountain ancestrally reserved for prayerful solitude and quiet, he noted their request that park officials "not permit tourists to photograph vision seekers, ceremonies, or religious objects; bring water and food on the Butte during a vision quest; operate cars, horns, motorcycles, radios, etc., during a vision quest; take religious offerings off the Butte; permit non-Indian women having their menstrual period to go on the Butte during a vision quest."[29] Following up on his premise of Bear

Butte as a park owned and managed by South Dakota, the judge sanctioned the state's right to bring tourists and campers onto its property and summarily rejected any obligation "to police" their actions in the form of requested protections. Claiming that the First Amendment protects against government action, Bogue would nevertheless not extend that protection against those violations of a long-established indigenous religious practice by those who were at the Butte through the auspices of the state government.

Judge Bogue supported his indulgence of South Dakota's irresponsible tourist policy at the Butte by relying on the decision of the court of appeals in *Badoni v. Higginson*, which had similarly exonerated government failure of tourist supervision at Rainbow Bridge National Monument. Without any attention to the significant difference between the relatively few Navajos and the occasional visits they made to the remote Rainbow Bridge and the thousand-fold presence of Lakota and Tsistsistas peoples at Bear Butte throughout the year, especially from spring through autumn, Judge Bogue simply intoned the self-serving admonition of the *Badoni* court: "We must accommodate our idiosyncrasies, religious as well as secular, to the compromises necessary in communal life [cites omitted]. Were it otherwise, the Monument would become a government-managed religious shrine."[30] Retaining its original offensive equation of indigenous religion with mere idiosyncrasy, the phrases' moralistic tone proved specious in its application. Marginal restrictions directed non-Indian tourists and campers to stay on certain identified hiking trails and the viewing platforms when they were on the Butte, which could be from eight in the morning to eight at night. Those minimal regulations could hardly compare to the intrusions inflicted on Lakota and Tsistsistas believers whose solitude, essential to the vision quest experience, was fundamentally compromised by the presence of tourists on the Butte throughout the day and the specific conduct engaged in by some of them that intruded upon, disturbed, or otherwise violated the beliefs and practices of tribal worshipers.

Harking back to his earlier remark about the apparent toleration of the Indian plaintiffs to coexist with the demands placed on them by Bear Butte's management as a state park, Judge Bogue dismissed the serious problem of distractions endured by tribal vision seekers from tourist presence and behavior through a serious misinterpretation and exclusive reliance upon the testimony of one of the plaintiffs. Grover Horned Antelope, a respected Lakota medicine man, long-practiced in the vision quest, had testified that despite the distractions he had encountered from tourist activity on the Butte, he had been able to complete his most recent vision quest. Ignoring the explicit language of the nations' complaint and the affidavits submitted with it on the interference and disruptions suffered from increased tourism during vision quests by members of both the Lakota and Tsistsistas traditions, and failing to qualify Grover Horned Antelope's exceptional status as an accomplished spiritual leader, Bogue seized on his testimony, not as an indication of the difficulty suffered even by such an experienced and gifted figure, but as the vindication for his conclusion "that defendants have not burdened the exercise of plaintiffs' religion by 'allowing' tourists to act on occasion in a manner which does not conform to the dictates of plaintiffs' religion."[31]

Judge Bogue's concern that protecting the religious practitioners on the Butte from the particular grievances of certain kinds of tourist behavior would turn the mountain into an illicit "government-managed religious shrine" was even more incongruous than its first coinage by the court of appeals in the *Badoni* case. When South Dakota took possession of Bear Butte in 1962 and added it to its forty-five other state parks, it did so fully cognizant of its singular significance within the religious landscape of the Lakota and Tsistsistas Nations. Precisely in its status as sacred land, not only in the remote past but as a current focus for indigenous belief and practice, the Butte offered a distinctive opportunity to the state for attracting tourists to observe Indian religion. Since the state had acknowledged that "the Indian religious tradition helps define the value and importance of Bear Butte to this region,"[32] it plainly admitted that it had purchased a preexisting Indian shrine. By turning it into parkland, and encouraging tourists with paved roads, a visitor center, hiking trails, viewing platforms, and overnight camping area, the state enmeshed itself in the very management that Judge Bogue had deemed impermissive. It was hardly appropriate, if not disingenuous, for the court to defend South Dakota's failure to prevent tourist offenses to the beliefs and practices at the religious shrine over which it had assumed patent managerial control to accommodate those non-Indian visitors.

The final issue Judge Bogue considered in the Lakota and Tsistsistas claim under the Free Exercise Clause illustrated yet another aspect of the administrative authority that South Dakota exercised over the Indian shrine. While it proceeded with the offensive construction projects, the state unilaterally closed for overnight camping the area traditionally used by the tribes for sweat lodge purification ceremonies, ritual drumming, and song by those who would later ascend the Butte for the vision quest and those who would remain in prayerful vigil until their return. Although the tribes were permitted to use the traditional ceremonial area during the day, the state required them to pass the night at another campground some two miles away, where they were prohibited from building sweat lodges. Thus this important purification ritual could not be celebrated at night as was customary for vision-quest ceremonies. But the court's response to this other interruption of Indian religious practice was to evaluate it solely in terms of a partial and temporary exclusion of the tribes from their traditional site. The court then relied on the submersion of sacred lands permitted by the courts in *Sequoyah v. Tennessee Valley Authority* and *Badoni v. Higginson*. Since they stood as precedents for the judicial approbation of government acts of flooding that permanently severed access to sacred Cherokee and Navajo sites respectively, Bogue adopted those decisions to justify the exclusion of the Lakota and Tsistsistas from their ceremonial campsite without any acknowledgment that this prevented the sweat lodge purification ritual from being conducted during the night. Although the judge failed to recognize the infringement upon tribal religious freedom, he nevertheless determined that South Dakota had demonstrated a compelling state interest for its construction projects at the Butte that would absolve it for any restraint it may have imposed on Lakota and Tsistsistas religion.

Confirming his allegiance to the perspective of Bear Butte as state property, Bogue ruled that the paved roads, parking lots, and other construction were compelling enhancements to a valuable environmental resource, "preserving [it] from further decay and erosion . . . protecting the health, safety, and welfare of park visitors, and . . . improving public access to this unique geological and historical landmark."[33] With no mention of the uncontested contribution of Native American religion to the historic significance defining the landmark status vaunted by the state, the district court was blind to the ironic tragedy that the unique feature drawing increased tourism to Bear Butte was being hindered in its free expression by that very tourism and South Dakota's efforts to promote it.

Having elevated tourism to a compelling state interest, the district court quickly dismissed the tribal complaint against the requirement that they register at the visitor's center and be issued a permit before entering Bear Butte State Park for the purpose of the vision quest. So thoroughly had the court adopted the view of the Butte as government property, assigned and administered for recreational and religious uses, that the imposition of a licensing scheme with the potential of restricting the number of Lakota and Tsistsistas worshipers and limiting the duration they would be allowed to pray on land immemorially held sacred by them was given scant judicial scrutiny. Noting only that its requirements of themselves did not violate any tenet of Indian religion and had not yet been applied to deprive any Indian access to the Butte, Judge Bogue determined them "to serve valid state interests in controlling traffic at the park and in providing the means to contact visitors in case of emergency."[34] In addition to betraying the problem of regulating increasing numbers of visitors at the Butte, thus unwittingly reinforcing the Lakota and Tsistsistas complaint against an invasive tourist intrusion during their vision quests, the judge's remark confirmed the managerial prerogative that the court would permit South Dakota to exercise in administering its property interest in the Butte.

Once the court had ruled that no violation of religious free exercise had been inflicted upon the tribal plaintiffs, it dispatched the remaining grounds on which they had sought relief. Alluding to Judge Richey's analysis of the American Indian Religious Freedom Act in his district court opinion in the case of *Wilson v. Block*, Judge Bogue agreed that the act did not create a distinct cause of action in federal courts for alleged violation of Indian religious freedom. So long as the government, in any particular incident, is found to have complied with the dictates of the First Amendment, the policy concerns of the act are satisfied. Similarly, the court dismissed Articles 18 of the Universal Declaration of Human Rights and the International Covenant on Civil and Political Rights as documents that did not create any legal rights in addition to those recognized by the First Amendment. Thus, Bogue concluded that the three additional bases on which the Indian plaintiffs sought relief were without merit, since he had found no infringement on their First Amendment Rights.

As an indication of how distant he was from understanding the heart of the Lakota and Tsistsistas claim, Judge Bogue ended his opinion by raising a list of ways in which he considered South Dakota had afforded "special treatment and special privileges to American Indian religious practices at the Butte."[35] Suggesting that the state ran the risk of violating the Establishment Clause by granting favored treatment to the tribes, he noted that they generally used a special camping area from which the public was excluded and at which the state provided free firewood, outdoor bathroom facilities, and garbage disposal; they enjoyed the option of seeking a five-day extension to their camping permit, not available to the public; they had not been charged the usual fee when they had been forced to camp at Bear Butte Lake along with the general public; they were not confined to the use of the hiking trails or viewing platforms that had been designated for public access on the Butte; and they were able to remain on the Butte during the nights of their vision quests when the general public had to be off by eight o'clock. Granting summary judgment for the government defendants, Bogue ended by characterizing as "privileges" the very restrictions that the state's administration of Bear Butte as a tourist attraction had imposed on the Lakota and Tsistsistas Nations.

ON APPEAL TO THE EIGHTH CIRCUIT

The tribal plaintiffs appealed the decision of the district court to the United States court of appeals for the Eighth Circuit. Since the district court had concluded its ruling with an intimation that granting relief to the Indian nations might constitute further state support for Indian religion in addition to the considerations already accorded them as distinct from the general public, the tribes argued that there was no such impermissive transgression of the Establishment Clause. Countering the insinuation that South Dakota was already "advancing" tribal religion by allowing marginal exceptions to the administrative regime it had imposed upon them by turning Bear Butte into yet another state park, the Lakota and Tsistsistas pointed out that it was not an Establishment issue if state authorities accorded religious worshipers the same privacy, security, and freedom of speech and assembly enjoyed by other religious groups and traditions. They contended that, on the contrary, the denial of those same rights and freedoms accorded to practitioners of all other religions was a clear violation of the Free Exercise Clause.

The tribal appellants criticized the district court's failure to distinguish between the Free Exercise Clause as a negative right and the Establishment Clause, which forbids the bestowal of a positive right. They argued that Free Exercise as a negative right generally connotes a freedom from government intrusion, whereas the Establishment Clause generally prohibits the government from providing preference or subsidy for religious purposes at public expense. The nations claimed that all they sought was the negative right of being left to pursue their ancestral beliefs and practices at Bear Butte, free from the desecrations and intrusions of the state's construction projects that attracted and accommodated increased tourism that further burdened their religion. They had sought neither government assistance nor state expenditures, and rather than any affirmative modifications of Bear Butte, they asked only that the state cease its own modifications before its construction and attendant tourism rendered impossible their religious practice. The tribes analogized their situation to one that might arise if a conventional church opposed the demolition of an indispensable cathedral for the construction of a playground. If the government agreed to locate the playground elsewhere and thus minimize the conflict with the religious liberty of the church members, it would not raise an Establishment problem because it would have involved no affirmative financial aid or privilege. That would not have been the case had the congregation petitioned public authorities to declare a parkland or plant trees around the cathedral to make it more attractive; in such a scenario the state would be positively aiding, rather than merely protecting the religion of the congregation. Similarly, the Lakota and Tsistsistas peoples reasoned that Bear Butte was their living cathedral, their mountain-altar for the practice of a most intimate religious experience, which they petitioned the state to respect and protect by refraining from construction projects that desecrated the sacred integrity of the Butte and attracted a tourist population that increasingly infringed upon the ceremonial propriety and solitude of the vision quest and its ceremonialism. Asking nothing more than freedom from such government intrusion, the Indian nations noted the paradox of the district court's insinuation that granting such relief to freely exercise their religion would raise Establishment problems. Recalling South Dakota's claim that it was building a parking lot and access road to better allow the tribes access to the Butte and that it had built the hiking trails and viewing platforms to protect their privacy from tourists, the tribal appeal stressed that the original complaint and submitted affidavits had explicitly rejected all such assistance, noting that the claimed government "benefits" violated their beliefs and facilitated the tourist population's access to their otherwise isolated sacred Butte. Their appeal stated:

> The paradox is an interesting one in this area of criticism of misguided but purportedly benevolent social policy. Can government take costly public action to "help" parishioners of one religion, over their protest, and then hide behind the Establishment Clause to defend its actions? It is all too contradictory. Surely freedom from unwanted government "help" in protecting and preserving religious beliefs is a Free Exercise right, rather than an Establishment Clause transgression.[36]

The appeal also protested the registration requirements imposed by the state park officials each and every time a tribal member went to Bear Butte to pray. Once registered, they had to wait for a permit to be issued, which was solely at the discretion of a park official. Initially granted for a period of five days, an extension was possible upon request and by administrative discretion but was not to exceed another five days. No written policy or guidelines existed, however, to inform, standardize, and thus protect the process against arbitrary abuse. The district court had paid scant attention to the subjugation of individual freedom to pray where, when, and for what duration to a licensing scheme like the one that burdened the Lakota and Tsistsistas religions. Contesting the district court's assertion that the registration and permit requirements were harmless regulations for the control of visitor traffic at the state park, the tribal appeal proposed that similar restrictions be placed on all churchgoers in South Dakota: that they be stopped at a roadblock, fill out a form, and await a discretionary permit before they be allowed to proceed to their church building to pray for a predetermined number of hours as limited by the permit. "We suspect that such a restriction, though no more than what has been imposed upon the appellants here [i.e., the Lakota and Tsistsistas Nations], would be decried as a most substantial infringement by all church organizations in the United States."[37]

The appeal relied on two Supreme Court decisions to ground its legal argument. In *Shuttlesworth v. City of Birmingham*,[38] the Court condemned a city ordinance granting "unbridled and absolute power" to a city commissioner charged with the authority to grant or deny parade permits. The ordinance was ruled unconstitutional because it made the exercise of free speech contingent upon the mere will of an administrative commission whose unfettered discretion to deny a permit could effectively censor and restrain a fundamental freedom. The Lakota and Tsistsistas argued that under *Shuttlesworth*, the unpublished and non-existent policy statement and principled guidelines that thus vested total authority in a state park official to accept or deny them access to their undisputed place of worship was an unconstitutional threat to their religious freedom. Even if no worshipers had yet been denied a permit, the tribal appeal contended, the very existence of such a discretionary administrative power to limit First Amendment religious rights should not be permitted to stand.

Similarly, the appeal turned to the then recent decision by the Supreme Court in *Larson v. Valente*[39] to criticize the discriminatory impact the registration and permit requirements had on the two indigenous religions. In that case, the Court had invalidated portions of a Minnesota law exempting some, but not all, religious organizations from the law's registration and reporting requirements, which had originally been imposed on all charitable organizations to prevent fraud. The exemption was later extended to those religious organizations receiving more than half of their total contributions from members. The Supreme Court found that such an exemption protected well-established churches that had achieved strong but not total financial support from their members, but discriminated against new churches and religious groups lacking constituencies or those that favored public solicitation of funds rather than relying on financial support from their members. Ruling that the exemption scheme favored certain religious groups but burdened others with recording and disclosure requirements, the Supreme Court struck it down as a violation of the Establishment Clause.

In their appeal, the Lakota and Tsistsistas Nations maintained that South Dakota's intrusive registration and permit demands, monitoring their attendance and length of stay at their ancestral place of prayer and worship, was not imposed on any other religious community within the state. The information taken from them in the registration procedure identified them as ceremonial users of the Butte, and thus, the permission subsequently granted or denied them; subjecting their religious belief to an administrative review not endured by members of any other denomination seeking entry into their respective churches or religious buildings. The district court's failure to scrutinize the discriminatory impact as well as the unchecked bureaucratic discretion of the registration and permit requirements demanded of the Lakota and Tsistsistas was a flaw they asked the court of appeals to address.

But the fundamental issue raised for the appellate court's consideration was the question of what constitutes an unconstitutional burden on Native American religions when their belief and practice is centered on land their traditions consider a sacred reality. The district court in *Crow v. Gullet*, like all of the courts, both district and appellate, in the previous related cases, refused to acknowledge the threshold issue, which prevented further analysis: harm is inflicted on tribal religion when government action not only denies access to the land in question, but initiates changes that alter the land's natural integrity. Land as itself a religious entity, a holy presence, was beyond the pale of judicial conception and was subjugated to the notion of property. In such a framework, seeing Bear Butte solely in terms of state parkland purchased and managed by South Dakota, it was more than sufficient that the state permitted the Lakota and Tsistsistas peoples to enjoy physical access to pursue their religious quests on land they did not own. However offensive to their sensibilities the registration and permit requirements might be, and however annoying the presence of tourists might prove, these never rose, in the district court's eyes, to anything more than inconveniences that had to be tolerated as conditions attendant to the state's designation of its land as available for public recreational use. The district court's uncritical allegiance to its conception of Bear Butte as state property was fundamental to its summary determination that the tribal religions had suffered no harm of constitutional significance.

Had the district court stopped there, it would have remained the responsibility of the court of appeals to carefully evaluate the lower court's refusal to recognize that any injury had been inflicted on the Lakota and Tsistsistas' exercise of their religious freedom from government construction projects at Bear Butte; their restrictions from the use of their traditional campground during the construction period; their subjection to registration and discretionary permits each and every time they prayed at the Butte; and the interference they endured from the state's accommodations for increased tourist access to the sacred site. In its review, the court of appeals would have to respond to the tribal allegation that the district court had concluded that none of these actions had violated their religious belief and practice by ignoring the explicit attestations of their complaint and the affidavits submitted in its support. But the court of appeals would have a further issue to scrutinize that the district court had irregularly raised by its contention that the religious interests of the Lakota and Tsistsistas Nations, however they might have been burdened, were outweighed by South Dakota's "compelling state interests" in enhancing and improving the Butte as an important state resource for the health, safety, and accessibility of park visitors. In considering this determination, the court of appeals would first have to correct the district court's erroneous procedure. In traditional free-exercise jurisprudence, the court looks first to see if the contested government action does in fact violate the plaintiff's constitutionally protected freedom of religious exercise. If a violation is found, the court proceeds to examine whether or not the government has a compelling state interest in pursuing its activity, the importance of which must be of such a magnitude as to justify the burden it inflicts on the religious freedom of the plaintiff. The irregularity of the district court was its gratuitous opinion that South Dakota's tourist interest at the Butte was sufficiently compelling to override any harm to the tribal religions. Having first concluded that no judicially cognizable burden had been imposed on them, the district court exceeded the accepted procedure with its presumptive judgment that even if no religious harm had been suffered by the Indian nations, South Dakota's interest in tourism at the Butte was of such significance as to compellingly outweigh any complaint raised against it.

Having identified the procedural error in the district court's opinion, the court of appeals would be free to assess the lower court's substantive claim advancing the compelling nature of South Dakota's tourist interest in Bear Butte. The tribal appellants had countered that government actions that had been sustained in the past as sufficiently compelling to override the protections otherwise accorded to the free exercise of religion were rare and had involved threats of imminent jeopardy to public health and safety, the requirements of national defense, and the need for maintaining the national Social Security system. The infrequency of such overriding state interests that had passed judicial scrutiny reflected the high threshold that had to be met before a government action could be considered "compelling." It was not enough that the state's particular interest be reasonable or merely legitimate.

In its ruling in *Sherbert v. Verner*, the Supreme Court in 1963 had emphasized that "[i]t is basic that no showing merely of a rational relationship to some colorable state interest would suffice; in this highly sensitive constitutional area 'only the gravest abuses, endangering paramount interests, give occasion for permissible limitation'."[40] Almost a decade later in *Wisconsin v. Yoder*, the high court reiterated that "[t]he essence of all that has been said and written on the subject is that only those interests of the highest order and those not otherwise served can overbalance legitimate claims to the free exercise of religion. We can accept it as settled, therefore, that, however strong the State's interest . . . it is by no means absolute to the exclusion or subordination of all other interests."[41] In *Sherbert*, South Carolina's interest in protecting its unemployment compensation fund from fraudulent claimants feigning religious objections was insufficient to deny such compensation to a Seventh-day Adventist whose Sabbath beliefs prevented her from accepting work requiring her to work on Saturday. In *Yoder*, Wisconsin's substantial interest in maintaining universal educational standards, requiring children to attend school until reaching the age of sixteen, was yet not of a sufficient magnitude to transgress the religious beliefs of Old Order Amish communities who declined to send their children beyond the eighth grade. If even such weighty state interests as those found in the *Sherbert* and *Yoder* cases were nevertheless deemed to lack the paramount significance to justify the harms they would cause to the constitutionally protected freedoms of Seventh-day Adventist and Amish believers respectively, how could South Dakota's interest in tourism ever qualify as "compelling"? The Lakota and Tsistsistas appeal denied that it could ever muster the requisite gravity, and faulted the district court for failing to address the issue and engage in a searching examination of the state's claim. Since the court had irresponsibly denied the existence of any constitutionally recognizable harm to the Indian religions, it managed to bypass the detailed analysis of carefully weighing the burdens that the tribes had stated in their complaint against the interests of South Dakota. But since the court had presumed to characterize those interests as "compelling," it was insufficient that it did so in the unsubstantiated, conclusive fashion it had used. By doing so, the court injudiciously exonerated South Dakota of its burden to demonstrate how its stake in adding yet another site to its existing forty-five state parks of more than 90,000 acres and of promoting public access and use of it in the way it had chosen were "of the highest order," protecting such "paramount interests" that would justify its interference with a site as sacred as Bear Butte to the Lakota and Tsistsistas religious traditions.

In their appeal, the two Indian nations sought the appellate court's correction of this failure by the district court to probe the state's claim that tourist development of Bear Butte was of such significance that it permitted South Dakota to ignore the necessities of quiet, solitude, and undisturbed natural features enjoyed by the very religious quest that it featured as a unique attraction of Bear Butte. Even if, in the district court's balancing, the state had been able to demonstrate a compelling interest for turning the Butte into state parkland and overriding the religious burdens placed upon the tribal religions, South Dakota still had to prove that no alternatives for managing the Butte existed that were less restrictive of Lakota and Tsistsistas religious observance than the construction of access roads, parking lots, viewing platforms, and other buildings and the imposition of registration and permit requirements. More fundamental yet was the state's failure to show that no alternatives for public hiking, camping, and enjoyment of nature existed among the 90,000 acres of other state parks, the 272,000 acres of national parks, and the two million acres of national forests that South Dakota already afforded. The lack of penetrating judicial inquiry into this important question permitted South Dakota to avoid its burden of proving that its interests in tourism could not be met by any other means less restrictive of indigenous constitutional freedoms than by appropriating and managing the land mass considered most sacred to the Lakota and Tsistsistas religions.

A further issue for review by the court of appeals derived from this same point concerning Bear Butte's undisputed importance in the belief and practice of the two Indian nations. In its opinion, the district court relied on the three precedents that had treated the closely related question of Native American religion and land. Without any sustained analysis and with no instructive application, the district court merely cited *Sequoyah v. Tennessee Valley Authority, Badoni v. Higginson,* and the district court opinion in *Wilson v. Block* to support its ultimate dismissal of the Lakota and Tsistsistas claim. But what the district court completely overlooked in the three previous decisions was the claim by those courts that the lands in question were not "central" or "indispensable" to the religious practices of the particular tribes. However unfounded and unjust such a standard was, it remained a critical factor in the rulings by those courts that no religious harm would be suffered respectively by the Cherokees from the submersion of the Little Tennessee Valley, by the Hopis and Navajos from the flooding of Rainbow Bridge and its canyon, or by the Navajos from the ski resort development on the San Francisco Peaks. Having arbitrarily determined that the various sites lacked sufficient centrality and indispensability and that the particular tribes were free to conduct their religious practices elsewhere, the courts in *Sequoyah, Badoni,* and *Wilson* refused to acknowledge any violations of Indian religious freedom.

But if the district court in *Crow v. Gullet* conveniently adopted those precedents to support its own determination that South Dakota had not transgressed the religious exercise of the Lakota and Tsistsistas peoples, it did so without regard for logical consistency or principle. Those same precedents directed the very opposite conclusion from the one asserted by the district court. If it had allowed itself to be genuinely guided by the rule they had pronounced rather than merely appropriate the dismissals they sustained, the district court should have upheld a finding of religious harm inflicted on the Lakota and Tsistsistas believers by state government actions at Bear Butte. Beyond question, Bear Butte satisfied the centrality and indispensability standards of the *Sequoyah*, *Badoni*, and *Wilson* courts. It had never been challenged by the state that the Butte had been and continued to be anything but the most sacred site for some 35,000 Lakota and Tsistsistas peoples. As already noted, South Dakota had admitted that "the Indian religious tradition helps define the value and importance of Bear Butte to this region"[42] as justification for incorporating it into its park system and attracting tourist visitors to the unique site. The Butte's centrality and indispensability to the Lakota and Tsistsistas religions was the very feature the state had heralded. Additionally, the *Wilson* court had specified that claims for protection of religious freedom on government-held lands would be recognized when "the government's proposed land use would impair a religious practice that could not be performed at any other site."[43] The district court knew the state's admission of Bear Butte's singular importance as the most sacred site of the two Indian nations, and it had received their own testimony that government construction projects were desecrating its holy integrity even as the increased tourist populations that the government attracted and accommodated were interfering with the silence, solitude, and ritual purification required by the vision quest. The district court's refusal to find government impairment of Indian religion at a site as central and indispensable to Lakota and Tsistsistas belief and practice was a distortion of the very judicial authorities on which the court had claimed to rely. *Sequoyah*, *Badoni*, and *Wilson* directed the district court to uphold, not dismiss, the Lakota and Tsistsistas claim of an unconstitutional government burden on their free exercise of religion as practiced at Bear Butte. This inconsistent misapplication of the legal precedents it had invoked was yet another flaw marring the district court decision from which the two Indian nations sought appellate relief.

Shockingly, the Court of Appeals for the Eighth Circuit, represented by a three-judge panel of then Chief Judge Donald P. Lay and Circuit Judges Myron H. Bright and Donald R. Ross, declined to address any of the issues raised by the Lakota and Tsistsistas appeal. In a terse recapitulation of the rudimentary facts and procedural history, the court of appeals issued a mere *per curiam* announcement, reiterating the district court's opinion and, without elaboration or explanation, affirmed its decision.[44] In doing so, the court of appeals abdicated its prerogative to provide clarification and guidance to the questions posed by the Indian appellants. Its mere affirmance without comment left unresolved important questions concerning the relationship between the Establishment and Free Exercise Clauses of the First Amendment and the appropriateness of registration and permit schemes imposed upon Native American religious believers seeking access to sacred sites to pray and worship. More importantly, the court of appeals left unanswered the fundamental question of what standard should be followed in determining when governmental activity constitutes a burden on the free exercise of Native American religions when the sacred reality that evokes their responses in prayer and ceremonial activity is land held by the government or to which it lays claim.

The rubric fashioned and imposed by the court of appeals in the *Sequoyah* case and invoked by the courts in *Badoni* and *Wilson* was a showing by Native American plaintiffs that the contested sacred land was "central" and "indispensable" to their way of life and to their religious practices. Yet when the district court in *Crow v. Gullet* relied on those cases to support its summary judgment against the Lakota and Tsistsistas claim, it severely and indefensibly limited the extent to which it would permit the uncontested centrality of Bear Butte for the silence and solitude of the vision quest to support the tribal claim against efforts by South Dakota to turn the Butte into a tourist attraction. Claiming that physical access alone was sufficient to protect the tribal free exercise, the district court completely minimized the indispensability of its relative remoteness and quiet for the effective pursuit of the vision quest, which was so clearly jeopardized by South Dakota's efforts to accommodate increased tourist presence at its recently declared state park. This failure by the district court to consistently apply the standard used in the cases that it nominally cited as its authorities was an incongruity the court of appeals unreasonably ignored. More irresponsible, however, was its mute response to the issue of what constitutes a "compelling state interest" that would justify a burden imposed on Native American religions. Government interest in recreation and tourism had been a secondary issue in the flooding of Rainbow Bridge in the *Badoni* case, but had become a salient point of inquiry in the *Wilson* case with the construction of a privately operated ski resort on the San Francisco Peaks of Coconino National Forest. Because the court of appeals in *Wilson* ruled that the Hopis and Navajos would suffer no religious burden from the resort, it never addressed the question of whether or not the government's interest in sponsoring the commercial development for recreational skiing was sufficiently "compelling" to warrant an intrusion on a mountain they had long held sacred. Although the court of appeals cut off a formal consideration of the issue, it remained for careful scrutiny. The district court in *Crow* provided the opportunity by its explicit determination that South Dakota's concern to enhance Bear Butte for greater public access and enjoyment was a "compelling state interest" that took priority over the demands of the Lakota and Tsistsistas religions practiced at the Butte. Challenged on appeal to identify the constitutional grounds that would support tourism at Bear Butte as the requisite "paramount" importance and "highest order" of significance, incapable of being satisfied through the extensive acreage of already existing state and national park and forest land in South Dakota, the Eighth Circuit court of appeals refused to respond. Its inarticulate approval of the district court's decision left the Lakota and Tsistsistas religions subjugated to the vagaries of South Dakota's interest in them as mere tourist attractions. But within two weeks of its decision, the United States District Court for the Northern District of California reversed the trend begun in *Sequoyah* and perpetuated in *Badoni*, *Wilson*, and now *Crow* by recognizing the constitutional harm to Native American religions from proposed government actions that threatened to violate the integrity of land whose sanctity was upheld and protected by the court against government claims of managerial authority. Affirmed by the court of appeals for the Ninth Circuit, the decision profoundly challenged the prevailing paradigm of land as property, a challenge the United States Supreme Court would tragically proscribe.

5

༄

Lyng v. Northwest Indian Cemetery Protective Association: *The Supreme Court and the Triumph of Property over Religion*

The far northwestern corner of California, in an area including Del Norte, Humboldt, and Siskiyou Counties and encompassing both the Six Rivers National Forest and the adjoining Klamath National Forest and the surrounding communities of Eureka, Arkata, McKinleyville, Klamath, Crescent City, Gasquet, Hoopa, Orleans, Happy Camp, and Yreka has been the traditional homeland of the Yurok, Karok, Tolowa, and Hupa tribes. Historically, the Yurok occupied the Klamath River canyon from Bluff Creek (some six miles above the modern hamlet of Weitchpec) downriver to its mouth. Their territory also stretched along the Pacific coast from a village on Little River (four miles south of modern Trinidad), to a village at Wilson Creek, some six miles north of the mouth of the Klamath. In all, the Yurok occupied some forty-three miles of Pacific Ocean frontage, forty-four miles of the Klamath River shore and the lower seventeen miles along Redwood Creek. Most village sites were traditionally located along the river or near the coast. They reserved the back country primarily for hunting and gathering of supplementary food resources, basketry materials, firewood, and for religious purposes.[1]

Karok villages traditionally stretched along seventy miles of the Klamath River (from Bluff Creek upriver to Seiad Valley) and some eight miles of the Salmon River (from the junction with the Klamath at Somes Bar). At the same time, the Tolowa occupied coastal and riverine villages north of the Yurok, with the greatest village concentration near present-day Crescent City and Point St. George. Other villages were situated at the mouth of the Smith River and by Lake Earl. Before the nineteenth century, they occupied thirty-two miles along the Pacific Ocean shore and another thirty-five miles along the banks of the Smith River. They also possessed hunting resources and religious use areas in the mountains. Finally, the Hupa occupied the area of the Trinity River upriver from the hamlet of Weitchpec on the Klamath River for some thirty-nine miles. Their most populous villages lay in the level eight-mile stretch of Hoopa Valley.

Although archeological evidence suggests human habitation of this area of northwest California for at least 2,000 years and possibly for as long as 4,300,[2] the first recorded expedition of white fur trappers into the region of the Trinity and Klamath Rivers to encounter groups of Yurok people dates to 1828. The meetings indicated that the Yuroks were friendly and willing to trade, especially for blankets and metal tools. The following twenty years witnessed tentative relations between the native peoples of northwest California and non-native fur traders. But with the discovery of gold in 1848, the relative isolation of the tribes changed drastically. The Klamath River region was rich in gold, and by the summer of 1850, miners were present on the Klamath and Salmon Rivers. Mining towns throughout the ancestral territories of the Yurok, Karok, Tolowa, and Hupa peoples grew quickly during the 1850s. In their pursuit of gold, miners often claimed and exploited Indian lands before they had been legally ceded to the United States. Until 1855, the United States Army was largely ineffective in protecting the native tribes from the degradations inflicted on them by ever-increasing numbers of gold miners.

In November 1855, President Franklin Pierce approved the Klamath River Indian Reservation, relegating a mere strip of land one mile wide on each side of that river from its mouth and extending upstream about twenty miles. But the formal establishment of the reservation and the removal to it of many of the Indians in the Klamath River region did not improve the welfare of the Indian peoples in northwestern California. One factor that exacerbated tension was that the reserved land was within the traditional homeland of the Yurok Indians. They objected to the enforced presence of other tribal groups such as the Karok and Tolowa, who were placed among them and competing for the limited fishing and hunting resources on the 25,000-acre reservation. Additionally, congressional appropriations for promised supplies for reservation Indians were grossly insufficient. Although it was generally safer for Indians on the reservation, where they were relatively protected from indiscriminate murder at the hands of white miners and other settlers who were bent on removing them from their lands, overcrowding and lack of food induced many non-Yurok Indians to flee. When they returned to their former homelands, they found that whites were now living there who took the Indians' flight from the reservation as justification to hunt them down, killing those who resisted and shipping those captured to areas in southern California.

During the Civil War, many of the 16,000 volunteers for the Union remained in California, where the army attempted to forcefully remove all Indians onto reservations. In 1862, after winter floods devastated the Klamath Indian reservation, the army relocated its inhabitants to a smaller reservation on the Smith River, upstream from Crescent City. But within two years, the majority Yurok population fled the reservation to return to their traditional homeland on the Klamath River. The government chose to leave them there without further interference, evidently determining that the frequently flooded region was undesirable for any further investment purposes. In 1869, the army closed the Smith River reservation and transferred those Indians still there to the only other reservation in northwestern California in Hoopa Valley. There, the government had agreed in 1864 to permit the Hupa people to remain within certain limited boundaries of their ancestral regional homeland. Thus, after some twenty years of open aggression from gold miners and other settlers, and generally ineffective but highly destructive relocation efforts by the federal government, the Yurok, Karok, Tolowa, and Hupa peoples nevertheless remained within the general areas of their customary territories. They were, however, greatly diminished in numbers, victims of murderous gold rush greed and army campaigns against them. Those Yuroks who lived off of the Hoopa reservation and had moved back into the area of the original 1855 Klamath River reservation were given the opportunity under the allotment system beginning in 1883 and continuing into the 1890s to own 160 acres per family head, 80 acres to a single Indian over eighteen years of age, and 40 acres to Indian orphans under eighteen years of age. The land remaining within the boundaries of the old 25,000-acre reservation after the Indians received their allotments was returned to the public domain. The resulting allocation saw the distribution of only 10,000 acres to the Yuroks, with the remaining 15,000 of the most valuable timbered acreage sold to white settlers and timber companies.

Throughout the turbulent invasion of their homeland by gold miners, the failed attempt by the army to relocate them, and the subsequent period of settling back into the regions of their ancestral villages and extending into the present, the Yuroks, Karoks, Tolowa, and certain of the Hupa continued to adhere to an ancient and generally held religious belief in the sacredness of "the high country," an area of peaks and rocks, roughly between the towns of Gasquet and Orleans, in the Blue Creek vicinity of the Siskiyou Mountains, which rise more than 7,000 feet above the Klamath River. Central to the religious ceremonialism of the tribes is the celebration of periodic dances, most notably the White Deerskin Dance and the Jump Dance, which have been designated as "world renewal" rituals whose purpose is the stabilization and preservation of the earth from catastrophe, and of humankind from disease.[3] The dances can be performed only in the presence of medicine men or women who preside by virtue of their spiritual power or medicine granted them during their initial training and periodic return to the high country, the most efficacious place of communication with the Creator, and the home of prehuman supernatural beings who remain responsive to the needs of those who seek their aid. The world renewal dances are tribal affirmations of the continuous power of those beings to grant health and remove evil from the world by establishing harmony and balance to the earth. Specific healing power derived from the high country is also dispensed through the mediation of the medicine men and women in other ceremonies such as the Brush Dance and Kick Dance, as well as through curative treatments rendered directly to individual patients.[4]

Although the high country is the indispensable source of the psychic and physical energies that might be transmitted through the relatively few "doctors" who feel called to complete the arduous self-discipline and isolation of successfully ministering to others, any member of these northwestern California tribes can make private pilgrimages into the high country for prayer, guidance, or the favorable resolution of specific needs and concerns. It is also in the high country that young men and women receive training in tribal religious traditions and ceremonies: the mountainous region of the high country preserves tribal identity as it instructs the generations in the significance of tribal belief and practice.

Whatever the reason for ascending to the high country, be it anticipation for celebrating one of the world renewal dances by a recognized spiritual leader; the periodic summoning of healing power to be exercised for communal or individual well-being by a tribal doctor; the personal search for wisdom or strength by any tribal member; or the initiation into tribal customs and rituals by young men or women, approaching the high country was itself a religious act. Individuals usually precede the ascent with a ten-day purification period of fasting and praying, confessing their mistakes, ridding themselves of grudges and bad feelings, removing themselves from the company of others, and usually waiting for some indication in a dream, vision, or portent that the supernatural beings in the high country acknowledge the sincerity of their quest and sanction its pursuit.[5]

Setting off, the individual may proceed to any number of sacred sites in the high-country region. It is generally understood that the holiness of a particular site coincides with its relative altitude; the most sacred and powerful locales are those higher in elevation. For those who aspire to be medicine doctors, there is a correlation between the sites where one prays in the high country and one's progress in the spiritual journey. Three of the most sacred sites within the high country are Doctor Rock, Chimney Rock, and the outcropping known as Peak 8. At each of these locations and throughout the region of the high country, "prayer seats" (or *tsektsels* in Yurok) have been used throughout the generations where the individual enters states of profound and intense prayer, experiencing a heightened sense of the physical beauty and awesome silence of the entire high-country region. The privacy and vantage afforded by these ancient, semicircular enclosures of piled rocks, varying from four to twenty feet in diameter and generally opening toward the east, fosters a sense of intimacy with and receptivity to the supernatural beings and their powers abiding within the high country. Perhaps sitting quietly, at times entering into trance, or otherwise dancing their responsiveness to the sacred energies that they seek for personal, communal, and world-renewing medicine, individuals spend their chosen time at their designated site within the confines or the near vicinity of these prayer seats.[6]

The remoteness and undisturbed solitude of the high country and the physical isolation of those praying within it are essential features in the religious experience of those indigenous peoples living in this northwestern corner of California. The exchange of healing power, defining the relationship of those who are drawn in prayer to spend time in and with the holy region, is sustained by the perception of the high country's integrity as a holy reality and the individual's capacity to dispose themselves to its spiritual and physical animation. This dynamic intercommunion could be disrupted by changes in the features of the high country or by distractions interfering with the individual's awareness of and receptivity to the beauty and silence through which its healing energies are manifested. "[I]n Northwest California culture, the environment as a whole has important religious significance. There is a physical-psychological interaction that takes place between those who go to get medicine and the sacred place which furnishes this medicine. If one feature of this interaction is disturbed, the flow of power is blocked."[7]

It was, with the gravest sense of alarm and threat that members of the

Yurok, Karok, and Tolowa tribes responded to the 1977 disclosure by the United States Forest Service of its plan for a road construction project that would replace an existing dirt road and connect two paved sections of road, one leading south from the town of Gasquet and the other going north from the town of Orleans. The proposed road would directly traverse the Blue Creek vicinity of the sacred high country, separating Chimney Rock to the north from Peak 8 and Doctor Rock to the south. It was later revealed that the Forest Service plan would permit the private, commercial harvesting of some 733-million board feet of timber from the same Blue Creek area during the next eighty years. The combined road construction project and timber cutting would have brought an estimated average of some 168 vehicles a day, including 76 logging vehicles, 84 administrative vehicles, and 8 recreational vehicles, into the sacred area.[8]

The authority of the Forest Service to contemplate such a project stemmed from the creation in 1951 of the Six Rivers National Forest, whose 987,920 acres encompassed much of the traditional, non-reservation homelands of the Yuroks, Karoks, and Tolowas in Del Norte and Humboldt Counties of California's northwestern corner; within its borders lay their sacred high country, whose 67,500 acres, designated by the Forest Service as "the Blue Creek Unit," was slated for road building to facilitate the logging of the high country's virgin Douglas fir forest and other valuable timber trees. In proceeding with its plan, the Forest Service resisted mounting testimony that the steep ridges of the Siskiyou Mountains, with their generally shallow and fragile soil, although marginally stable when bound up by forest roots, had historically been subject to mountain slides even without excessive rain or snow. The impact of road construction and subsequent tree removal would significantly increase the scope and destructiveness of erosion. According to one of its own studies, the Forest Service recognized that some 83 percent of the land area in the Blue Creek Unit of the national forest was deemed "moderately unstable or worse." Additional evidence showed that in one area of the Siskiyous that already endured clear-cutting, soil loss from such timbering could reach twenty-two tons per acre, per year. Given the estimation that losing only one inch of topsoil reduces productivity of the denuded land by some eighty percent, and that in this area of northwestern California, thousands of years were required for the formation of new topsoil, the prospects for reforestation were extremely dim.[9]

But the scarring of the land was not the only environmental threat posed by the Forest Service plan. The eroded soils would fall into the waters of Blue Creek, a tributary to the Klamath River and an important spawning habitat for adult anadromous fish returning from the Pacific to lay their eggs. Chinook, coho, and king salmon as well as steelhead trout covered their fertilized eggs with the gravel from Blue Creek's waters, providing them protection and allowing the necessary oxygen to circulate with the consistently cold waters requisite for embryo development. The danger of increased erosion from road construction and subsequent logging on the ridges above would be manifest in the perilous sedimentation that would slide into and smother the life-protecting gravels of Blue Creek. Already, in areas along the Klamath River that sustained heavy commercial clear-cut logging, a severe decline in fisheries had been noted. Yet against mounting warnings and complaints of biologists, geologists, commercial, and sports fishing advocates, and several established as well as grassroots environmental groups, the Forest Service pressed forward with its road construction and timbering plan.

As early as the 1960s, the Forest Service had been aware of the religious significance of the high country to the region's indigenous peoples. Its response to recommendations by its local district rangers that the area needed to be protected was to issue in 1969 a Multiple-Use Plan in which it identified certain isolated rocks within the Blue Creek Unit as ceremonially significant for local Indians. Subsequently, the supervisor of the Six Rivers National Forest proposed that adequate protection for each discrete holy site could be afforded by fencing off forty-five acres around each of the identified rocks. Evidently, such delineated safety zones were considered sufficient gestures of respect while not deterring the planned road, which would run under the south side of Chimney Rock and on across the north side of Peak 8; the route would be only three miles north of what would be administratively referred to as Doctor Rock Recreation Area, Zone 7-11A Recreation Area, Primitive Experience.[10] The Forest Service proceeded accordingly, building one section of the road south from Gasquet and the other north from Orleans, and by late 1977, there remained only 6.02 miles that would connect the two segments. It was that area, designated the Chimney Rock section, that would run right through the most sacred of the high country. A number of alternative routes had been proposed, including two that would run outside the Chimney Rock corridor, and another proposal argued that the road construction project be discontinued altogether.

While the Forest Service considered these alternatives, Congress enacted the American Indian Religious Freedom Act in 1978. With its direction that federal agencies evaluate their policies and procedures to protect and preserve Native American religious cultural rights and practices, the act prompted the Forest Service to commission a comprehensive and final study to provide definitive information on the impacts that construction of the road and subsequent actions would have upon the Indian religious culture of the high country. Completed in April 1979, "Cultural Resources of the Chimney Rock Section, Gasquet-Orleans Road, Six Rivers National Forest" authored by Dr. Dorothea J. Theodoratus, Dr. Joseph L. Chartkoff, and Ms. Kerry K. Chartkoff (hereinafter cited as the Theodoratus Report) was a 450-page study with some 125 additional pages of appendices, presenting ethnographic, historic, and archeological data identifying the cultural properties of the proposed Chimney Rock Section of the Gasquet-Orleans Road and their significance to the Native American population of the area, especially its effects on the religious beliefs and practices among the Yurok, Karok, and Tolowa peoples. The report described various impacts that could be expected from the proposed changes in the high country and offered recommendations as to how the Forest Service should proceed.

Revealing the distorted conceptualization behind the Forest Service plan to simply fence off the primary locations of Doctor Rock, Chimney Rock, and Peak 8 in 45-acre zones, the Theodoratus Report addressed the indigenous tribal understanding of the high country as more than merely an enumeration of specific locales. Speaking of the integrity of the region in its physical beauty and natural silence, the report warned against the conventional tendency to speak of "sites" as discrete, isolated locations. "In this report religious site descriptions are given in terms of the perceptions of local Native Americans and therefore may include psychological, visual, and other sensory aspects of a particular area. Another element of perceptual difference, the idea fundamental to local Native Americans, that sacred sites are used qualitatively rather than quantitatively, also defines site locations in a manner which is unconventional to many non-Indian Americans. In order to understand what a site means to Native American residents of this area, a mental shift must be made away from the purely physical aspect of a site to an extended definition which includes various qualitative, psychological and sensory aspects."[11] The notion of fencing off relatively small, circumscribed areas to which the native peoples would continue to enjoy physical access, while ignoring the structural changes to the regional features that a road would exact and the noise that its construction and subsequent traffic and timbering activity would inflict was the kind of fundamental distortion of tribal religious experience that the Theodoratus Report censured.

More broadly, the report cautioned against the determination of the words *religious* or *sacred* to apply merely to a set of ritual behavior performed at certain specific locations within the region of the high country. Emerging from a similar mythology shared among the region's indigenous peoples, the high country was itself a holy reality, the center of the world, and the place of contact with the powers of the universe whose healing and world-renewing energies could be sought and communicated to those properly disposed to receive such psychic and physical "medicine" at customarily designated locations. Although the efficacy of such sites varied in terms of the intensity of power that might be experienced at their respective ascendency among the region's heights, they all participated in and testified to a sacred reality whose presence suffused the whole of the high country, endowing it, in its totality, with a holy, religious significance. Any attempt to isolate, fence in, and reserve the designation of "sacred" or "religious" to a mere handful of known Indian places of prayer, while constructing a road and lumbering the trees around them, was to seriously misperceive the Yurok, Karok, and Tolowa conception of the high country. Even as the Theodoratus Report began a detailed geographic description, archeological analysis, and anthropological explanation of innumerable sites found throughout the trails and ridges of the region, and the ritual conduct associated with them, it warned against the tendency to fragment the sacred landscape of the high country by invidious distinctions that would not reflect the local tribal apprehension of the area:

> The most important aspect of the present study has been the examination of those beliefs and practices which must be subsumed, although inadequately, under the discrete classification "religion." The "religious" aspect of the lives of Native Americans can be only roughly categorized into separate considerations. Because of the particular nature of the Indian perceptual experience, as opposed to the particular nature of the predominant non-Indian, Western perceptual experience, any division into "religious" or "sacred" is in reality an exercise which forces Indian concepts into non-Indian "categories," and distorts the original conceptualization in the process. . . . It is also important to realize for the purposes of this study, that descriptions which single out specific cultural sites as isolated (e.g., Doctor Rock, Chimney Rock, Peak 8) are distortions of Indian conceptualizations of these important cultural properties.[12]

From the start, the Forest Service was thus on notice, through the report it had commissioned, that its proposal to construct a road through the high country by merely detouring around the three primary Indian prayer sites, separated from the road by only a margin of acreage, would be based on a severely inadequate understanding of local tribal religious belief and practice, which would be violated by the road and the consequent lumbering it would facilitate.

Discussing the religious culture shared by the Yurok, Karok, and Tolowa peoples as one centered on and described as "world renewal," the report, based on interviews with 166 tribal representatives complementing its detailed ethnogeographic fieldwork examination of the high country, explained the function and training of the religious "doctors" as principal figures frequenting the sacred region. For them, as well as for those members of the tribes who sought supernatural help for any number of personal reasons, the report emphasized the importance of the natural silence, the undisturbed and pristine features, and the solitary privacy of the high country. The noise from the initial blasting and construction, and the subsequent traffic from commercial lumbering and tourism would jeopardize those inherent aspects of the region critical to the religious experience of Indian believers. The report revealed that in addition to the principal sites of the most prominent significance for prayer and ritual—Doctor Rock, Chimney Rock, and Peak 8—there were many other additional stone outcroppings throughout the high country used for the same purpose. In addition, the network of ancient Indian trails going into, ascending, and traversing the ridges of the high country were themselves holy, with innumerable places among them for contact with supernatural power. Bearing the names of the Golden Stairs, Elk Valley Trail, Blue Creek Trail, Doctor Rock Trail, Williams-Eightmile Ridge Trail, Sawtooth Mountain Trail, Chimney Rock Trail, Little Medicine Mountain Trail, the Boundary Trail, South Red Mountain Trail, and Red Mountain Trail, "[t]hese trails are not only the routes to important ritual places, they are significant ritual sites in their own right because of the hundreds of ritual features that occur along them."[13] The pouring of pavement along any of the nine alternate routes running through the Chimney Rock section of the high country as proposed by the Forest Service would have included the movement of heavy machinery and the disturbance of land beyond the designated corridor of concrete roadway. To support the construction process, more terrain would be affected by the need for water connections, parking, campfires, trash accumulation, and dump and borrow sites as well.

According to the Theodoratus Report, even if the road's path skirted the three principal prayer sites, it would have a destructive impact, through its initial construction and subsequent use, on the host of individual locations within the network of the region's sacred trails that would be torn up, eroded, or otherwise degraded. The loss would be a significant archeological tragedy as well as a religious desecration, since the area provided an important and unique source of information on the evolution of northwest California indigenous culture from prehistory to the present. "The archeology of the project area reflects a dimension in the prehistory of Northwest California for which no other data exists: the relationship between coast and highland in prehistory and the changing role of the highland in the development of the distinctive Northwest California cultural tradition. The prehistoric archeological sites in the Chimney Rock section and surrounding areas establish the antiquity of the Native Californians in this region. The sites form part of their national patrimony as well as that of all Native Americans, and of all Americans in general. These data are not repeated in the lowland sites of the lower Klamath River and adjacent sea coast, nor are they repeated in other mountain ranges, because of the unique conditions of this region."[14]

In its final recommendations, the Theodoratus Report criticized the Forest Service's ignorance of the physical features, historical significance, and religious importance of the area it slated for road construction. Any attempts to ameliorate damage from the project would utterly misconstrue the Yurok, Karok, and Tolowa perception of the interdependent totality of ridges, creeks, plants, bushes, lakes, meadows, trees, soil, and rocks whose pristine beauty, solitude, and tranquility manifest the high country's sacred healing power. Having been essential several thousand years ago for the subsistence needs of the first peoples to occupy northwest California, the area's distinction gradually evolved from one of providing essential natural resources for physical sustenance to its preeminence as the spiritual center for the peoples living in the Klamath River region. Hailing the high country as the seat for "one of the great flowerings of Native American culture anywhere in the United States . . . of signal importance to national culture as well as to the Native Americans of Northwest California and their own ongoing traditional ways of life,"[15] the Theodoratus Report not only warned the Forest Service against the ruinous impact of road construction and its subsequent logging and mining operations, but bluntly faulted the whole administrative philosophy that conceived the high country as a natural resource to be managed and improved, rather than as the site of primary religious experience indispensable to the spiritual lives of the traditional peoples whose reverence for the region had been traced over the span of prehistory into the present. The very "land resource improvements" initiated by the Forest Service would become the very process that would destroy the religious reality central to Yurok, Karok, and Tolowa belief and practice. The only appropriate management of such land was its preservation in its natural state:

> These ridges, trails and peaks cannot be enhanced by Forest Service improvements. Research indicates that there is a direct relationship between active Forest Service involvement with these sites and the degrading of Native American religious life in these mountains. We urge the Forest Service not to take action to try to improve these sites and trails.

On the contrary, the most effective management technique would be the prevention of interference with Native American religious activities by prohibiting those activities that would bring physical harm to the sites.

Ridges and peaks should be placed in land-use categories that would prohibit commercial activities such as mining, logging, road building, administrative movement of machinery or prospecting on or around any of these ridges, trails or peaks. We recommend that no permanent Forest Service or other government installation be established in the vicinity of any of these sites. The protection of the physical sites is separate analytically from the preservation of traditional Native American religion, but the two are linked and neither can be preserved in isolation. The immediate concern is for the preservation of the sites whose significance comes from traditional religious observances. These sites cannot be preserved if mining, logging, road building, or government installations and their attendant activities are allowed.[16]

Not only did the Theodoratus Report argue against the completion of the six-mile Chimney Rock section of the road connecting Gasquet and Orleans, but it recommended that the sections already built be torn up so that the cross-mountain route through the high country be rendered impossible and rendered "closed to machinery movement of any kind for any purpose, commercial, extractive or administrative."[17] Although the report urged that the high-country region was of such singular importance to an understanding of the evolution of northwest California cultural processes from the prehistoric to contemporary period that it be included in the National Register of Historic Places, its consistent concern was its authentication not only of sacred sites within the high country, but its determination "that although specific religious sites are identified within this region, the entirety of the region possesses a generalized sanctity which is necessary for the proper use of the specific sacred sites."[18] The report certified that the construction of the proposed Forest Service road through any of the nine possible routes into the high country would so intrude upon the integrity and pristine visual and aural conditions of the sacred region that it would jeopardize and ultimately destroy the indigenous religious cultures of the Yurok, Karok, and Tolowa peoples:

Field data indicate that increased intrusion into this sacred region would adversely affect the ability and/or success of the individual's quest for spiritual power ... intrusions into the area have already caused such impairments.... [T]he spiritual, moral and physical viability of the practitioner's home community will be diminished in proportion to the diminished ability of that practitioner to seek and attain power within the high country.... [T]he Indian concept of world renewal is inextricably related to religious practice in the high country. Intrusions on the sanctity of the Blue Creek high country are therefore potentially destructive of the very core of Northwest religious beliefs and practices.[19]

In none of the cases preceding it, in which the identity of land as a sacred reality had been raised by Native Americans to prevent government actions from altering or destroying it, had such a comprehensive study been engaged and such a clear, unambiguous challenge been issued for government restraint than in the Theodoratus Report. Upon its submission, Dr. Joseph Winter, forest archeologist for the Six Rivers National Forest, evaluated it and concluded that it was a "sound and professional analysis of high methodological quality" and concurred with its conclusion.[20] Then, in 1981, the secretary of interior listed an area generally encompassing the high country on the National Register of Historic Places, and in January 1982 the Advisory Council on Historic Preservation found that construction of the Forest Service road would have "devastating effects on an historic property of great cultural value to the native peoples of the area" and refused to sanction "a project whose planning has been so badly segmented as to hardly constitute planning at all."[21]

Nevertheless, in March 1982, ignoring the Theodoratus Report—which it had itself commissioned—and the new designation accorded the high country on the National Register, the Forest Service, through its regional forester, selected a route for its proposed road that would take it right through the sacred land. Intending to implement its plan to harvest more than 700 million board feet of timber from the area during the next eighty years, the Service justified its road construction as providing better access to the trees; permitting efficient administration of the area; potentially increasing the price of bids on future timber sales by reducing hauling costs to mills; stimulating employment in the regional timber industry; and allowing increased public recreational access to an area of the Six Rivers National Forest.

Having exhausted their administrative appeals of the Forest Service decision, representatives of the Yurok, Karok, and Tolowa peoples sued R. Max Peterson, chief of the Forest Service, and John R. Block, secretary of the U.S. Department of Agriculture, to protect their sacred land from the road construction and timbering scheme. Joining them as plaintiffs were the state of California; the Sierra Club; the Wilderness Society; California Trout, a non-profit corporation; the Siskiyou Mountains Resource Council; the Redwood Region Audubon Society; the Northcoast Environmental Center; and the Northwest Indian Cemetery Protective Association, a non-profit organization comprising Tolowa, Yurok, Karok, and other Northwest California Indians dedicated to protecting Indian burial grounds, ceremonial sites, and areas of religious, cultural, and historical significance. Claiming violations of the religious protections of the First Amendment, the American Indian Religious Freedom Act, the National Environmental

Policy Act, the Wilderness Act, the Federal Water Pollution Control Act, the water and fishing rights reserved to American Indians on the Hoopa Valley Indian Reservation and the government's trust responsibility toward those rights, the Administrative Procedure Act, the Multiple-Use Sustained-Yield Act, and the National Forest Management Act, the plaintiffs filed their suit with the United States District Court for the Northern District of California. The ten-day trial was held before District Judge Stanley A. Weigel, who issued his decision in May 1983.

DECISION OF THE U.S. DISTRICT COURT

Judge Weigel relied substantially on the Theodoratus Report ultimately to rule that the proposed Forest Service road construction and timber-harvesting plan would unconstitutionally violate the religious freedom of the plaintiff tribes. Although the courts, which had previously heard related claims, consistently granted summary judgment to the government and its agencies, refusing to recognize any harm to Indian religious interests, Weigel found abundant evidence from the Forest Service's commissioned but ignored Theodoratus Report to inform and sustain his ruling. Reflecting the tribal conception that the whole of the high country in its integrity was the sacred reality, and not mere individual, discrete sites, the judge characterized the Forest Service management plan as a desecration of the ancestrally revered land, noting the importance of the solitude, quiet, and pristine environment for the "emotional and spiritual exchange with the Creator" to those who prayed in the high country. Likewise, the judge recognized the critical link between those who frequented the high country and the larger communities of the tribes and indeed, the whole world. Whether it be for the physical, psychic, or spiritual healing administered through the medicine men and women to tribal members in the Brush and Kick Dances or the ceremonial renewal and harmony of the earth in the White Deerskin and Jump Dances, the power of the high country extended beyond those relatively few who visited its ridges to keep vigil in its stone prayer seats and other hallowed locations. "For the Yurok, Karok, and Tolowa peoples, the high country constitutes the center of the spiritual world. No other geographic areas or sites hold equivalent religious significance for these tribes."[22]

Having identified the status of the high country and the threat to its pristine visual, aural, and structural integrity from the proposed road and logging, Judge Weigel reviewed the rulings of the four judicial precedents and their unanimity in finding no harm to Indian religious belief and practice. Rather than criticize or argue against the decisions in *Sequoyah v.*

Tennessee Valley Authority, Badoni v. Higginson, Wilson v. Block, and *Crow v. Gullet,* the judge adopted "the central and indispensable" standard those courts had questionably crafted and then wielded against the claims of the Cherokee, Navajo, Hopi, Lakota, and Tsistsistas peoples. For Weigel, there was no question that the "use of the high country is 'central and indispensable' to the Indian plaintiffs' religion [and that] the Forest Service's own study concluded that 'intrusion on the sanctity of the Blue Creek high country are . . . potentially destructive of the very core of Northwest Indian religious beliefs and practices'."[23]

Concluding that the proposed Forest Service actions would constitute an unlawful burden on the free exercise of the tribal religions, Weigel next addressed the question of whether the service's interests were of sufficient magnitude and importance that they could override the constitutionally protected religious beliefs and practices of the Yurok, Karok, and Tolowa peoples toward the high country. Systematically reviewing each of the reasons given by the Forest Service for the planned road and timber harvesting, the judge exposed the tenuous claims for the proposal's justification and ruled that they did not constitute the requisite "interest of the highest order," which alone could intrude upon the free exercise of religion.

At trial, the Forest Service had conceded that the six-mile segment of road it sought to build would not significantly improve access to the timber resources it targeted in the Blue Creek Unit of the Six Rivers National Forest. If it were to proceed with harvesting those trees, those sections of the road already completed leading south from Gasquet and north from Orleans provided sufficient access. Judge Weigel further concluded that the Forest Service had not proven that completion of the road would result in any net increase in the number of jobs in the northwestern regional timber industry; at most, it would simply have shifted a certain number of jobs from Humboldt County in the south to Del Norte County in the north. Nor was the judge persuaded by the argument that the six-mile segment through the high country was essential for recreational purposes. The public already enjoyed access to the general region for camping and hiking, and the very completion of the Gasquet-Orleans road, although facilitating vehicular traffic between the towns, would result in "environmental degradation [that] would decrease the area's suitability for primitive recreational use."[24] Moreover, the Forest Service's own projection indicated that the majority of the road's use would go to support logging and administrative vehicles, with only marginal recreational traffic: of the average 168 vehicles projected on the road daily, seventy-six would be for logging purposes, eighty-four for administrative matters with only eight qualifying as using the road for recreational interest.[25] With such evidence, the judge would not permit tribal religious freedom to be jeopardized by so questionable a claim of recreational necessity. Judge Weigel similarly dismissed the Forest Service contention that the planned road would allow for a more efficient administration of Six Rivers National Forest. Better insect control, habitat improvement, road maintenance, fire protection, and monitoring of visitors along a stretch of road that would be used primarily for industrial cutting and hauling of timber could not justify the destruction of the high country whose "complex of sites, trails and features is unique . . . absolutely unique in North America and perhaps in the world . . . a priceless historical heritage for the entire nation."[26] Additionally, it had been demonstrated during the trial that a majority of those administrative functions were to be shared by the district forest rangers stationed in Gasquet and Orleans, whether the proposed road through the high country was constructed or not. Thus, the actual administration of such activities would not be changed and could not be used as justifications for completing the road, which would infringe on the free exercise of the tribal religions. Though not so commented by the judge, the notion of building a road so as to provide better road maintenance betrayed a preoccupation as ludicrous as it was insensitive to the religious values it was willing to destroy. But a related bureaucratic concern with closing the gap and joining the two roads running south from Gasquet and north from Orleans did receive explicit though brief judicial attention. The judge found that past investment in the already existing paved roads did not justify the construction of a connecting link, and certainly not one running through the sacred precinct of the high country. The Draft Environmental Statement submitted by the Forest Service had already exposed a highly casual, if not haphazard, approach to building the paved routes out of the two towns: proceeding segment by segment, decisions on whether, or where, to make any further advances had always awaited completion of preceding sections, a severely fragmented approach already noted in the Advisory Council on Historic Preservation's sharp criticism of it. But despite their rather happenstance routing, Judge Weigel found that in and of themselves as they stood, the roads from Gasquet and Orleans had independent, practical utility. Providing "improved and useful access to vast recreational, timber, and other resources in the region,"[27] the two roads had functional significance not dependent on the six-mile section that the Forest Service planned through the high country.

As for the claim that construction of the section would increase competition for timber in the Orleans area of the Six Rivers National Forest and thereby increase Forest Service revenues, the judge saw no evidence whatsoever during the trial to substantiate any such effect on the regional timber market. "Such speculative and diffuse goals as these cannot provide the basis for denying plaintiffs' free exercise claim."[28] Finally, Weigel concluded that there was no compelling interest even to harvest timber from the Blue Creek Unit of the Six Rivers National Forest, which encompassed the high country. The trees from that region were but a fraction of the timber available from other sections of the 987,920-acre forest. Its trees would make but a scant contribution to the regional timber industry, which would "not suffer greatly without access to timber in the Unit."[29] Ruling that none of the reasons offered by the Forest Service for constructing the road through the high country qualified as the requisite "paramount interests," which alone could justify government action that would burden constitutionally protected religious freedom, the judge reminded the service that even if it had been able to muster evidence of such interest, its forest management plan would still have been legally deficient. For even when the government can advance compelling interests of the highest order, it must demonstrate that no other means of serving that interest exists that would be less restrictive of the free exercise of religion that the government's proposed action would harm. Under that well-established rubric of First Amendment jurisprudence, the Forest Service would have been challenged by its failure to adopt one of two existing alternatives that would have permitted timbering in the Blue Creek Unit, while avoiding the Chimney Rock corridor of the high country and thus sparing the harm which it imposed on the tribal religions.

Clearing the way to sustain the First Amendment claim against the Forest Service, Judge Weigel quickly dispatched the final argument, which the Government had applied consistently in each of the preceding related cases. The Forest Service contended that accommodating Yurok, Karok, and Tolowa beliefs about the sanctity of the high country would transgress the Establishment Clause by turning the region into a "government-managed religious shrine." Weigel scored this trite slogan as without merit. "Actions compelled by the Free Exercise Clause do not violate the Establishment Clause. In the present case, the Forest Service failed to accommodate the Indian plaintiffs' religious practices to the extent required by the Free Exercise Clause. Government actions having the goal and effect of such accommodation and which do not result in excessive government entanglement with any religion are consistent with the Establishment Clause."[30] Relying on the well-established Supreme Court rulings in *Sherbert v. Verner* and *Wisconsin v. Yoder,* Weigel demonstrated the principle of accommodation granted for legitimate religious practices permitting exemptions to laws fixing eligibility standards for employment compensation (*Sherbert*) and laws requiring compulsory school attendance (*Yoder*). The nature of the accommodation that the Yurok, Karok, and Tolowa peoples sought would not entail excessive government entanglement with their religious traditions, nor were they asking the Forest Service to exclude recreational users from the high country or regulate their behavior in any way. They simply sought relief from a Forest Service decision to construct a demonstrably inessential road through land that they immemorially held sacred and that would be destroyed as a central and indispensable place of prayer and communion if the service proceeded, ignoring the findings of its own commission detailing the ethnographic, historic, archeological, and religious losses the road would inflict.

It is interesting that although Judge Weigel relied on the Theodoratus Report to sustain the First Amendment claim against the Forest Service, he simultaneously ruled that its commission by the service, along with hearings that had been held at which representatives from the tribes testified, was sufficient to show compliance by the Forest Service with the American Indian Religious Freedom Act (AIRFA), which the tribal plaintiffs had raised as a separate cause of action. Noting that the most the act required was that the federal agencies "evaluate their policies and procedures with the aim of protecting Indian religious freedoms," the judge had no basis to rule that it required the Forest Service to accept the evaluation and recommendation of the Theodoratus Report against building the road. Although the wealth of information on Indian belief in and practice upon the high country and the destructive impact that road construction and logging operations would wreak upon local indigenous religion was critical for the determination of a free-exercise violation, the Forest Service decision to ignore the Theodoratus Report was not a breach of AIRFA.

Turning from the constitutional claims alleged by the plaintiffs, Judge Weigel next addressed the charge that the Forest Service project was in violation of the National Environmental Policy Act (NEPA) because of inadequacies in the Final Environmental Impact Statement (FEIS) and the Draft Environmental Statement (DES). The plaintiffs complained that the two statements failed to adequately discuss the impact of the road on geologic and soil stability and on Indian cultural resources; that they inadequately discussed the possible alternatives; that no supplemental Environmental Impact Statement (EIS) had been prepared after the Forest Service had been apprised of new information concerning the road's impact on Indian cultural resources; and that they failed to disclose the road's impact on water quality and sedimentation in Blue Creek and to describe proposed measures needed to mitigate those adverse impacts.

As he began his examination of these claims, the judge noted the relatively limited role courts could play in reviewing the adequacy of Environmental Impact Statements. So long as they reasonably set forth sufficient information to allow the decision maker to consider environmental factors and make a reasoned decision, such statements were to be upheld. Accordingly, the judge found that the FEIS had adequately revealed the existence of slope stability problems with the presence of dormant and active landslides along the proposed route, indicating that they were comparable to those found all along the two roads coming out from Gasquet and Orleans. Such disclosure was sufficient.

Similarly, the NEPA was deemed not to require anything more than the frank acknowledgment in the FEIS and the Theodoratus Report that the road project would have harsh, adverse impacts on Indian cultural resources. That both sources did so straightforwardly only to be given little weight by the Forest Service did not transgress the minimal demands of the NEPA that the evaluation be made and published. The NEPA did not insist that the disturbing information be acted upon, merely noted. On the same basis, the judge could not fault the discussion in the FEIS of the alternative routes that might have been taken, avoiding the high country. It evaluated and ultimately rejected them based on several factors that included their length, their construction and maintenance costs, the steepness of their gradient, the size of the area disturbed, the cost of hauling timber on them, and their driveability. The judge declined to rule that these considerations were inadequate to allow a reasoned decision to have been made and so ruled against the plaintiffs' criticism that a supplementary EIS was necessary to include further information on Indian cultural resources. Since the FEIS had incorporated the findings of both the Theodoratus Report and Dr. Winter's review and support of it, "studies which are the most comprehensive available of Indian religious beliefs and practices," Judge Weigel found no need for further supplemental studies.[31]

But when it came to considering the failure of the Draft Environmental Statement (DES) and the Final Environmental Impact Statement (FEIS) to sufficiently disclose the cumulative impact road construction and subsequent logging activities would have on the waters of Blue Creek, there were serious deficiencies. Weigel found that the evidence established that the construction of the high-country road would result in as much as a 500 percent increase in sediment loads in Blue Creek, a disclosure the DES and FEIS had failed to make. It had been revealed at trial that given the steep elevation of the high country, which ranged from 1,200 to 6,000 feet above sea level, and the heavy annual rainfall, the ridges of the high country were easily erodable. "A single minor landslide along the proposed route would dramatically raise sediment levels in Blue Creek, thereby violating state water quality standards and endangering fish spawning habitat downstream."[32]

The FEIS and DES failure to discuss the risk of such a significant event was compounded by their silence on describing measures to mitigate adverse impacts on water quality and fish habitat in the Blue Creek. Not registering the potential for slope failures and thus not alerted to the significant increase in the creek's sedimentation, the documents failed to address the issue of inadequate oxygen for the fish eggs buried under its shallow layers of gravel. Even if some of the eggs were able to survive, the young fish hatching from them would not be able to emerge from the layers of sediment covering the gravel. Judge Weigel faulted the FEIS and the DES for merely invoking highly generalized, and thus empty, phrases that asserted through technical, non-specific terms that the use of "Best Management Practices" should minimize any harm to Blue Creek. The NEPA was held by the judge to require much more specific description, analysis, and proposed mitigating measures for the project's otherwise understated threats to Blue Creek's water quality and spawning capacity. The same findings on the increased sediment levels and the reduced survival rate of the fish eggs in the spawning gravels of Blue Creek were also held to violate the Federal Water Pollution Control Act. Additionally, the adverse impact on water quality and fish habitat was ruled a violation of the water and fishing rights of Indians on the Hoopa Valley Indian Reservation, since the condition of the water and fish in Blue Creek directly affected those portions of the Klamath River that flow through the Hoopa Reservation. That violation in turn was held to constitute a violation of the government's trust responsibilities toward the Indians of the Hoopa Reservation.

Judge Weigel also ruled with the plaintiffs on their allegation that the Forest Service was required by the NEPA and the Wilderness Act to assess the impact of timber harvesting in the general area of the high country on the region's potential suitability with two other contiguous areas, for designation as a single wilderness area. The NEPA required that an EIS disclose the impact of a proposed action on the wilderness resource potential of any area eligible for inclusion in the National Wilderness Preservation System. Likewise, the Wilderness Act required the Forest Service to review for preservation as wilderness each area in the national forests classified as primitive. What the plaintiffs objected to and what Weigel agreed with was an apparent bias by the Forest Service against preserving as wilderness the Blue Creek Unit of the Six Rivers National Forest, which included the high country. Evidence of the bias was found in the artificial separation of the Blue Creek Unit from two adjacent units known as the Eightmile and Siskiyou roadless units, also within the Six Rivers National Forest. Rather than evaluate the impact of the timber-harvesting plan on the wilderness potential of the three areas as one single, contiguous region, the Forest Service had departed from its customary practice and considered the wilderness potential of each of the three regions as separate, distinct areas. Judge Weigel ruled that this "separation of these roadless areas for evaluation as potential wilderness artificially lowered the wilderness 'ratings' given these areas by the Forest Service in the Final Environmental Statement (FES), and thus reduced the likelihood that the Forest Service would recommend the Blue Creek roadless area for preservation as wilderness. This bias against preservation of the Blue Creek Unit as wilderness renders the FES inadequate under NEPA."[33] The judge also held that the violations of the NEPA, the Wilderness Act, the Federal Water Pollution Control Act, Indian water and fishing, and tribal First Amendment rights constituted violations of the Administrative Procedure Act.

Judge Weigel did not agree, however, with the contention that the Forest Service's plan to construct the road through the high country and permit harvesting of timber in the Blue Creek Unit transgressed either the Multiple-Use Sustained-Yield Act or the National Forest Management Act of 1976. Although the eventual decision was offensive on other counts, most significantly as an infringement upon the constitutional protections of Native American belief and practice, the Forest Service showed evidence of sufficient attempts to balance competing values for the use of the Blue Creek Unit so as not to be so insensitive to environmental concerns that violated either of the two statutes in the ways the plaintiffs had alleged.

The final result of Judge Weigel's analysis was his order that the Forest Service be permanently enjoined from constructing the proposed road through the high country and from engaging in commercial timber harvesting and/or from constructing any logging roads in the high country. He further ordered an injunction of road construction and timber harvesting in any of the 31,100 acres of the Blue Creek Unit of the Six Rivers National Forest until the Forest Service prepared an Environmental Impact Statement that adequately evaluated the wilderness resource potential of the combined Blue Creek, Eightmile, and Siskiyou Roadless Areas of the same national forest. Likewise, an injunction would stand against road construction and/or timber harvesting until the Forest Service adequately specified effective measures to mitigate the adverse impact of those proposed activities on the water quality and fish habitat of Blue Creek and demonstrated that the proposed logging would not violate the Federal Water Pollution Control Act and would not reduce the supply of anadromous fish in those portions of the Klamath River that flowed through the Hoopa Valley Indian Reservation.

DECISION OF THE U.S. COURT OF APPEALS FOR THE NINTH CIRCUIT

The government appealed Judge Weigel's decision to the United States Court of Appeals for the Ninth Circuit where arguments were heard on July 9, 1984, before a panel consisting of Judges Benjamin C. Duniway, William C. Canby, and Robert R. Beezer. While the court's ruling was pending, Congress enacted the California Wilderness Act, which was signed by President Ronald Reagan on September 28, 1984. The Act placed in wilderness some 26,000 acres of the Blue Creek Unit of the Six Rivers National Forest, including most but not all of the high country.[34] Because wilderness designation prohibits commercial activities, most of the timber harvesting within the high country that had been enjoined by Judge Weigel's ruling was now prohibited by the California Wilderness Act. But the act did not foreclose the construction of the paved road. Even though Congress in setting aside the area as wilderness had expressly recognized its "critical importance to Native Americans for cultural and religious purposes,"[35] it nevertheless left a 1,200-foot-wide corridor through the newly created Siskiyou Wilderness for the possible completion of the road between Gasquet and Orleans. Taking no position on the merits of that project, Congress simply made provision for it, "but only if it is determined permissible under other laws."[36] In its decision issued on June 24, 1985, the Court of Appeals of the Ninth Circuit affirmed Judge Weigel's ruling that the road would not be permissible under the Free Exercise Clause of the First Amendment. That decision remained unchanged even after the court granted the Forest Service its petition for rehearing and issued a new opinion on July 22, 1986.

In that second, comprehensive review, the court of appeals again affirmed the district court in all respects except the wilderness claim, which had been rendered moot by the California Wilderness Act, and the charge that the Forest Service project violated the water and fishing rights of the Hoopa Valley Indian Reservation. Since the Hoopa Valley Tribe was not a named plaintiff in the suit, the court of appeals concluded that the case was not an appropriate vehicle to rule on an issue regarding their rights.

In its review of the First Amendment issue, the court of appeals reiterated that the amendment prohibits government actions that burden the free exercise of religion "unless those actions are necessary to fulfill a governmental interest of the highest order that cannot be met in a less restrictive manner."[37] The Forest Service had challenged the district court's conclusion that its management decisions regarding the Blue Creek Unit of the Six Rivers National Forest impermissibly burdened tribal religious freedoms. The service further countered that even if its project did impose such a burden, it had demonstrated a governmental interest sufficient to override the Indians' religious interests. Thus, the court of appeals first considered whether the Yurok, Karok, and Tolowa plaintiffs had successfully met their initial responsibility of demonstrating that the Forest Service plans for the construction and use of the road through the high country would in fact burden their constitutionally protected right of religious exercise.

More readily than the district court, the Ninth Circuit Court of Appeals adopted the perspective as well as the standard that had been crafted and applied by the courts in *Sequoyah, Badoni, Wilson,* and *Crow*. The orientation is to view land in terms of its use; its value derives not from any inherent worth, but the contribution it makes to and the role it plays in human activity. Without elaboration, but with explicit directness, the Ninth Circuit panel rejected the sufficiency of a claim that the high country was a holy reality in and of itself, worthy of protection from the desecration of an unnecessary road and the destructive impact of logging. If it were to be spared in the name of religion, the tribal communities would have to demonstrate its usefulness to their religious practices. In adopting the standard first formulated in *Sequoyah v. TVA*, the Ninth Circuit perpetuated the notion of land as merely the background entity, the location for the performance of human ceremonial behavior—land not as primary religious reality, holy in itself, but as that which has significance primarily as the locale where religious activity is engaged and performed. Land would be protected not on a claim that it was sacred in itself, but only on a showing of its "indispensable and central" usefulness to the performance of religion. "That the Indians . . . consider the area sacred is not enough to characterize the contemplated Forest Service actions as a burden on free exercise rights. The Indians have to show that the area at issue is indispensable and central to their religious practices and beliefs, and that the proposed governmental actions would seriously interfere with or impair those religious practices."[38]

But even under the restrictive rubric that accorded religious significance to land only to the extent to which its usefulness for some human religious behavior could be demonstrated, the Ninth Circuit Court of Appeals upheld the district court's finding that such use was clearly evident in the Yurok, Karok, and Tolowa tribal traditions. Looking to the record and finding across the generations that members of the tribes had traveled the high country to pray, perform rituals, and prepare for medicinal and other ceremonies, the court of appeals affirmed the "central and indispensable" character of the land to the Indian plaintiffs. Noting that there was ample evidence to illustrate the belief that the high country, in its unitary pristine nature, endowed tribal representatives and leaders with the requisite power to serve "the religious lives of many other Indians," the appellate court relied substantially on the Theodoratus Report and its conclusion that the construction of the road between Gasquet and Orleans and/or the harvesting of timber would be "intrusions on the sanctity of the Blue Creek high country [that] are ... potentially destructive of the very core of Northwest [Indian] religious beliefs and practices."[39] Accepting the characterization "that the proposed government operations would virtually destroy the plaintiff Indians' ability to practice their religion,"[40] the court of appeals affirmed the district court's ruling that the Forest Service's plans were a severe threat to the constitutional protections of tribal free exercise. Nor would the Ninth Circuit countenance the government's suggestion that logging and road building on public lands was a mere internal administrative decision beyond judicial constitutional scrutiny. For the court, any government action that makes the exercise of First Amendment religious rights more difficult or impedes religious observances is subject to challenge, even though the burden is only an indirect consequence of governmental activity; constitutional protection is not implicated only in cases of explicit governmental penalization of religious beliefs or practices, as the Forest Service had argued.

The court of appeals similarly rebuffed the long-used refrain that accommodation to tribal religious interests would effectively turn land sites into government-managed religious shrines and thus violate the separation of church and state enjoined by the Establishment Clause. The appellate panel exposed the exaggeration of Forest Service rhetoric by insisting that the injunction against road construction and timber harvesting still left the service free to administer the high country for all other designated purposes, including outdoor recreation, range, watershed, wildlife and fish habitat, and wilderness. The injunction against road building and commercial tree cutting didn't prevent or restrict the Forest Service from maintaining an active managerial presence within the area. Instead, it represented judicial insistence that the government, in its agency of the Forest Service, refrain solely from those actions that threatened not merely a burden upon, but the eventual destruction of, Northwest Indian religious beliefs and practices. Ensuring that government management of public land respects the constitutional stricture against harming religion could not, according to the court of appeals, be held as an impermissible endorsement or advancement of the particular religious beliefs and practices being protected. If the Free Exercise Clause of the First Amendment is to be effective, remedies against its violation must be fashioned that actually address the harm. If every attempt to correct a recognized infringement against the exercise of religious freedom is met by the claim that doing so violates the Establishment Clause, constitutional protection of religion will be nullified as a hollow slogan. Thus, the court of appeals upheld the district court's imposition of an injunction against building the road through, and timbering activity within, the high country as a legitimate, evenhanded accommodation between the constitutional responsibility of protecting the free exercise of the Yurok, Karok, and Tolowa religions from government-sponsored destruction on the one hand, and avoiding the sponsorship, financial support, advocacy, and partiality enjoined by the Establishment Clause on the other. For the appellate court, the injunction "evidences a policy of neutrality" between the mandate of the Free Exercise Clause and the prohibitions of the Establishment Clause.[41]

Curiously, the court of appeals suggested that the district court injunction, which it would sustain as an appropriate and valid response to the threatened destruction of the tribal religions, might nevertheless not meet the three-fold requirements of the test enunciated by the Supreme Court in *Lemon v. Kurtzman*.[42] Yet despite the misgivings that the court of appeals had and did not elaborate, the facts argue that all three demands of the *Lemon* test were met to satisfy that the injunction did not violate the Establishment Clause. As originally formulated in *Lemon*, the three-prong test was applied by the Supreme Court in its consideration of laws passed by the state legislatures of Rhode Island and Pennsylvania providing state aid to church-related elementary and secondary schools. Both programs were ruled constitutional violations of the Establishment Clause, and the *Lemon* test has subsequently been applied by the courts in their determinations of claims based on that First Amendment Clause.

In its appeal, the Forest Service had claimed that the district court injunction amounted to an unconstitutional establishment of the tribal religions. Under the *Lemon* test, the court of appeals could well have shown that the injunction was free of such a charge, since it (1) had a secular purpose, (2) its principal or primary effect neither advanced nor inhibited religion, and (3) it did not foster an excessive government entanglement with religion.[43] The district court had imposed the injunction for reasons in addition to the concern for the tribal religious beliefs and practices. Judge Weigel had ruled that the proposed road construction and subsequent timbering were significant threats to the stability and coherence of the soil in the ridges of the high country, dramatically increasing its susceptibility to erosion and landslides, which would in turn precipitously raise the risk of sedimentation levels in the waters of Blue Creek, and thus violate state water quality standards and endanger fish-spawning habitats. Those findings were not only flaws in the Forest Service's draft and final environmental impact statements, but were held to be violations of the Federal Water Pollution Control Act as well as violations of the water and fishing rights of Indians on the Hoopa Valley Indian Reservation. Additionally, the Forest Service was found to violate the National Environmental Policy Act and the Wilderness Act in its apparent bias against preserving as wilderness the Blue Creek Unit of the Six Rivers National Forest, which included the high country. So it was that Judge Weigel's imposition of the injunction forbidding road construction and timbering in the high country was grounded on quite explicit statutory, non-sectarian, "secular" policy determination of environmental protection; there was a purpose and motivation for the injunction beyond the purely religious concern for tribal religion, thus satisfying the first demand of the *Lemon* test.

The "principal or primary effect" of the injunction was to preserve the high country in a pristine natural state, protected from the structural deformations and the incidental consequent degradations imposed by the construction and use of a road running through it and timber stripped and hauled from it. Leaving the land alone, free from the distress of construction, traffic, and commercial taking of its tree cover, was the physical preservation the injunction directed. Clearly, that result effected no inhibition of Yurok, Karok, and Tolowa traditions. But that very freedom from molestation and hindrance did not support the claim that the injunction "advanced" the tribal religions. The destruction of the high country's soil and water integrity, the disturbance of its stone outcroppings, the uprooting and loss of its woods and foliage were what the injunction primarily enjoined; neither advancement nor inhibition of Native American religion could be argued as logically prior to and assuming precedence over the principal environmental stability and conservation the injunction safeguarded. Without that as the primary effect and condition, the inhibition of tribal belief and practice would have quickly followed. Similarly, the protection of the high country was the fundamental consequence of the injunction which, rather than advance Yurok, Karok, and Tolowa religion, permitted them to coexist and perdure along with the landscape it spared. Thus the injunction neutrally avoided the joint prohibitions of the second of the *Lemon* criteria.

Finally, the district court injunction against road construction and timber harvesting posed no threat to the third requirement of the *Lemon* test. Fostering no "excessive government entanglement with religion," the injunction imposed no administrative duties on the Forest Service beyond those it was statutorily authorized to assume for the whole of the Six Rivers National Forest. As already noted, the injunction made no attempt to sever or delimit the Forest Service responsibilities within the high country for purposes including outdoor recreation, range, watershed, wildlife and fish habitat, and wilderness. In addition, neither the original tribal suit nor the terms of the injunction sought or imposed any requirement that the Forest Service exclude or police non-Indian hikers, campers, or other people entering the remote region of the high country. Absent any such call for or imposition of Forest Service ongoing surveillance and oversight patrolling of the high country to ensure an exclusive tribal religious use of the area, there were no grounds to sustain an argument that prohibition of road building and timbering would lead to any "entanglement," let alone an "excessive" one between the government and the religions of the Yurok, Karok, and Tolowa peoples.

Had the injunction not been issued, the Forest Service scheme to erect buffer zones in the Chimney Rock Section of the high country around some eleven sites it designated as having historical and ritual significance would have been a far greater entanglement with tribal religions. Rather than an appropriate avoidance of the entire region held sacred to the Native American beliefs, the service was prepared to weave its road and allow logging of trees near and around sites selectively identified as worthy of being spared the right of way, its traffic and lumbering. That approach ignored the tribal belief in the sanctity not merely of certain discrete prayer locations, but of the entire high country in its integrity. Instead of avoiding an offensive selection of particular sites that alone it deemed of sufficient religious significance to isolate with its artificial and meaningless zones of protection, the Forest Service insinuated itself into tribal religious understanding. Disregarding the indigenous sensibility and belief in the whole of the high country, imposing instead its determination of what sites were more deserving of religious designation than the excluded remainder, the Forest Service usurped tribal experience concerning the very nature of the holy reality in the Yurok, Karok, and Tolowa religious traditions by refusing to countenance and accord respect to the whole of the high country revered by tribal belief. That level of government involvement, selectively choosing to recognize and protect only partial fragments of the claimed religious reality, is the kind of incursion into religious affairs the third criterion of the *Lemon* test condemns. The injunction against road construction and timbering in the high country obviated the kind of meddlesome interference by government in strictly religious determinations that the criterion demands. It removed the entire area from the offensive calculations by the Forest Service to designate and theoretically insulate islands of ritual significance, thrusting itself into the realm of religious evaluation and administrative control that both of the religion clauses of the First Amendment were designed to prevent. Thus, far from posing a threat to the protections of the Establishment Clause, the district court injunction safeguarded them by its satisfaction of the requisite terms of the *Lemon* test: it had a secular purpose, with a primary effect that neither advanced nor inhibited the tribal religions, and that avoided the kind of government entanglement with those religions that the Constitution sought to prohibit.

The court of appeals next chided the government for its cavalier inattention to the standard that had to be observed in cases alleging violations of the Free Exercise Clause. Specifically, in its defense of the action against which the claim is made, the government must establish that the burden it imposes furthers a state interest of the highest order and magnitude capable of outweighing the constitutional protection of religious freedom that it threatens. The government must also show that no means to further its overriding state interest is available that would be less restrictive of the religious liberty that it burdens. The court of appeals faulted the government's inadequate attempt to demonstrate its compelling interest in completing the section of road running through the Indian high country, and its failure to even engage the question of whether its interests could have been met in other ways that would have interfered less with tribal religious rights. The court found no comparison between the interest of the Forest Service in constructing six miles of roadway through tribal sacred land and the kind of multi-state concerns for water and energy sources that were used to justify the Glen Canyon Dam and Lake Powell in the case of *Badoni v. Higginson*.[44] The physical magnitude of that project, along with the congressional and state legislative ratifications for the uses to which the dam and its reservoir would be put, were arguably of a compelling stature. Although making no reference to the toll exacted by that project from Navajo religious freedom, the Ninth Circuit found nothing to approach its eventual overriding significance in the Forest Service rationale for the logging road that threatened the Yurok, Karok, and Tolowa religions. The court of appeals upheld the district court's findings that on all counts, the road's alleged justifications proved wanting. There would be no improved access to timber resources, no statewide net gain in employment, no enhanced recreational benefits, no significant improvements in forest management functions, and no confirmed contributions to Forest Service revenues from the road. Far from demonstrating paramount interests of the highest order, the road's inadequacies revealed its marginal significance and unworthiness to permit its destructiveness to the tribal religions. Accordingly, the Ninth Circuit affirmed the district court's ruling that the Forest Service should be enjoined from constructing the road through, and harvesting timber in, the high country as an unjustifiable violation of the free-exercise rights of the Yurok, Karok, and Tolowa peoples. The court of appeals further upheld the district court's ruling on the inadequacies of the Forest Service's Environmental Impact Statements and the demand for supplemental or new statements that would adequately specify effective measures to mitigate the adverse impact of road construction and logging on the water quality and fish habitat of Blue Creek, as well as providing a demonstration that those activities would not violate the Federal Water Pollution Control Act.

It is significant to note that one of the judges on the appellate panel dissented from granting constitutional protection to the tribal plaintiffs. Virtually ignoring the unequivocal warnings contained in the Theodoratus Report against the construction of the road because of its destructive impact on "the very core of Northwest [Indian] religious beliefs and practices," Judge Beezer insisted that the report did not sustain the conclusion "that the mere existence of the G-O Road would impair the Indian plaintiffs' religious practices."[45] Admitting that the report focused concern for the threats posed to certain "sites" by road construction through the high country, the judge explicitly rejected the report's instruction against restricting the words *religious* or *sacred* as applicable only to a set of ritual behavior performed at certain specific locations within the region of the high country. Unwilling to engage in "the mental shift" that the report suggested was necessary to correctly understand the local Native American perception of the high country as a holy reality in its geographic integrity, Judge Beezer pointedly dismissed such a perception as excessively broad and, for that reason, a concept of religion not recognized by the Constitution. The judge's mere assertion was bald of any substantiation or the pretense to any. His remarks, however, intoned the refrain that had been heard throughout the cases that had preceded it, and simultaneously exposed an injudicious preoccupation with preserving governmental dominion over public lands.

For Beezer, the nature of the tribal religions, while oriented to land, was essentially reduced to the series of rituals, observances, and practices performed at any number of discrete locations within the region of the high country. The notion of that area in its indivisible wholeness as itself the holy reality, indeed, the sacred center of the world and the place of contact with the regenerative and healing powers of the universe, which alone evokes and gives meaning to the pilgrimages, prayers, and rituals among its trails and along its ridges, was never reflected in his dissent. For him, the high country was simply the place where the Yuroks, Karoks and Tolowas had traditionally practiced their religion; the land didn't sanctify their practices, it merely situated them. The dissociation between religion and land with the simultaneous equivalence drawn between religion and Indian practices is apparent in the judge's remarks concerning the alleged offensiveness of the road. Of potential concern was not that the very presence of the road would be an invasive desecration of the high country, but that it might remotely impair visual and auditory conditions conducive to tribal religious practices. Against that threat, Judge Beezer responded to the adequacy of the Forest Service's plans to minimize the road's visibility, but ultimately suggested that the tribes simply conduct their religious observances elsewhere in the high country farther from the road. Not only did the judge's position ignore the road's close proximity to three of the most hallowed rock formations within the high country's sacred landscape, but it betrayed a notion of religion as a set of behavior, distinct and separable from the places of its performance: if the road impinged on the performance, move the performance and let the religion be practiced at a different location.[46] For Judge Beezer, the defining character of the high country was not in its status as a religious reality. Holiness was not inherent to its land, whose religious significance was merely derived from the tribal practices conducted within its borders.

For the judge, the determinative feature of the high country was its condition as government property by virtue of its incorporation into the national forest system. Judge Beezer's dissent was a defense of the government's authority to dispose of its land as it chose. Faulting the district court for not giving "proper respect to the government's ownership rights in public lands,"[47] the judge suggested the near-absolute nature of those rights. By virtue of its position as landlord, the government enjoyed a compelling authority to exploit its lands that would brook no challenge from any alleged religious significance claimed for those lands. "The government's interest in putting public lands to productive use must be weighed carefully in the balance. While the government has many obligations that are not shared by private landowners, the government retains a substantial, perhaps even compelling, interest in using its land to achieve economic benefits."[48]

Although it referred to a balancing of interests, it was clear that Judge Beezer's allegiance to the notion of property was the foundational concept against which he viewed the tribal claim investing land with religious significance. For him, the high country existed primarily as government property, and any First Amendment protection demanded by Native

The Triumph of Property over Religion

American experience threatened to divest the government of its authority and control. The judge's adherence to that position accounts for his unworthy characterization of the constitutional issue raised by the tribal suit: "The Indian plaintiffs are attempting to use the free exercise clause to bar the development of public lands."[49] Having relegated religion to the realm of human practices, discrete and transposable from one location to another, and having confined land to the category of property, Beezer distorted the Yurok, Karok, and Tolowa claim as merely an attempt to dispossess the government's property interests in the high country. Consistent with those joint perspectives on religion and property, the judge was begrudgingly willing to make the barest concession to Native American religious freedom, which was largely sacrificed to his injudicious policy determination of preserving intact the government's ownership and disposition of public lands. Inappropriately responding to the specter of wholesale loss of government property with its "compelling" economic benefits, Judge Beezer, unwilling to grant judicial recognition to an alternative valuation of land as sacred reality, would countenance only the possibility of designating small allotments from government-held land on which Native Americans could perform their religious practices. "Although it may be appropriate in some limited circumstances to order the preservation of discrete parcels of land to accommodate Indian religious exercises, the courts should guard against the creation of private religious preserves covering vast expanses of our public lands."[50] Although it urged a judicial caution, Beezer's dissent was motivated by an unambiguous intent to defend government ownership of land. Threatened by the prospect of massive disfranchisement through Native American claims of sacred landscape, the judge refused the convergence of religion and land. The high country as a component of the Six Rivers National Forest was federal property, and although the Yuroks, Karoks, and Tolowas were free to keep their religious observances there, they should not be permitted to deter the government's managerial prerogatives to construct a road or permit logging on its land. Though Judge Beezer's position was a dissenting one, his subservience of religion to property was the critical issue that would figure in the Supreme Court's review, to which the government appealed the Ninth Circuit's majority ruling.

DECISION OF THE UNITED STATES SUPREME COURT

Hearing oral arguments on November 30, 1987, the United States Supreme Court issued its ruling on April 19, 1988.[51] In an utter and dismal failure to acknowledge any constitutional harm to tribal belief and the exercise of traditional religion, the Court reversed the decisions of the two lower courts, permitting the government to proceed with its development of the high country. In rendering its decision, the Supreme Court understood quite clearly the intimate relationship between religion and land the case posed. Writing the majority opinion,[52] Justice Sandra Day O'Connor noted "that the logging and road-building projects at issue in this case could have devastating effects on traditional Indian religious practices. Those practices are intimately and inextricably bound up with the unique features of the Chimney Rock area, which is known to the Indians as the 'high country'.... [W]e can assume that the threat to the efficacy of at least some religious practices is extremely grave."[53] The Court even went so far as to assume that the government road would "virtually destroy the Indians' ability to practice their religion."[54]

In Justice William J. Brennan's dissenting opinion, the connection between religion and land, clearly implicated in the majority opinion, became most explicit. Justice Brennan, informed by the Theodoratus Report and the congressional record relating to the passage of the American Indian Religious Freedom Act of 1978, noted that for most Native Americans,

"the area of worship cannot be delineated from social, political, cultural and other aspects of Indian lifestyles." . . . A pervasive feature of this lifestyle is the individual's relationship with the natural world; this relationship, which can accurately though somewhat incompletely be characterized as one of stewardship, forms the core of what might be called, for want of a better nomenclature, the Indian religious experience. . . . In marked contrast to traditional western religions, the belief systems of Native Americans do not rely on doctrines, creeds, or dogmas. . . . Where dogma lies at the heart of western religions, Native American faith is inextricably bound to the use of the land. The site specific nature of Indian religious practice derives from the Native American perception that the land is itself a sacred, living being. . . . Rituals are performed in prescribed locations not merely as a matter of traditional orthodoxy, but because land, like all other living things, is unique, and specific sites possess different spiritual properties and significance.[55]

Finally, almost at the end of a decade, land as alive and holy had been judicially noted by the highest court in the country. Yet having made that recognition, and having closely understood the logic that government alteration of the land would severely interfere with, if not destroy, the religion of the Yuroks, Karoks, and Tolowa Indians, the Supreme Court irresponsibly refused to apply the constitutional protections the case mandated. In a shocking repudiation of First Amendment jurisprudence, the Court retreated to the most literal interpretation of the Free Exercise Clause in a position unsubstantiated by its own precedents.

In a disturbing refusal to apply its own established case law, the Supreme Court's majority opinion claimed that the Free Exercise Clause of the First Amendment is implicated only when the government makes outright prohibitions of or places indirect coercions and penalties upon the exercise of religion. All other "incidental effects of government programs, which may make it more difficult to practice certain religions but which have no tendency to coerce individuals into acting contrary to their religious beliefs"[56] are outside the protections of the Constitution. In an alarming distortion of logic, the Supreme Court baldly asserted that although the government's development of the California high country would gravely affect and even doom the tribal religions, it could not be said that the building of a road or the lumbering of trees were explicit actions that would coerce the Indians into violating their religious beliefs, nor did it deny the Indians any rights, benefits, or privileges enjoyed by other citizens. In the twisted reasoning of the Court, the government could desecrate and even obliterate the object of a people's religious belief so long as it did not proscribe them from holding to that belief. To contend in this way that the government's land-use policies did not infringe on the tribes' right to religious freedom amounted, in the words of Justice Brennan's dissent, "to nothing more than the right to believe that their religion will be destroyed."[57]

The Supreme Court's departure from the standard it should have applied to the case is egregious. In a long line of precedents, the Court had determined that in claims relating to the free exercise of religion, a determination should first be made that the contested government action would interfere with the belief or practice of religion. Once it could be shown that governmental action would in fact burden the free exercise of religion, it would be incumbent upon the government to prove that it had a state interest of such magnitude and of the highest order that it would outweigh the legitimate claims to the free exercise of religion. Even if the government could advance such a compelling interest, it would have to demonstrate that no other means of serving that interest existed that would be less restrictive of the First Amendment right.

Because the Court did not follow its own well-established procedure for the analysis and determination of free-exercise claims, it discredited itself in the shameful absurdity that although the government's proposed development of the high country could be assumed to have such "devastating effects on traditional Indian religious practices" as to "virtually destroy the Indians' ability to practice their religion," their plight nevertheless warranted no constitutional protection as a violation of the Free Exercise Clause. Had it been faithful to its own standard of review, the

Supreme Court should have noted the American Indian value of land, and specifically the Yurok, Karok, and Tolowa understanding of the high country as a sacred reality. Then it should have explicitly determined what it clearly assumed: that the Forest Service proposal to construct the logging road through the high country would constitute a severe interference with the ability of the California tribes to exercise their religion. Finally, it should have insisted, according to the third step of its own procedure, that the government proceed with its land-use plan for the high country only on a showing that the proposed road and ensuing lumbering were interests of sufficient magnitude and of the highest order. On this point, the Supreme Court should have relied upon the findings of the two lower courts that the government would have failed the test.

It was a well-settled rule of federal procedure that the Court would not disturb findings of facts agreed upon by both the district court and the court of appeals unless those findings were clearly erroneous. Since no complaint or suggestion of error had been raised, the Supreme Court should have allowed itself to be informed by the lower courts that the construction of the Forest Service road would not improve access to timber resources in the Blue Creek Unit of the Six Rivers National Forest; that it would not increase the number of jobs in the regional timber industry; that recreational access to the area already existed, and the road would in fact degrade the pristine quality of the land that made it attractive for recreational use; that the road would not greatly improve the efficient administration of the Six Rivers National Forest; and finally, that the harvesting of timber in the affected area was but a small fraction of trees in the entire national forest, and that the local timber industry would not suffer seriously without access to the lumber in the affected areas.

It should therefore have been abundantly clear to the Court that far from having the required "paramount interests" of the highest order, the government's plan was of only marginal importance and would fail the test of proving a compelling state interest necessary to justify the infringement on the tribes' freedom of religion.

Irresponsibly, the Supreme Court never applied its own test, and the government never had to prove any overriding interest. What was it that so distorted the majority's decision that it could capitulate so blindly in the destruction of religious freedom? The Court was confronted with two competing conceptions of federal land: on the one hand, "a sacred, living being ... unique [with] specific sites possess[ing] different spiritual properties and significance," and on the other, property to be used and managed as a purely internal administrative function of the government. The

The Triumph of Property over Religion

Court's refusal to comply with its own procedural analysis betrayed its indefensible suasion by the latter dominant paradigm.

The majority's notion of land as governmental property lies behind its rigid insistence that *Bowen v. Roy* 476 U.S. 693 (1986) should control the outcome in *Northwest Indian Cemetery Protective Association*. But aside from the fact that the plaintiffs in the two cases were Native Americans who based their claims on the Free Exercise Clause, *Roy* and *Northwest Indian Cemetery Protective Association* are thoroughly disparate. That the Supreme Court imposed *Roy* as the precedent that determined its analysis and decision for *Northwest Indian* was so strained and contrived that it clearly exposed the majority's inappropriate bent toward the northwest California high country solely as a holding of the federal government, which should enjoy unquestioned discretion in its use and disposition of that land.

In *Roy* the Court had considered a challenge to a federal statute that required the states to use Social Security numbers in administering certain welfare programs. Stephen J. Roy, a Native American descendant of the Abenaki Tribe, objected to the use of a Social Security number for his two-year-old daughter, Little Bird of the Snow, as a condition for receiving benefits under the Aid to Families with Dependent Children program (AFDC), and the food stamp program. Upon his refusal to obtain the number for her, the Pennsylvania Department of Public Welfare terminated AFDC and medical benefits payable to Roy on his daughter's behalf and moved to reduce the number of food stamps Roy's family had been receiving. Roy sued the Secretary of the Pennsylvania Department of Public Welfare, the Secretary of Health and Human Services, and the Secretary of Agriculture, contending that the Free Exercise Clause of the First Amendment entitled his daughter to an exemption from the Social Security number requirement. At trial, Roy asserted a sincere religious belief "that control over one's life is essential to spiritual purity and indispensable to 'become a holy person'."[58] In conversations with an Abenaki chief, Roy had come to believe that technology was robbing the human spirit. In the face of that threat, he attempted to prepare his daughter for greater spiritual power by keeping "her person and spirit unique and that the uniqueness of the Social Security number as an identifier, coupled with the other uses of the number over which she [would] have no control, [would] serve to 'rob the spirit' of his daughter and prevent her from attaining greater spiritual power."[59] Roy clarified his belief when it was learned during the trial that the Social Security Administration had, in fact, already issued a Social Security number for Little Bird of the Snow pursuant to a policy of assigning numbers to those who are required by federal law to have one but decline to complete an application. With this disclosure, Roy had been recalled to the stand and testified that Little Bird of the Snow's spirit would be robbed only by use of the Social Security number by the federal or state governments in their computer systems or by other dissemination. Since no known use of the number had yet been made, Roy expressed his belief that his daughter's spirit had not been damaged. Nevertheless, he claimed the protection of the Free Exercise Clause to enjoin the government from making any use of the Social Security number that had been issued to Little Bird of the Snow and from transmitting the number to any agency, individual, business entity, or any other third party. Likewise, he pressed for protection from federal and state refusals to grant cash assistance, medical assistance, and food stamps on behalf of his daughter because of his religious belief that he should not submit to the regulations requiring that he provide the particular welfare agencies with the Social Security number that had at any rate been issued to Little Bird of the Snow. The district court agreed, but the Supreme Court, noting its probable jurisdiction, heard the case and reversed the lower court.

The Supreme Court rejected Roy's argument that the Free Exercise Clause of the First Amendment compelled the government to accommodate a religiously based objection to the congressional requirement that the state welfare agencies utilize Social Security numbers in the administration of the Aid to Families with Dependent Children program. Chief Justice Warren Burger, writing the majority opinion, was joined in his conclusions by all the other justices, except Justice Byron White, who dissented. In reaching its decision, the Court ruled that the Social Security system, in its assignment and use of Social Security numbers, was a purely internal administrative function of government record keeping. The Court noted that Roy's objection to the government's reliance on Social Security numbers was not from any restrictions the numerical system imposed on what he could religiously believe or practice; his complaint rather was that the use of a numerical identifier might harm the spiritual development of his daughter. Alluding to the government's organizational infrastructure and operational mechanism of its day-to-day functioning, the Court asserted that it had never "interpreted the First Amendment to require the Government *itself* to behave in ways that the individual believes will further his or her spiritual development or that of his or her family. The Free Exercise Clause simply cannot be understood to require the Government to conduct its own internal affairs in ways that comport with the religious beliefs of particular citizens."[60]

The Court further found that the statutory requirement that applicants provide a Social Security number as a condition of eligibility to receive benefits from a state AFDC plan was wholly neutral in religious terms and uniformly applicable. It created no danger of censorship; did not intrude on the organization of religious institutions or schools; placed no direct burden on the dissemination of religious views; and did not compel benefit recipients, by threat of sanctions, to refrain from religiously motivated conduct or to engage in conduct they found objectionable for religious reasons. Although several justices argued forcefully for the principle that would have sustained a religious exemption for Roy from this otherwise inoffensive requirement,[61] they concurred that he had no grounds to challenge the Social Security system in its reliance on numerical designations. The Court stressed that aspect of the system's operational configuration as a purely "internal" component through which the government processed information and administered record-keeping functions. As such, the Court held that "Roy may no more prevail on his religious objection to the Government's use of a Social Security number for his daughter than he could on a sincere religious objection to the size or color of the Government's filing cabinets. The Free Exercise Clause affords an individual protection from certain forms of governmental compulsion; it does not afford an individual a right to dictate the conduct of the Government's internal procedures."[62]

The distinction between the complaints in *Bowen v. Roy* and *Lyng v. Northwest Indian Cemetery Protective Association* is glaring: *Roy* objected to the application of a Social Security number, *Lyng* sought the preservation of sacred land. Yet in reaching its majority decision in *Lyng*, the Supreme Court rigidly fixed *Roy* as the sole determinative precedent for its reversal of the two lower courts, which had extended constitutional protection for the tribal high country. The analogy that the Court forced between the two cases is strained to the point of distortion. What the Court repudiated in *Roy* was the attempt of a single individual, motivated by a desire to protect his daughter's unique spiritual identity and to ensure her reception of greater spiritual power, to challenge a federal system of administering welfare programs. Although it did not question the authenticity of the religious belief animating the father's concern, the Court characterized it as one involving a "private person['s] ability to pursue spiritual fulfillment,"[63] and the harm to his daughter through the use of a Social Security number as an "incidental interference with an individual's spiritual activities."[64] Similarly, in alluding to the government's reliance on the numerical system as an internal administrative affair, the Court affirmed the system's legitimacy against a challenge like Roy's, which was based merely "on a religious objector's spiritual development."[65] The Supreme

Court's phrasing thus suggested that the alleged harm from a Social Security number derived not from any threat to Abenaki tribal religion, but only from its perceived interference with the personal reception and cultivation of spiritual power asserted for one tribal member's daughter. Such a claimed impediment to individual holiness was ruled insufficient to dictate the design and implementation of the government's own administrative procedures.

But no such singular claim of personal spiritual development and fulfillment was at state in the Yurok, Karok, and Tolowa attempts to prevent the Forest Service from constructing the six miles of paved road for timber harvesting through the high country. Unlike *Roy*, in which the complaint rested on conversations that Roy had with an Abenaki chief concerning spiritual power and the threat of an identification number to his two-year-old daughter, the plaintiff in *Lyng* represented some 5,000 members of three northwest California Indian tribes seeking to protect the integrity of land long revered as sacred to them from the destructive impact of government road construction and lumbering. That they were joined in their action by the state of California and such organizations as the Sierra Club, the Wilderness Society, and the regional Audubon Society which, among others, supported their First Amendment argument, was a further distinction from the individual, non-tribal suit brought in the *Roy* case. Yet in the majority opinion in *Lyng*, the Supreme Court exercised a highly selective reading of the Theodoratus Report to include a severely abbreviated passage which, referring to the high country as a place of prayer used by members of the three tribes, included phrasing similar to language found in the *Roy* decision.

Editing two sentences from a report of more than 500 pages, the Court suggested that the tribes objected to the road because it would "create distractions that will interfere with 'training and ongoing religious experience of individuals using [sites within] the area for personal medicine and growth . . . and as integrated parts of a system of religious belief and practice which correlates ascending degrees of personal power with a geographic hierarchy of power'."[66] Seizing upon the phrases "religious experience of individuals," "personal medicine and growth," and "degrees of personal power," the majority opinion dismissively asserted, "The Court rejected this kind of challenge in *Roy*."[67] But to read the relevant section of the Theodoratus Report that provided the context from which the Court excised the clauses it chose, is to witness the Court ignoring evidence that the Forest Service road threatened an entire religious worldview and lifeway and not simply the spiritual development of a two-year-old child at issue in *Roy v. Bowen*:

The Triumph of Property over Religion   157

> The ethnographic component of this report has demonstrated the existence of an ongoing indigenous religious system, shared by contemporary Northwest California Indian people since before the time of Indian/non-Indian contact. This belief system has been shown to incorporate elements of daily life, ritual practice, geographic locale, and ideas of origin and World Renewal into a conceptualization of sacredness. This concept is foreign in many ways to western European categories of thought. Further it has been demonstrated that the Blue Creek high country (and the G-O Road project area within it) is significant as an integral and indispensable part of Indian religious conceptualization and practice. Specific sites within the project area are necessary to the *training and ongoing religious experience of individuals using the area for personal medicine and growth*, curing medicine, deviltry, and medicine affecting the well being of local communities as well as (today) the broader world community. These sites are necessary both as specific sites for specific medicines *and as integrated parts of a system of religious belief and practice which correlates ascending degrees of personal power with a geographic hierarchy of power*. Individuals progressively use sites of increasing power and this progression is a necessary part of religious growth. Experience at the lower levels of medicine is a prerequisite for attainment of power at the higher levels. Research has also shown that successful use of the high country is dependent upon and facilitated by certain qualities of the physical environment, the most important of which are privacy, silence, and an undisturbed natural setting.... Based on the ethnographic findings summarized above, it is the conclusion of the ethnographic researchers that the construction of the Chimney Rock Section of the G-O Road, along any of its alternative routes (I-9), would cause serious and irreparable damage to the sacred areas which are an integral and necessary part of the belief systems and lifeway of Northwest California Indian peoples. It is, therefore, the recommendation of the ethnographic researchers that the Chimney Rock Section of the G-O Road, along any of its alternate routes (I-9) not be constructed.[68]

In *Roy* the Supreme Court discounted the relative significance of a parent's concern for the spiritual development of his child as insufficient to prevent the government from relying on numbers to administer its Social Security system. Seeking to force a groundless analogy, the Court in *Lyng* accentuated language from the Theodoratus Report on the religious experience of those who prayed in the high country, suggesting that the religious interest at issue was, like that in *Roy*, of too personal and individual a character to halt the government's interest in constructing its road. In making that insinuation, the Supreme Court deleted reference to the shared intertribal extensions of the belief in the high country long held by the Yurok, Karok, and Tolowa peoples. But minimizing the tribal scope and long-standing persistence of their belief was not as egregious as the Court's refusal to recognize any distinction between the harm threatened by the government against Little Bird of the Snow in *Roy* and the destruction it would wreck on the three indigenous cultures of Northwest California in *Lyng*. The Court asserted that "[i]n both cases, the challenged government action would interfere significantly with private persons' ability to pursue spiritual fulfillment according to their own religious beliefs."[69] Although "the pursuit of spiritual fulfillment" may have been adequate to represent Stephen Roy's quest to protect the unique identity and autonomy of his daughter from the intrusion and dissemination of a Social Security number, it utterly failed to characterize the jeopardy the government would inflict on tribal belief and practice with the construction of its logging road through the high country.

No mere "pursuit of spiritual fulfillment," but the protection of their very religion itself was at the heart of the Yurok, Karok, and Tolowa constitutional claim. All reference to their spiritual growth, development, or fulfillment would be rendered superfluous if the integrity of the high country as the locus and manifestation of sacred reality were itself desecrated through the invasive alterations and consequent degradations the government road would exact. Without the sanctity of the land, disclosing itself to tribal perceptions in the natural contours of its rocks and ridges, trees and waters, addressing them in the silence of its remote solitude as well as in the voices of its birds and other creatures, the tribal acknowledgment of it, through their array of prayers and rituals, would be meaningless. Pilgrimages, preparatory feasts and sweats, prolonged vigils of concentrated awareness, and persistent dancing in and around stone prayer seats, quiet prayer or personal songs and traditional chants, healing and world-renewing dances and ceremonialisms, were all so many derivative tribal responses to the primordial holiness revealing itself to them in and through the land of the high country. It was the land as sacred entity, the animating and evocative presence for all the religious practices celebrated and centered upon it, that would be ravaged by the Forest Service management plan; to harm the land, even before any consideration of the subsequent interference with the tribal activities inspired by and oriented toward it, was to violate the very heart of the Yurok, Karok, and Tolowa religions.

Precisely because it refused to grant judicial recognition to that notion of land as sacred reality, the Supreme Court irresponsibly abandoned First Amendment protection not only to those three indigenous religions of northwest California, but to the entirety of those Native American beliefs—indeed to any sincerely held religious convictions—that revere land as holy. No matter how serious the threat of diminishment or even destruction, religious beliefs and practices inspired and evoked by land, if claimed and held by the government, could be sacrificed to whatever development scheme the government chose. Even if its actions threatened to completely doom an entire religious way of life, the government was now exempt and no longer obligated to demonstrate a compelling interest of the highest order, nor was it required to show that the means it had adopted to meet the interest was the least restrictive to religion. Ultimate government discretion in the disposal of land, not religion, was the value the Supreme Court protected with its ruling in *Lyng*.

It is remarkable that Justice O'Connor would write the majority opinion that exonerated so completely government behavior that could devastate religious beliefs and practices so critically. For it was she, in *Bowen v. Roy*, joined by Justices William Brennan and Thurgood Marshall, who sharply resisted Chief Justice Burger's move to dispense with the compelling interest test. The chief justice had suggested that in cases, such as *Bowen*, in which religious challenges are made to the eligibility requirements imposed by the government before a person can receive government benefits, the government could meet its burden on a mere showing that its requirements were "reasonable means of promoting a legitimate public interest."[70] Although Justice O'Connor had agreed that Stephen Roy's concern for his daughter's spiritual development was insufficient to dictate how the government designed and implemented the numerical system for administering its Social Security System, she rebuffed the chief justice's attempt to lower the standard under which the government would have to justify an offense against the free exercise of religion. A showing of mere reasonableness, she argued, would jeopardize religious freedom by making it too easy for the government to vindicate its religiously offensive actions.

> Such a threat has no basis in precedent and relegates a serious First Amendment value to the barest level of minimal scrutiny that the Equal Protection Clause already provides. I would apply our long line of precedents to hold that the Government must accommodate a legitimate free exercise claim unless pursuing an especially important interest by narrowly tailored means.... Once it has been shown that a governmental regulation burdens the free exercise of religion "only those interests of the highest order and those not otherwise served can over-balance legitimate claims to the free exercise of religion." *Wisconsin v. Yoder* 406 U.S. 205, 215 (1972). This Court has consistently asked the Government to demonstrate that unbending application for its regulation to the religious objector "is essential to accomplish an overriding governmental interest," *United States v. Lee* 455 U.S. 252, 257–258 (1982), or represents "the least restrictive means of achieving some compelling state interest," *Thomas v. Review Board* [450 U.S. 707, 718 (1981)]. Only an especially important governmental interest pursued by narrowly tailored means can justify exacting a sacrifice of First Amendment freedoms as the price for an equal share of the rights, benefits, and privileges enjoyed by other citizens.[71]

Justice O'Connor's firm insistence, in her dissenting remarks in *Bowen v. Roy*, that where government action threatens religious freedom the government must be held to "the compelling interest and least restrictive means test," was altogether abandoned in her majority opinion in *Lyng*. Her reversal is shocking, given her explicit recognition of the harm the Forest Service plan posed to the tribal religions and yet her preemptory and unpersuasive contention that the destruction did not warrant First Amendment protection: "The Government does not dispute, and we have no reason to doubt, that the logging and road-building projects at issue in this case could have devastating effects on traditional Indian religious practices. . . . Even if we assume that we should accept the Ninth Circuit's prediction, according to which the G-O road will 'virtually destroy the Indians' ability to practice their religion,' 795 F. 2d, at 693 (opinion below), the Constitution simply does not provide a principle that could justify upholding respondents' legal claims. However much we might wish that it were otherwise, government simply could not operate if it were required to satisfy every citizen's religious needs and desires."[72] The statement is flawed by the incoherence of its initial acknowledgment of the devastation of traditional Indian practices and even the destruction of Indian religion and its subsequent cavalier dismissal of mere "needs and desires" having no constitutional significance. The Yuroks, Karoks, and Tolowas were not petitioning the government for its bestowal of any supernumerary benefits or privileges, nor were they animated by some vague spiritual need or desire that they were looking to the government to fulfill. Rather, their claim was grounded in a First Amendment obligation that the government refrain from action that had been judicially recognized as destructive to their religion. Far from seeking any government subsidy or largess, the tribal suit sought only to enjoin the Forest Service from an intrusive alteration of land they had held sacred for generations before the government annexed it into the national forest system. Not demanding title or exclusive use of the high country region, the tribes asked only that the government leave its sacred presence alone and follow the recommendations of the Forest Service's own commissioned study—the Theodoratus Report—not to disturb its authentic status as a tribal sanctuary for the sake of a six-mile logging road that ultimately had no justification.

Probed by both the district court and the Ninth Circuit Court of Appeals, the lack of justification for the project was upheld on all counts: the road would not improve access to timber resources in that area of the national forest; it was not necessary even for the harvesting of timber in that unit; it would make no significant contribution to improved administration of the national forest; the marginal increase it might bring for recreational access would be at the very expense of destroying the pristine natural setting that made the area attractive for primitive recreational enjoyment; and it would not generate new jobs in the local timber industry, which had access to other areas of the national forest and was found not to suffer serious harm if deprived of taking the trees growing in the tribal high country.

Justice O'Connor, who only two years previously had argued forcefully for the necessity of retaining the compelling interest standard in First Amendment challenges to government action, should have been keenly attentive to and instructed by the factual determinations from the two lower courts. Not only did the Forest Service threaten the gravest harm to the tribal religions, but its project had only the most marginal significance, falling far short of anything even approaching a compelling state interest of paramount importance. Justice O'Connor's awareness of the governmental harm, even while ignoring the scant rationale that rendered it indefensible, her willingness to abandon her previous position and to so openly forfeit religious protection is shocking. Yet her position was not idiosyncratic or singular. As the author of the majority opinion in *Lyng*, she was joined by Chief Justice William Rehnquist and Justices Byron White, John Paul Stevens, and Antonin Scalia. Collectively, that majority refused to extend First Amendment religious protection to the tribal high country out of an injudicious policy determination based on an allegiance to the notion of land as property.

For the majority of the Supreme Court in *Lyng*, land existed fundamentally as property. Accordingly, the high country, having been incorporated into the Six Rivers National Forest, had become property of the federal government. Inappropriately, the majority moved against the Yurok, Karok, and Tolowa claim for religious protection to safeguard the government's property interest in the high country. Fearing the implications of granting judicial recognition to a religious valuation of land, the Court's majority was willing to sacrifice the religious liberties of some 5,000 tribal believers. To uphold the sanctity of the native land, enjoining the Forest Service from the desecration of its superfluous road project, threatened to dispossess the government of its claim to public lands. Abdicating its responsibility to adjudicate conflicting claims often arising from divergent values and perceptions, the Supreme Court in *Lyng* chose rather to annul the tribal claim by ignoring the spiritual and religious value of land, heeding only its status as property and subsequently granting complete discretion to the government as landlord. Even as it admitted that the tribes were not seeking exclusive ownership or use of the high country, the Court indulged in reckless speculation that such a claim would be encouraged if it were to shield the remoteness of the high country for the undisturbed practice of the tribal religions. Exploiting its own hypothetical specter of extensive governmental disfranchisement from control of public lands, the Supreme Court simply voided the Indian threat by an unworthy and injudicious assertion of the primacy of land as property. Referring to the tribal beliefs as practiced in the high country, the Court ruled: "No disrespect for these practices is implied when one notes that such beliefs could easily require *de facto* beneficial ownership of some rather spacious tracts of public property. Even without anticipating future causes, the diminution of the Government's property rights, and the concomitant subsidy of the Indian religion, would in this case be far from trivial. . . . Whatever rights the Indians may have to the use of the area, however, those rights do not divest the Government of its right to use what is, after all, *its* land."[73]

In the Court's underlined emphasis on the unquestioned proprietary interest the government enjoyed in its control over the high country, its insistence on rigidly following *Bowen v. Roy* as the sole dispositive precedent becomes clear. In *Roy*, the Court would not recognize a religious challenge to the use of numbers for the implementation and administration of the Social Security system. The Court deemed that the design and reliance upon identification numbers was a purely "internal procedure" related to the government's routine operational functioning and no greater significance than "the size or color of the government's filing cabinets." *Roy* stood, then, for the Supreme Court's deference to a certain limited number of domestic government processes and habitual practices, such as reliance on number systems or the choice of bureaucratic furniture, that the Court would not allow to be constrained even by claims of religious objection.

With its allegiance to the paradigm of land as property, the majority of the Supreme Court in *Lyng*, through its reliance on *Bowen v. Roy*, affirmed the absolute discretion it invested in the government as landlord and the total diminishment to which such a conception reduced the status of land. Stripped of any religious or spiritual significance, land became but a cipher in the government's managed disposition of its multiple holdings. Land's utter degradation and minimal significance is starkly apparent in the Court's astounding statement that "[t]he building of a road or the harvesting of timber on publicly owned land cannot meaningfully be distinguished from the use of a Social Security number in *Roy*."[74] Confined to the category of property, the Indian high country remained just so many acres of federal forest; the paving of its ridges and the falling of its trees, excluded from the language of the sacred and its desecration, were but the "internal procedures" of governmental administration, arranging the contours of its domain with the casual disposition and scant accountability of replacing office fixtures.

Scoring the majority's forfeiture of First Amendment religious protection for all Native Americans whose land-centered beliefs were jeopardized by its ruling, Justice Brennan's dissent identified the very heart of the case. "[It] represents yet another stress point in the longstanding conflict between two disparate cultures—the dominant western culture, which views land in terms of ownership and use, and that of Native Americans, in which concepts of private property are not only alien, but contrary to a belief system that holds land sacred."[75] The severity of Justice Brennan's rebuke was leveled at the majority's "embrace" of the government as landowner and its capitulation to the government's assumption that as landlord it enjoyed the prerogative of always taking precedence over claims that a particular use of its property infringed upon religious liberty. For Brennan, the majority's refusal to carefully balance and weigh the competing values of land as federal holding on the one hand and sacred reality on the other, by simply denying the tribal claim of any constitutional significance was an "indefensible abdication" of judicial responsibility. The majority had attempted to justify its dismissal of the Yurok, Karok, and Tolowa claim by insisting that the Free Exercise Clause is not implicated by federal land-use decisions, because such decisions neither coerce conduct inconsistent with religious belief nor penalize religious activity. According to that rationale, the Forest Service decision to construct a logging road through the high country was religiously innocuous: it didn't force the tribal believers to do anything inimical to their religious beliefs, and it didn't punish or castigate them for making pilgrimages, maintaining their prayer vigils, or otherwise engaging in religious conduct within the area. That the road and subsequent logging would indelibly scar the natural being and hallowed condition of the high country as the sacred presence that evoked and gave meaning to the tribal prayers and ceremonialism addressed to it was completely exonerated by such a narrow reading of constitutional religious protection. Justice Brennan pilloried the absurd incoherence of the majority's reading of the Free Exercise Clause that indemnified the Forest Service destruction of the very reality without which the tribal religion would not endure. Even as it cut down, paved over, and put traffic on the land revered by tribal belief and celebrated in tribal ritual, the Forest Service was found to commit no religious harm, since it didn't deprive the Indian believers from still holding to the holiness of the high country and expressing that belief in their traditional ways. Rebuking such a proposition as logically untenable and "cruelly surreal" in its result, Justice Brennan wrote:

Today, the Court holds that a federal land-use decision that promises to destroy an entire religion does not burden the practice of that faith in a manner recognized by the Free Exercise Clause. Having thus stripped respondents [i.e., the Yurok, Karok, and Tolowa tribes] and all other Native Americans of any constitutional protection against perhaps the most serious threat to their age-old religious practices, and indeed to their entire way of life, the Court assures us that nothing in its decision "should be read to encourage governmental insensitivity to the religious needs of any citizen." I find it difficult, however, to imagine conduct more insensitive to religious needs than the Government's determination to build a marginally useful road in the face of uncontradicted evidence that the road will render the practice of respondents' religion impossible. Nor do I believe that respondents will derive any solace from the knowledge that although the practice of their religion will become "more difficult" as a result of the Government's actions, they remain free to maintain their religious beliefs. Given today's ruling, that freedom amounts to nothing more than the right to believe that their religion will be destroyed. The safeguarding of such a hollow freedom not only makes a mockery of the "policy of the United States to protect and preserve for American Indians their inherent right of freedom to believe, express, and exercise their traditional religions," it fails utterly to accord with the dictates of the First Amendment.[76]

In Justice Brennan's view, the precedent that should have guided the Court in its disposition of *Lyng* should have been *Wisconsin v. Yoder* 406 U.S. 205 (1972) and not *Bowen v. Roy*. In *Yoder* the Supreme Court struck down a state compulsory school attendance law on free-exercise grounds because the Court recognized "the *impact* that compulsory high school attendance could have on the continued survival of Amish communities."[77] Justice Brennan noted that the Amish, like the Native Americans implicated in *Lyng*, shared a pervasively religious view of life and that their faith dictated their entire lifestyle. Although no Amish rule explicitly proscribed attendance at public school beyond the eighth grade, the Amish parents had objected to Wisconsin's regulation because "the *values* . . . of the modern secondary school are in sharp conflict with the fundamental *mode of life* mandated by Amish religion."[78] In *Yoder* the Supreme Court had clearly responded to prevent the gradual erosion and disintegration of the Amish way of life, which they had persuasively argued would be threatened by forcefully exposing their children to the secularizing influence and pressures toward conformity with the broader American culture from which Amish religious beliefs obliged separation. Although Justice Brennan admitted that the threat to Amish life against which the Supreme Court intervened arose from the compulsory nature of Wisconsin's education law, "it was the 'impact' on religious practice itself, not the source of that impact that led us to invalidate the law."[79] The predicted harm to Amish community life and religious practice was the object of the Supreme Court's constitutional protection in *Yoder*. All the more reason, argued

The Triumph of Property over Religion 165

Brennan, that the Court should apply the same protection to the tribal religions threatened by the Forest Service construction and logging project in *Lyng*. The Yuroks, Karoks, and Tolowas faced a religious destruction of greater immediacy and without the choice the Amish, had the Supreme Court failed to intervene, might yet have entertained of leaving Wisconsin to preserve their religious way of life in some more tolerant region.

> Respondents here have demonstrated that construction of the G-O road will completely frustrate the practice of their religion, for as the lower courts found, the proposed logging and construction activities will virtually destroy respondents' religion, and will therefore, necessarily force them into abandoning those practices altogether.... Here ... respondents have claimed—and proved—that the desecration of the high country will prevent religious leaders from attaining the religious power or medicine indispensable to the success of virtually all their rituals and ceremonies.... Here the threat posed by the desecration of sacred lands that are indisputedly essential to respondents' religious practices is both more direct and more substantial than that raised by a compulsory school law that simply exposed Amish children to an alien value system. And of course respondents here do not even have the option, however unattractive it might be, of migrating to more hospitable locales; the site-specific nature of their belief system renders it non-transportable.[80]

In *Yoder* Justice Brennan likewise found precedent for a requirement that tribal religions would have to show that the land in question had some central significance to their belief and practice. Aware that Native American religious traditions generally consider all land as sacred, he addressed those circumstances where particular sites, currently held as federal property, were historically deemed by respective tribes to be more directly related to their religious beliefs and practices than other land. Brennan contended that it would not be necessary to demonstrate, as had the Yuroks, Karoks, and Tolowas, that the government's land use would "assuredly eradicate their faith." In *Yoder* the Supreme Court had treated the objection to the compulsory school attendance of adolescents as "central" enough to the Amish community and its religious way of life to accord it immunity from the state law. Even though the mandatory schooling regulation would not have prevented or otherwise rendered Amish religion from being practiced, its threat of undermining that religious way of life was sufficiently clear that the Court granted it constitutional protection. From that precedent, Justice Brennan proposed that where a religious challenge is raised to a federal land-use decision, those making the claim "should be required to show that the decision poses a substantial and realistic threat of frustrating their religious practices. Once such a showing is made, the burden should shift to the Government to come forward with a compelling state interest sufficient to justify the infringement of those practices."[81] In the following paragraph of his dissent, Brennan elaborated that the proposed standard was one of showing that government action would *frustrate or undermine* Indian religious practices. In speaking of the judicial responsibility in such sacred land cases, he contended that "like all other religious adherents, Native Americans would be the arbiters of which practices are central to their faith, subject only to the normal requirements that their claims be genuine and sincere. The question for the courts, then, is not whether the Native American claimants understand their own religion, but rather, whether they have discharged their burden of demonstrating, as the Amish did with respect to the compulsory school law in *Yoder*, that the land-use decision poses a substantial and realistic threat of undermining or frustrating their religious practices."[82]

As Justice Brennan himself noted, the dictionary can't be the final word on the meaning of constitutional language, but it is nevertheless significant.[83] Thus, the meaning of *undermining* includes the act of weakening or causing the collapse of something by removing an underlying support or foundation, and the act of injuring or destroying something in imperceptible stages. Similarly, "to frustrate" means to nullify, thwart, or to render something worthless or unavailing. As applied to their attempts to protect sacred lands in *Sequoyah v. TVA, Badoni v. Higginson, Wilson v. Block, Crow v. Gullet,* and *Lyng v. Northwest Indian Cemetery Protective Association*, the Native American plaintiffs could well have met Justice Brennan's *Yoder* standard. Whether it was the flooding of the Little Tennessee River Valley, the submersion of Rainbow Bridge and its vicinity in Utah, the development of a ski resort on the San Francisco Peaks in Arizona, the tourist accommodations at Bear Butte in South Dakota, or the six-mile logging road in northwest California, all were significant government operations that threatened to frustrate and undermine Native American religious belief and practice. In each case, state action altered the contours and invasively changed the natural integrity of landscapes whose historical and structural presence had addressed tribal religious sensibilities and evoked tribal responses in prayer and ritual over generations. In each case the sacred, embodied and manifest in land, would be ignored and degraded by government projects that would innundate the entire area or otherwise segregate and selectively develop delineated segments for secular use. From the tribal faith perspectives, such government acts destroyed or injured the foundational reality, the holy presence that sustained and gave meaning and worth to their religious practices. Whether it was its dramatic disappearance under the floodwaters at issue in *Sequoyah* and *Badoni*, its commercial and recreational development in *Wilson* and *Crow*, or its exploitation for the road and logging operations in *Lyng*, the despoliation of land "undermined" its sacred character and clearly "frustrated" tribal religious expression. Had Justice Brennan's *Yoder* standard been applied to each of the five cases under consideration, the respective Native American plaintiffs would have met the threshold burden of showing that government activity posed a substantial and realistic threat to their constitutionally protected freedom of religion. In all five cases the burden would then have shifted to the government to identify a compelling state interest sufficient to justify the infringement its actions threatened.

In *Yoder* Wisconsin had a persuasive argument that its compulsory school attendance law was a compelling state interest. Its importance was recognized as such by the Supreme Court: "There is no doubt as to the power of a State, having a high responsibility for education of its citizens, to impose reasonable regulations for the control and duration of basic education. Providing public schools ranks at the very apex of the function of a State."[84] Nevertheless the Supreme Court proceeded to hold that "however strong the State's interest, in universal compulsory education, it is by no means absolute to the exclusion or subordination of all other interests."[85] Noting that the Religion Clauses of the First Amendment had specifically and firmly fixed the right to free exercise of religious beliefs long before a general acknowledgment of the need for universal formal education, and that the Amish did in fact prepare their children through informal vocational training to be self-reliant and self-sufficient members of their own community and that of the larger society, the Supreme Court ultimately ruled that Wisconsin's interests were not sufficiently paramount to override the religious liberties upon which its law would clearly infringe.

If as lofty and convincing a state interest as Wisconsin's educational law was yet determined to lack the necessary import to outweigh the religious freedoms of the Amish community in *Yoder*, the state interests in the *Sequoyah, Wilson, Crow,* and *Lyng* cases were all the more inadequate. Abundant evidence of congressional disapproval and attempts to halt the Tellico Dam, which was funded only through the technical ruse of a secretive, last-minute rider on an energy appropriations bill, testifies to the utter lack of compelling interest for the government action that destroyed Cherokee sacred land in *Sequoyah*. Had the compelling interest test been applied in *Wilson* and *Crow*, the state interest in the private commercial development of a ski resort or the inducements and accommodations for tourists could never have qualified as paramount, overriding justifications for the respective infringements against the Navajo and Hopi religions and those against the Lakota and Tsistsistas peoples.

In the *Badoni* case, even though the Tenth Circuit Court of Appeals relied on a notion of compelling interest, its procedural application was seriously flawed. The court inappropriately presumed from the outset that the Glen Canyon Dam forming Lake Powell was of compelling state interest. With that conclusive determination, the court dismissed the Navajo complaint without proper recognition that the floodwaters of Lake Powell, submerging the surrounding area and the base of Rainbow Bridge, constituted a religious harm to Navajo belief and practice. Designed to shift the burden to the government to show overriding justification for infringing on religious exercise, the compelling interest standard was egregiously misused by the court to preemptively strike judicial recognition and comprehensive consideration of an alternative notion of land as sacred reality.

But if the court of appeals in *Badoni* inappropriately invoked the compelling interest standard, the infamy of the Supreme Court's majority ruling in *Lyng* was its complete abandonment of that standard altogether. Refusing to countenance a valuation of land as sacred, diminishing it instead through its unilateral categorization as property, the Court's majority invested the government with an unfettered discretion in its disposition of public lands. In so doing, it repudiated its institutional responsibility as arbiter between claims rising from different perspectives and values, arriving at a final determination through the application of appropriate law and rule and the prudent and principled evaluation of the competing interests. In matters of constitutional significance, such as claims grounded on the Free Exercise Clause of the First Amendment, the Court's obligation to properly balance and weigh religious concerns against authority asserted in governmental actions is fundamental to the Court's integrity. In *Lyng* that integrity was seriously compromised.

Assuming the injudicious role as warden of government land holdings, the Supreme Court forfeited its identity as guardian of constitutionally protected religious freedom. The Court recognized the unambiguous threat to the Yurok, Karok, and Tolowa religions from the Forest Service logging road through the high country. Had it been faithful to its own procedural analysis, the Court should have next shifted the burden to the government to demonstrate what compelling interest of paramount significance was at stake that could possibly justify the religious harm it would wreck on the tribal traditions. Ignoring the uncontested evidence from the lower courts that the road was of negligible significance, having only bare bureaucratic rationale to support its construction, the Court never put the government to the test. Instead, the Court insulated the government from ever having to respond to claims alleging the sacred character of lands it held. In its reductive conceptualization of land as property and its reckless presumption to serve the interests of the government as landlord, the Court rashly departed from its own standard and completely dispensed the government from all obligation to show the compelling interest for the particular land use it devised. The government's utter discretion in the disposition of the northwest California high country reflected the Court's constriction of federal lands to mere holdings where features could be submerged, uprooted, paved over, or otherwise changed as merely the "internal procedures" of a purely administrative routine whose alterations of landscapes had no greater significance than changes in governmental office furniture. The Supreme Court's degradation of land in *Lyng* and its acquiescence in governmental hegemony over it were the results of the Court's refusal to grant full recognition and thorough judicial evaluation of the tribal religious claim.

Threatened by the celebration of land as the animate presence of sacred reality, the Court dismissed the testimony of tribal prayer and ritual as constitutionally insignificant. By refusing the witness of tribal belief and practice, the Court silenced a singular voice capable of articulating a value of land beyond the idiom of mere property and exploitation. Minimizing the constitutional gravity of the tribal claim, the Court reinforced the rhetoric and consolidated the paradigm that consigned land to a thing of bare utility and proprietary value. But in its capitulation to that ancient bias, the Court discredited itself through the distorted incoherence of its flawed justification. Although admitting the destruction of the Yurok, Karok, and Tolowa religions from the proposed logging road, the Court nevertheless refused to extend the protection of the First Amendment. Asserting that the Free Exercise Clause was implicated only when the government coerced or prohibited religious belief or practice, the Court condoned government actions that would reduce religious expression to empty cant and meaningless gesture: the government could violate or otherwise infringe upon the sacred reality that called forth and gave significance to the variety of religious practice and ceremony so long as it didn't proscribe or directly constrain those activities; the government could desecrate the primordial source and inspiration of religious behavior with constitutional immunity, provided it left that behavior intact. Even then, as its *Lyng* decision reductively impoverished land through a sterile and univocal fixation of it as property, the Supreme Court similarly debased religion by diluting it to the mere shell of empty formality, severed from the holiness that grounded and animated its original expression. Finally, the Supreme

Court's mutual diminishment of land and religion reflected its corresponding inhibition of the Constitution itself: adopting the most literal and restrictive reading of the Free Exercise Clause, the Court abandoned its own jurisprudence to sacrifice indigenous cultures to the expediency of government dominion over land, and by so doing, reduced constitutional protection of religion to a hollow sanctuary.

Epilogue

The convergence of religion, law, and land is uniquely illustrated by the Supreme Court's ruling in *Lyng v. Northwest Indian Cemetery Protective Association* and the four lower court cases that preceded it. Together they represent a disturbing failure of the judiciary as interpreter of constitutional law to apply the protections of the Free Exercise Clause of the First Amendment to Native American Indian claims to preserve sacred land. The immediate impact and ongoing repercussions from *Lyng* and its predecessors, whose rulings were unchallenged by the high court decision, have not been sustained just by the tribal plaintiffs in those respective cases. Additionally, *Lyng*, as the prevailing judicial precedent, thwarts all attempts by Native American Indians to challenge government land-use decisions that threaten the desecration of lands ancestrally revered as holy and as the object of their religious faith and practice. Ignoring the significance of tribal historical presence upon and spiritual affiliation with the particular land that has evoked and continues to provide meaning to their prayer and ceremonialism, the Supreme Court will refuse to recognize the constitutional status of indigenous religious claims, if the land that the tribes seek to preserve has been appropriated and held as government property. In *Lyng* the Supreme Court's reduction of public land to the univocal category of government property and its subsequent refusal to weigh an alternative religious valuation effectively denies First Amendment religious freedom to those Native Americans who would exercise their beliefs by objecting to the submersion, paving, deforestation, or any other development scheme to which the government would consign land they have traditionally revered as sacred.

As the controlling judicial impediment to the safeguard of fundamental free-exercise protections for Native Americans, the *Lyng* decision likewise confirmed the empty verbiage of the American Indian Religious Freedom Act, which had already been exposed by the lower courts. With scant review, the Supreme Court dispatched the legislation as having "no teeth in it" beyond mere evaluation of federal policies and procedures bearing on American Indian religion; nothing in the act mandated changes pursuant to the review process. In the *Lyng* case itself, the Forest Service was found to conform with the act by virtue of having commissioned the Theodoratus Report; nothing in the act compelled the service to follow the report's findings on the religious significance of the Indian high country and its recommendation that the service refrain from building a road that promised to destroy the religious cultures of the Yurok, Karok, and Tolowa peoples. *Lyng* is a glaring illustration that compliance with the review procedure prescribed by the American Indian Religious Freedom Act provides no assurance that substantive agency or judicial protections will be extended to Native American belief and practice, even when the very review process identifies serious jeopardy to Indian religion from proposed government action. No clearer nor more extensive a harm to Native American religious cultures could be found than in the Theodoratus Report's conclusion unchallenged by the Supreme Court, that the government road and logging project would "virtually destroy the Indians' ability to practice their religion." Nothing in the act, however, prevented the Forest Service from ignoring with impunity the destruction to the Yurok, Karok, and Tolowa religious traditions against which its own commissioned study had forewarned.

If the Supreme Court ruling in *Lyng* exacts its harshest and most immediate toll from the constitutional protections that would be afforded to Native American Indian religions, its significance is not restricted to those traditions alone. As the reflection and codification of a broader cultural orientation toward land and the natural world, the ruling is of exceptional historic consequence. At the close of the twentieth century, in a moment of growing awareness of and increasing concern for the well-being of the earth against the sheer density of human population and its exploitive depredations of the planet, religious, philosophical, and ethical thought systems, among others, are being intensively challenged to reflect upon and persuasively articulate the intrinsic value of the earth. In response, one of the most striking developments in global interreligious dialogue continues to be an emerging consensus from among the different faith perspectives and their developed traditions that the natural world and the innumerable communities of life that define its interdependent totality participate in a cosmos of spiritual as well as physical identity. That cosmos may be variously conceived as the tangible manifestations of absolute reality in itself; or as the divinely ordained and rhythmically sustaining harmony of primordial creative energies; or the plurality of mutually dependent and co-originating forms in and through which the absolute recognizes itself as differentiated wholeness; or the community of beings created and embodied by God to share an eternal relationship with him in love. Their exact specifications may differ, but religious cosmologies witness to a shared capacity and growing responsibility to identify the natural world as grounded in and expressive of a sacred creative reality; the cosmos, the earth, and the multitudes of beings that collaborate in its extraordinary community of life have a significance, dignity, and value beyond the mere utilitarian purposes or blatant indifference they suffer from the human species. However tardy and halting, religious traditions are responding to the plight and plunder of the natural world by reanimating it from within their respective cosmologies and evoking a transformed human consciousness of the earth as numinous, revelatory of the sacred by virtue of its origin from, manifestation of, or participation in its very being.

This process, which increasingly engages and probes the moral sensitivity and authority of religious traditions, is of singular, momentous significance. Never before in historic memory has the earth been so severely impoverished and jeopardized in its capacity to sustain the extraordinary diversity of its biological creativity; never before has it witnessed so rapid a wasting of its life-sustaining soils and fresh waters, so accelerated an increase in the industrial chemicals and gases that continue to accumulate in its atmosphere. Never before, then, have religious traditions been confronted by so urgent a challenge to exercise their capacity to reground and celebrate the goodness and integrity, the holiness, of the natural world. If the different religions continue to respond to the planetary dimensions of the threat, and address the profoundly entrenched anthropocentric assumptions and drives that evidence only negligible and remote awareness of the sanctity of the earth, those respective religions will realize a more profound and expansive dimension of their own identities. Faithful to their claim to discern the presence of the sacred and to acknowledge it through appropriate expressions of reverence and corresponding moral behavior, religious traditions that celebrate the holiness of the natural world and articulate principles of ethical conduct reflecting its dignity and worth affirm their own vital authenticity. Indigenous religions, including the diversity of Native American tribal traditions, have consistently and prominently testified to the spiritual character of all beings within the community of life itself, and have evoked patterns of thought, language, and behavior that give striking witness to a perception of the natural world as sacred. Other religions, notably Judaism, Christianity, and Islam, need yet to more effectively and thoroughly stimulate their fundamental cosmological orientations, and to foster and sustain new expressions of liturgy and prayer capable of disposing the minds and hearts of their adherents to the sacredness of the natural world and a corresponding care for its well-being and protections.

It is in this context of urgency and challenge that the Supreme Court's ruling in *Lyng v. Northwest Indian Cemetery Protective Association* must be more broadly evaluated. At a moment in earth history when the significant psychic energies from across the whole range of religious traditions is needed to inform and instruct the human community in the sacred dimension of the natural world, the highest court in the United States unworthily dismissed a claim grounded on that very proposition. Never had such an explicit argument been raised before the Court attesting to the holiness of the land itself. Never had an issue concerning the constitutional protections for Native American Indians illustrated so salient a perception of land as sacred reality. In refusing to acknowledge the legal status of that view, reductively subjugating public land to the sole category of property and then capitulating completely to governmental discretion in its subsequent disposition of the land, the Supreme Court indulged certain assumptions about religion that should be repudiated by those traditions that seek a more creative expression of themselves as they strive for a more fundamental response to the crisis confronting the earth.

The invidious delineation between religion and land, implicit in the *Lyng* decision, is not the result of any judicial craft. It is instead a broadly held cultural presumption found persistently in the lower court cases that preceded *Lyng*. *Sequoyah v. Tennessee Valley Authority*, *Baldoni v. Higginson*, *Wilson v. Block*, and *Crow v. Gullet* all variously manifested the minimal notion that religion consists of certain beliefs to which adherents give their credence, and a corresponding set of ceremonies, rituals, and/or prayers mandated or inspired by those beliefs. The courts followed the unremarkable proposition that so long as government does not prohibit or proscribe religious beliefs nor prevents, censures, or hampers the celebration of religious practices, no violation of the Free Exercise Clause will be perpetrated. Yet, in making the determination of when government action does in fact interfere with religious practice, courts must have some appreciation for the sense of the sacred that animates the religious faith, which in turn gives meaning to the practices under consideration. It is on this point that the courts, reviewing the respective tribal claims, betrayed a shallow and confined understanding of sacred presence intrinsic not only to Native American traditions but to the plurality of human religious experience. From *Sequoyah* through *Lyng*, the courts, having been petitioned to protect Indian religions, focused almost exclusively upon the extrinsic forms of tribal religious practice, with minimal or no regard for the fundamental belief in the sacred character of the land that evoked and inspired the various ceremonies, rituals, and prayers directed to it. Through their mute inattention to the numinous reality manifesting itself to Indian faith in and through the land, the courts effectively severed the vital connection between the central religious phenomenon and the responses addressed to it. Thus could the courts hold blameless government actions that altered the natural state of land, while not directly proscribing or preventing tribal practices from continuing at that same locale. For in the view of the courts, unresponsive to the fundamental claim of a holy presence consecrating it, land functioned as mere locale, the scene or setting, "the background" where religious practices were conducted in their various tribal expressions. No charge of desecration registered on courts whose utterly secular perspective fixed land not as the primordial subject of religious experience, but only as the site where religious behavior was performed. Government land use might dramatically reconfigure the structure of land without violating the First Amendment, provided it did nothing to prevent tribal practitioners from continuing to express their beliefs in the spiritual character of the recontoured government property. Thus, while their homeland with its ancestral burial sites had been submerged by the waters from the Tellico Dam, Cherokees were still free to visit, revere, and pray to its now sunken identity, as were Navajos who yet sought to attend with ceremony and prayer offerings the flooded precincts of Rainbow Bridge. The Hopis remained at liberty to instruct their young, and themselves to make pilgrimage, to honor and seek the life-sustaining blessings of the Kachinas abiding on the San Francisco Peaks, whose slopes were now entertainment for the clientele of a federally sponsored ski resort. The Lakota and Tsistsistas peoples, while ignoring the distractions and interferences from state-encouraged tourism and its accommodations, were nevertheless free to continue using Bear Butte as their most sacred altar upon which they could spend days and nights in prayerful vigil, crying for the vision that would bring spiritual wisdom and strength. Finally, the Yuroks, Karoks, and Tolowas could still ascend the California high country in preparation for their World Renewal dances and ceremonies by assuming their ancient prayer seats and disposing themselves to sacred healing power by resisting the visual and aural distractions that would come from the construction, lumbering, and subsequent traffic along the Forest Service road that would cut its way to the very peripheries of the once remote and silent sanctuaries of Doctor Rock, Chimney Rock, and Peak 8.

Non-Indian religious traditions need to censure a jurisprudence that could countenance so facetious a protection for Native American religions rooted in and oriented toward land. They should do so not just from a sense of solidarity with Indian believers and from their own moral imperatives to identify and condemn injustice worked in the name of legal principle. More fundamentally, those religions that seek to advance from within their own cosmologies and traditions a more effective response to the demise of the natural world must repudiate so sterile a notion of religion and religious protections as that found in the assumptions of the judicial opinions from *Sequoyah* through *Lyng*. Specifically, religions must reassert the integrity of religious practices and the experience of the Sacred that evokes, inspires, and gives meaning to them. They need to expose the incongruity of religious protection that claims to accommodate the survival of religious observances while ignoring the destruction of the holy reality without which those observances become hollow gestures and empty phrases. Disregarding the elemental claim concerning the sacred character of land, conceptually disconnecting the variety of religious practices from that radical and vital intuition, the courts refused to find harm of constitutional significance where tribal expressions of faith could still persist on and toward land government had inundated, commercially developed, on which it had constructed tourist accommodations, or planned to pave over and open to traffic in logging operations.

In the absence of the sacred, which their own distorted notion of religion helped to perpetuate, the courts from *Sequoyah* through *Lyng* acquiesced in the reductive fixation of land as property. Stripped of any essential religious significance, the land that had long addressed Indian cultures as a living, spiritual presence became in the ultimate view of the courts just so many governmental holdings. What for the Cherokees had been the embodiment of power, their place of origin, abode of their ancestors, and life-sustaining contact with the Creator, existed for the district court as so much acreage of the Little Tennessee River Valley legislated for the designs of the TVA. The awesome sandstone body of the holy Rainbow Couple, vaulting as one from the canyon floor in Utah to bless generations of Navajos with the life-enhancing moisture of clouds and rain, registered in the eyes of the district and appellate courts as a national monument created by presidential proclamation in 1910 and managed by the National Park Service. The San Francisco Peaks of Arizona, another embodied Navajo "Holy One" and the dwelling of the Hopi Kachinas who sent the snow and rain to nurture their villages with water and well-being, stood for the courts under its presidential designation as a forest reserve and then as an incorporated parcel of the Coconino National Forest under the auspices of the U.S. Forest Service. What in Bear Butte had revealed itself to the Lakota and Tsistsistas Nations as the "axis of the world," the living altar of the most efficacious and powerful contact with the Great Spirit and those beings who would respond in visions to those who sought wisdom and healing, had become for the courts a legal purchase by South Dakota to be added to its state park system and managed as a tourist attraction by its Department of Game, Fish, and Parks. Similarly, what had long been the mountainous sanctuary where the Yurok, Karok, and Tolowa peoples encountered and communed with the Sacred Presence, which animated their dances with "world renewal" energy and stabilizing harmony, was rendered by the Supreme Court as "the Chimney Rock section of the Six Rivers National Forest," held under the jurisdiction and discretion of the U.S. Forest Service since 1951.

The judicial reduction of sacred land to government property effected through an inadequate, artificially delineated conception of religion, and a deeply entrenched, culturally pervasive proprietary instinct toward land, was firmly consolidated by the Supreme Court's ruling in *Lyng*. In an egregious abdication of its responsibility to weigh competing claims, grounded on variant perceptions and values, to arrive at a final determination through the application of law and principled evaluation of the competing interests, the Supreme Court utterly capitulated to the possessory bias toward land. Explicitly identifying the tribal claim to the sacred nature of land as a threat to the government's interest as landlord, the Court abandoned its established procedural analysis for the adjudication of complaints against government infringement upon the free exercise of religion. Openly conceding that the projected government land use could virtually destroy the practice of tribal religion, the Supreme Court nevertheless dispensed the government from the prescribed rubric of demonstrating a compelling interest of paramount significance that might otherwise justify so destructive an impact on the Yurok, Karok, and Tolowa religions. From the district and appellate court records, it was clear that no such interest existed, but the Court absolved the government of any necessity to even attempt a justification beyond the mere administrative efficiency it asserted. In so doing, the Court irresponsibly invested an unqualified authority in the government's disposition of land, intensifying the grip of a paradigm that subjugates land under the restrictive and exclusive category of property.

Non-Indian religious traditions, standing in solidarity against the inequities worked against Native American beliefs, and seeking to invigorate their own capacities to celebrate the goodness and holiness of the earth, need to rebuke and reject the Supreme Court's aggrandizement and categorical elevation of government property interests in land. They are challenged to affirm the Constitution's ability to protect claims to the sanctity of land, to demonstrate not a failure in the Free Exercise Clause of the First Amendment, but a judicial flaw in its interpretation and application. Testifying to the coherence of religious practice and the sacred reality that evokes it, those traditions can authoritatively expose the distorted logic that would condone the desecration of land while claiming no harm to Indian religions. In defense of a religious valuation of land and the capacity of constitutional law to acknowledge and protect it, those traditions can effectively discredit the Supreme Court's unworthy embrace of government property interests through its ruling in *Lyng*, which yet stands as a pernicious burden against all who would revere the numinous dimension of land.

Notes

INTRODUCTION

1. 485 U.S. 439, 99 L. Ed. 2d 534, 108 S. Ct. 1319 (1988).
2. *Ibid.*, 485 U.S. 439 at 451 (citing the Ninth Circuit Court of Appeals, 795 F.2d at 693).
3. *Ibid.* at 473 (Brennan, J., dissenting).
4. *Ibid.* at 453 (emphasis in the original).
5. *Ibid.* at 476 (Brennan, J., dissenting).

CHAPTER ONE

1. Tennessee Valley Authority Act of 1933, 16 U.S.C. 831 (a–dd).
2. *Tennessee Valley Authority v. Hiram Hill et al.*, 437 U.S. 153, 98 S. Ct. 2279, 57 L. Ed. 2d 117 (1978).
3. See Congressional Record H4663 (daily ed. June 18, 1979); see also Congressional Record H7215 (daily ed. August 2, 1979)
4. *Ibid.*
5. Cong. Rec. S12272–12279 (daily ed. Sept.10, 1978)
6. See affidavit of Ammoneta Sequoyah, Cherokee medicine man and plaintiff, offered as Exhibit D as attached to the plaintiffs' complaint.
7. See affidavit of Dr. Duane H. King, offered as Exhibit H as attached to plaintiffs' complaint. See also affidavit of Iva Rattler of the Eastern Band of Cherokee offered as Exhibit CC as attached to the plaintiffs' complaint; affidavit of Ela Jackson of the Eastern Band offered as Exhibit DD as attached to the plaintiffs' complaint; affidavit of Willie Walkingstick of the Eastern Band of Cherokee offered as Exhibit EE as attached to the plaintiffs' complaint; affidavit of John Crowe, principal-chief of the Eastern Band of the Cherokee offered as Exhibit L as attached to the plaintiffs' complaint.

8. Affidavit of Dr. Robert K. Thomas, anthropologist trained at the University of Arizona and the University of Chicago and himself a Cherokee from Oklahoma. Offered as Exhibit MM as attached to the plaintiffs' complaint.

9. *Ibid.*

10. Plaintiffs' Memorandum in Support of Application for Temporary Restraining Order and/or Preliminary Injunction, p. 2.

11. Plaintiffs' Memorandum in Support of Application for Temporary Restraining Order and/or Preliminary Injunction. p. 25 (emphasis in the original).

12. *Ibid.* (emphasis added).

13. See Exhibit I of Plaintiffs' Memorandum, the testimony of Charles Hudson, professor of anthropology; see also Exhibit H, the testimony of Dr. Duane H. King, professor of anthropology.

14. See the affidavit of Dr. Duane H. King, anthropologist.

15. *Ibid.*

16. *Ibid.*

17. The testimonies of Lloyd Sequoyah (Exhibit F); Emmaline Driver (Exhibit X); Willie Walkingstick (Exhibit EE); and Lloyd C. Owle (Exhibit O) respectively.

18. See the analysis of the Cherokee anthropologist Dr. Robert K. Thomas in his affidavit, Exhibit MM as attached to the plaintiffs' complaint.

19. Testimony of Richard Crowe as quoted in Plaintiffs' Memorandum in Support of Application for Temporary Restraining Order and/or Preliminary Injunction, p. 10.

20. P.L. 95–341, 42 U.S.C. 1996. The act had been passed on August 11, 1978.

21. See *Ibid.*

22. *Ibid.*

23. See endnote 3 above.

24. 437 U.S. 153, 98 S. Ct. 2279, 57 L. Ed. 2d 117.

25. *Ibid.* at 190–191.

26. *Ibid.*

27. *Sherbert v. Verner*, 374 U.S. 398, 83 S. Ct. 1790, 10 L. Ed. 2d 965 (1963).

28. *Wisconsin v. Yoder*, 406 U.S. 205, 92 S. Ct. 1526, 32 L. Ed. 2d. 15 (1972).

29. *Sherbert v. Verner*, 374 U.S. at 407.

30. *Ibid.* at 408.

31. 406 U.S. 205 (1972).

32. *Ibid.* at 213.

33. *Ibid.* at 220.

34. Transcript of the First Meeting of the Endangered Species Committee of January 23, 1979, as quoted in *Environmental Law and Policy: Nature, Law and Society* by Plater, Abrams, and Goldfarb, p. 670.

35. See Cong. Rec. S12275 (Sept. 10, 1979).

36. TVA's Brief in Support of the Motion to Dismiss, or For Summary Judgment, and in opposition to plaintiffs' motion for restraining order or preliminary injunction, p. 6.

37. *Badoni v. Higginson*, 455 F. Supp. 641 (D. Utah 1977) was later upheld by the 10th Circuit Court of Appeals, 638 F.2d 172, which ruled that property rights was a factor to be weighed, but was not determinative of a First Amendment claim of freedom of religion with respect to land. This case is the subject of the following chapter.

38. TVA's Brief in Support of Its Motion to Dismiss. pp. 14–15.
39. See Peter Matthiessen's *Indian Country*, 117–118.
40. Affidavit of Ross O. Swimmer, as quoted in TVA's Brief in Support of Its Motion to Dismiss, pp. 18–19.
41. See Plaintiffs' Response to Defendant's Motion to Dismiss, or in the Alternative for Summary Judgment, p. 35.
42. TVA's Brief in Support of Its Motion to Dismiss, pp. 5–6.
43. *Environmental Defense Fund v. Tennessee Valley Authority*, 339 F. Supp. 806 (E.D. Tenn.), aff'd, 468 F.2d 1164 (6th Cir. 1972) (Tellico I). *Environmental Defense Fund v. Tennessee Valley Authority*, 371 F. Supp. 1004 (E.D. Tenn.), *stay pending appeal denied*, 414 U.S. 1036 (1973), aff'd, 492 F.2d 466 (6th Cir. 1974) (Tellico II).
44. TVA's Brief in Support of Its Motion to Dismiss, p. 6.
45. See *Ibid.* at 7.
46. Chief Oren Lyons, Note, *Native Americans Versus American Museums: A Battle for Artifacts*, 7 AM. INDIAN L. REV. 125 (1979).
47. See Howard Stambor, *Manifest Destiny and American Indian Religious Freedom: Sequoyah, Badoni, and the Drowned Gods*, 10 AM. INDIAN L. REV. 59 (1982).
48. *Sequoyah v. TVA* 480 F. Supp. 608, 610 (E.D. Tenn. 1979).
49. *Kunz v. New York*, 340 U.S. 290, 71 S. Ct. 312, 95 L. Ed. 280 (1951).
50. *Cantwell v. Connecticut*, 310 U.S. 296, 60 S. Ct. 900, 84 L. Ed. 1213 (1940).
51. *Ibid.* at 310.
52. 480 F. Supp. 608, 612 (E.D. Tenn. 1979).
53. *Ibid.*
54. See Memorandum to Chief Judge Edwards from Gary Petty, staff attorney on the Motion for Injunction, Case No. 79-1633 of Nov. 6, 1979.
55. Appeal from the United States District Court Eastern District of Tennessee, Northern Division. Appellants Reply Brief, p. 16 (emphasis added).
56. On Appeal from the United States District Court for the Eastern District of Tennessee, Northern Division. Brief of Defendant—Appellee Tennessee Valley Authority, p. 7.
57. *Kleppe v. New Mexico*, 426 U.S. 529, 96 S. Ct. 2285, 49 L. Ed. 2d. 34 (1976).
58. U.S. Constitution, art. IV, 3, cl. 2.
59. *Kleppe v. New Mexico* at 541 citing *Utah Power & Light Co. v. United States*, 243 U.S. 389, 405 (1917).
60. *Ibid.* at 531, citing *United States v. San Francisco*, 310 U.S. 16, 29 (1940).
61. *Ibid.* at 544, citing *Camfield v. United States*, 167 U.S. 518, 526 (1897).
62. *Adderley v. Florida*, 385 U.S. 39, 87 S. Ct. 242, 17 L. Ed. 2d 149 (1966).
63. *Ibid.* at 48–49.
64. *Op. cit. Brief of Defendant—Appellee Tennessee Valley Authority*, p. 14.
65. *Sequoyah v. Tennessee Authority*, 620 F.2d 1159, 1164 (1980).
66. *Ibid.* at 1165.
67. *Wisconsin v. Yoder*, 406 U.S. 205, 92 S. Ct. 1526, 32h. Ed. 2d 15 (1972).
68. *Frank v. Alaska*, 604 P. 2d 1068 (Alaska 1979).
69. *People v. Woody*, 61 Cal. 2d 716, 40 Cal. Rptr. 69, 394 P. 2d 813 (1964).
70. *Sequoyah*, 620 F.2d at 1164.
71. *Wisconsin v. Yoder*, 406 U.S. 205 at 216.
72. *Ibid.*
73. *Sequoyah v. Tennessee Valley Authority*, 620 F.2d at 1164.

74. Matthiessen, supra note 39, at 118.

CHAPTER TWO

1. *Badoni v. Higginson*, 455 F. Supp. 641, 644 (1977).
2. *Ibid.*
3. *Ibid.* at 643.
4. *Ibid.* at 644.
5. *Ibid.* at 645.
6. *Ibid.*
7. *Wisconsin v. Yoder*, 406 U.S. 205 (1972) at 216.
8. *Badoni*, 455 F.Supp. at 646.
9. *Ibid.*
10. *Ibid.*
11. *Badoni v. Higginson*, 638 F.2d 172, 176–177 (1980), quoting *Wisconsin v. Yoder*, 406 U.S. 205 at 214–215 (1972).
12. Brief of Appellants in their Appeal from the United States District Court for the District of Utah, Central Division to the United States Court of Appeals for the Tenth Circuit, p. 8.
13. *Badoni v. Higginson*, 638 F.2d at 178.
14. *Ibid.* at 179.
15. *West Virginia State Board of Education v. Barnette*, 319 U.S. 624, 63 S. Ct. 1178, 87 L. Ed. 1628 (1943).
16. *Committee for Public Education and Religious Liberty v. Nyquist*, 413 U.S. 756, 773, 93 S. Ct. 2955, 37 L. Ed. 2d 948 (1973).
17. *Badoni v. Higginson*, 638 F.2d at 179.
18. *Shuttleworth v. City of Birmingham*, 394 U.S. 147, 89 S. Ct. 935, 22 L. Ed. 2d 162 (1969).
19. *Cox v. Louisiana*, 379 U.S. 536, 85 S. Ct. 453, 13 L. Ed. 2d 471 (1965).
20. *Ibid.* at 558–559.
21. *Niemotro v. Maryland*, 340 U.S. 268, 71 S. Ct. 325, 95 L. Ed. 267 (1951).
22. *Hague v. CIO*, 307 U.S. 496, 59 S. Ct. 954, 83 L. Ed. 1423 (1939).
23. *Badoni v. Higginson*, 638 F.2d at 178.
24. *Ibid.* at 179, quoting *Hague v. CIO*, 307 U.S. 496, 51–516 (1939).
25. *Ibid.* at 178.

CHAPTER THREE

1. Affidavit of Faye B. Tso, submitted as Plaintiffs' Exhibit B-5 in the case of *Wilson v. Block*, 708 F.2d 735 (1983).
2. Affidavit of George Conway, ethnobotanist at the University of New Mexico Medical School, submitted as Plaintiffs' Exhibit O in the case of *Wilson v. Block*.
3. Affidavit of Nettie Nez, Navajo medicine woman, submitted as Plaintiffs' Exhibit B-3 in the case of *Wilson v. Block*.
4. See the affidavits of Fred F. Stevens Jr., a Navajo medicine man, submitted as Plaintiffs' Exhibit B-4; Frank Blue Horse, a Navajo medicine man, submitted as Plaintiffs' Exhibit B-7; Nettie Nez, a Navajo medicine woman, submitted as Plain-

tiffs' Exhibit B-3; and Faye B. Tso, a Navajo medicine woman, submitted as Plaintiffs' Exhibit N in the case of *Wilson v. Block*.

5. Affidavit of Abbott Sekaquaptewa, chairman of the Hopi Indian Tribe, submitted as Plaintiffs' Exhibit XIV, p. 9 in the case of *Wilson v. Block*.

6. *Ibid*.

7. Affidavit of Jerrold Levy, Ph.D., professor of cultural anthropology at the University of Arizona and submitted as Defendants' Exhibit XV, p. 8.

8. *Hopi Indian Tribe v. Block*, 19 ERC (BNA) 1215 (D.D.C. June 15, 1981 available on LEXIS, Gen fed library, Courts file, at 12 of printout).

9. *Ibid*. at 11 of printout.

10. *Ibid*. at 12 of printout. See also Opening Brief of Appellants Navajo Medicinemen's Association at pp. 30–31, fn. 10

11. *Hopi Indian Tribe v. Block*, 19 ERC (BNA) 1215, at 12 of printout.

12. Affidavit of Dr. Charlotte J. Frisbie, professor of anthropology at Southern Illinois University, offered as an expert witness in behalf of the Plaintiffs and submitted as Exhibit XIX, p. 4.

13. *Hopi Indian Tribe v. Block*, 19 ERC (BNA) 1215 at 12 of printout.

14. *Ibid*. at 14 of printout.

15. *Ibid*., citing H. Rep. 1308, 95th Cong., 2d Sess. (1978)

16. In his affidavit, the chairman of the Hopi Indian Tribe made the following analogy: "Numerous Hopi sacred shrines and sacred places are located in the Peaks area, and for at least some of those shrines and places, Hopi religious pilgrimage routes pass through the Snow Bowl permit area. . . . The present non-Hopi activities which are carried on within the permit area consist in part of such things as drinking alcoholic beverages, physical recreation and sports, and other merry-making and revelry, all of which is inconsistent with the spiritual purposes of such a pilgrimage. . . . For a non-Hopi this impact would be like being forced to pass through an amusement park as you enter a Church or a temple. The impact upon the worship within the sanctuary is substantial and adverse." See Narrative Direct Testimony of Abbott Sekaquaptewa, Plaintiffs' Exhibit XIV, pp. 6–7.

17. *Hopi Indian Tribe v. Block*, 19 ERC (BNA) 1215 at 22, quoting from the Multiple-Use Sustained-Yield Act of 1960, 16 U.S.C. section 528.

18. *Ibid*. at 12 of printout.

19. *Ibid*.

20. *Ibid*. at 11 of printout.

21. See Opening Brief of Appellants Navajo Medicinemen's Association, et al. No. 81-1956, No. 82-1705, p. 26.

22. *Sherbert v. Verner*, 374 U.S. 398, 83 S. Ct. 1790, 10 L. Ed. 2d 965 (1963)

23. *Thomas v. Review Board of the Indiana Employment Security Division*, 450 U.S. 707, 101 S. Ct. 1425, 67 L. Ed. 2d 624 (1981).

24. *Ibid*., 450 U.S. 707 at 717.

25. Brief of Richard F. Wilson and Jean Wilson as *amicus curiae* in the Appeals of the Hopi Tribe and the Navajo Medicinemen's Association p. 17, quoting the familiar formulation of the Supreme Court in *Wisconsin v. Yoder*, 406 U.S. 205 (1972) at 215.

26. *Wisconsin v. Yoder*, 406 U.S. 205 (1972) at 234, n. 22, as quoted in the Opening Brief of Appellants Navajo Medicinemen's Association, et al., p. 37.

27. *Lemon v. Kurtzman*, 403 U.S. 602 91 S. Ct. 2105, 29 L. Ed. 2d, 745 (1971).

28. Brief for Appellant, Hopi Indian Tribe, pp. 26–27.
29. *Wilson v. Block*, 708 F.2d 735, 743 (1983).
30. See, for example, the testimony of Dr. Charlotte J. Frisbie, professor of anthropology, in her affidavit submitted as Plaintiffs' Exhibit XIX, p. 4.
31. *Wilson v. Block*, 708 F.2d at 742, n. 3.
32. *Ibid.* at 742.
33. *Ibid.* at 744.
34. *Ibid.*

CHAPTER FOUR

1. According to the testimony of Arvol Looking Horse, nineteenth-generation Keeper of the Sacred Calf Pipe of the Lakota, the original pipe was first seen near Devil's Tower, just east of the Black Hills. Affidavit of Arvol Looking Horse in Support of Plaintiffs' Motion for a Preliminary Injunction, pp. 1–2. Also restated in Appellant's Reply Brief, Appeal from the United States District Court for the District of South Dakota, Western Division, pp. 1–2. It was then submitted that according to the Tenth Annual Report of the Bureau of Ethnology 1888–89 (GPO 1893), which was attached as Exhibit A to Appellants' Post Trial Memorandum of Points and Authorities, Docket Entry 19, the sacred pipe had been brought into the Black Hills area of Green Grass, S.D. in the year 901 A.D.
2. See Appellants' Reply Brief: Appeal from the United States District Court for the District of South Dakota, Western Division, pp. 1–3. See also Brief of State Appellees: Appeal from the United States District Court for the District of South Dakota, Western Division, pp. 9–10.
3. *Ibid.*
4. Brief of State Appellees, *op. cit.* at 10.
5. *Ibid.*
6. *Crow v. Gullet*, 541 F. Supp. 785, 789 (D.S.D 1982).
7. *Ibid.*
8. See, e.g., the Affidavit of Larry Red Shirt in support of Plaintiffs' Motion for a Preliminary Injunction, pp. 7–8.
9. For an itemized listing of tourist interruptions that the tribes attributed to South Dakota by not preventing such behavior, see Plaintiff's Post-Trial Memorandum of Points and Authorities, U.S. District Court of the District of South Dakota, Western Division, Civil No. 82-5047, p. 8.
10. For details of the camping restrictions, the alternative site, and the discomfort from tourist presence at the campsite, see, e.g., the Affidavit of Larry Red Shirt in Support of Plaintiffs' Motion for a Preliminary Injunction, pp. 8–9. He explained there the necessity for the purification of all persons at a ceremonial campsite. "Any person who has not gone through these purification ceremonies and does not have the proper frame of mind . . . interferes with all participants of the vision quest. It interferes because it distracts the person who is seeking the vision as well as his supporters; it interferes with communication with the spirit world; and destroys the strength of the ceremony itself."
11. For the hardship this caused certain tribal members and the necessity of canceling their vision quest plans as well as the offensiveness experienced at being

forced to pay for the right to worship at their ancestral sacred Butte, see, e.g., the Affidavit of Francine Nelson in Support of Plaintiffs' Motion for a Temporary Restraining Order and the Affidavit of Larry Red Shirt, *op. cit.* at 9.

12. Letter from Tony Gullet, park manager of Bear Butte State Park to Bill Red Hat, attached as Exhibit A to the Amended Complaint for Declaratory and Injunction Relief, and for Damages, for Deprivation of Civil Rights, Civil No. 82-5047 United States District Court for the District of South Dakota, Western Division.

13. *Ibid.*

14. Amended Complaint for Declaratory and Injunctive Relief, and for Damages, for Deprivation of Civil Rights, Civil No. 82-5047, pp. 6–7.

15. The Amended Complaint cited that part of AIRFA, 42 U.S.C. 1996, which stated that "it shall be the policy of the United States to protect and preserve for American Indians their inherent right of freedom to believe, express, and exercise the traditional religions of the American Indians, . . . including but not limited to access to sites" *Ibid.* at 7.

16. *Ibid.* at 8, citing United Nations' General Assembly Resolutions 217A (III), Dec, 10, 1948, and 2200A (XXI), Dec. 16, 1966.

17. *Ibid.*

18. *Ibid.* at 9.

19. *Ibid.*

20. *Ibid.* at 9–10.

21. Appeal from the United States District Court for the District of South Dakota, Western Division, Appellants' Brief, p. 16.

22. *Crow v. Gullet*, 541 F. Supp. 785, 791 (D.S.D. 1982).

23. *Ibid.*

24. See Appellants' Brief, *op. cit.*, at 21. It is also stated there that Judge Bogue disregarded a post-trial affidavit of Frank Fools Crow, a named plaintiff, explicitly refuting a statement attributed to him that he was "pleased" with the construction on the mountain.

25. *Crow v. Gullet*, 541 F. Supp. at 789.

26. "[Plaintiffs] are essentially claiming that anyone asserting a religious interest in government property . . . has a constitutional right to demand that the government grant them access to it, yet restrict the rights of the public to, and any development of, this property in order to facilitate the exercise of religious beliefs. This Court will not extend the First Amendment to such limits." *Ibid.* at 791, citing *Hopi Indian Tribe v. Block*, 8ILR 3073 (No. 81-0481, D.O.C., June 15, 1981, at 3075).

27. "At the same time we decline to follow those cases which have placed primary reliance upon the government's property interest and which have held, apparently, that the Free Exercise Clause can never supersede the government's ownership rights and duties of public management. . . . The government must manage its land in accordance with the constitution . . . which nowhere suggests that the Free Exercise Clause is inapplicable to government land." *Wilson v. Block*, 708 F.2d 735 (1983) at 744, fn. 5.

28. *Crow v. Gullet*, 541 F. Supp. at 790.

29. *Ibid.* at 792.

30. *Ibid.*

31. *Ibid.*

32. *Ibid.* at 794.

33. *Ibid.*
34. *Ibid.* at 793.
35. *Ibid.* at 794.
36. Appellants' Brief: Appeal from the United States District Court for the District of South Dakota, Western Division on the United States Court of Appeals for the Eighth Circuit, p. 26.
37. *Ibid.* at 15.
38. 394 U.S. 147, 89 S. Ct. 935, 22 L. Ed. 2d 162 (1969).
39. *Larson v. Valente,* 456 U.S. 228, 102 S. Ct. 1673, 72 L. Ed. 2d 33 (1982)
40. 374 U.S. 398, 408, 83 S. Ct. 1790, 10 L. Ed. 2d 965 (1963), quoting *Thomas v. Collins,* 323 U.S. 516, 530 (1945) (1963).
41. 406 U.S. 205, 216, 92 S. Ct. 1526, 32 L. Ed. 2d 15 (1972).
42. *Crow v. Gullet,* 541 F. Supp. at 794.
43. *Wilson v. Block,* 708 F.2d 735, 744 (D.C. Cir. 1983).
44. See *Crow v. Gullet,* 706 F.2d 856 (8th Cir. 1983).

CHAPTER FIVE

1. This information and that which follows on the other three tribal groups is from the extensive study titled *Cultural Resources of the Chimney Rock Section, Gasquet-Orleans Road, Six Rivers National Forest* commissioned by the United States Forest Service and written by Theodoratus Cultural Research of Fair Oaks, California, pp. 18–20. Hereafter, this study will be referred to as the Theodoratus Report.
2. *Ibid.* at 402.
3. See *Ibid.* at 45–50.
4. See Brief for the Indian Respondents at 6, *Lyng v. Northwest Indian Cemetery Protective Association,* 485 U.S. 439, 99 L. Ed. 2d 534, 108 S. Ct. 1319 (1988).
5. See Theodoratus Report at 61. See also *Ibid.* at 7.
6. See Theodoratus Report at 76–79.
7. *Ibid.* at 75.
8. See Brief for the Indian Respondents at 8, *Lyng v. Northwest Indian Cemetery Protective Association,* 485 U.S. 439.
9. See "The High Country" chapter in *Indian Country* by Peter Matthiessen, pp. 167–188 for an excellent description of the hazards posed by the Forest Service plan.
10. See *Matthiessen, op. cit.* at 182.
11. See Theodoratus Report at 10–11.
12. *Ibid.* at 44.
13. *Ibid.* at 367.
14. *Ibid.* at 388.
15. *Ibid.* at 409.
16. *Ibid.* at 403–405.
17. *Ibid.* at 413.
18. *Ibid.* at 419.
19. *Ibid.* at 419–420.
20. Brief for the Indian Respondents at 9, *Lyng v. Northwest Indian Cemetery Protective Association,* 485 U.S. 439.
21. *Ibid.*

22. *Northwest Indian Cemetery Protective Association v. Peterson*, 565 F. Supp. 586, 594 (1983).
23. *Ibid.* at 594–595.
24. *Ibid.* at 596.
25. *Ibid.* See also Brief for the Indian Respondents at 8, *Lyng v. Northwest Indian Cemetery Protective Association*, 485 U.S. 439.
26. *Theodoratus Report op. cit.* at 413.
27. *Northwest Indian Cemetery Protective Association v. Peterson*, 565 F. Supp. at 595.
28. *Ibid.*
29. *Ibid.*
30. *Ibid.* at 597.
31. *Ibid.* at 599.
32. *Ibid.* at 600.
33. *Ibid.* at 603.
34. See California Wilderness Act of 1984, Pub. L. No. 98-425, 98 Stat. 1619 et seq.
35. H. R. Rep. No. 98-40, 98th Cong., 1st Sess. 32 (1983); S. Rep. No. 98-582, 98th Cong., 2d Sess. 28-29 (1984).
36. Statement of Congressman John Seiberling, chairman of the House Subcommittee on Public Lands and National Parks which produced the California Wilderness Act of 1984, as quoted in Brief for the Indian Respondents at 14, *Lyng v. Northwest Indian Cemetery Protective Association*, 485 U.S. 439.
37. *Northwest Indian Cemetery Protective Association v. Peterson*, 795 F.2d 688, 691 (9th Cir. 1986).
38. *Ibid.* at 692.
39. *Ibid.*, citing *Cultural Resources of the Chimney Rock Section, Gasquet-Orleans Road, Six Rivers National Forest* (1979) (Theodoratus Report).
40. *Ibid.* at 693.
41. *Ibid.* at 694.
42. *Lemon v. Kurtzman*, 403 U.S. 602, 91 S. Ct. 2105, 29 L. Ed. 2d 745 (1971)
43. See *Ibid.* at 614.
44. 638 F.2d 172 (10th Cir. 1980). See chapter 2 of this work for the more complete analysis of that case.
45. *Northwest Indian Cemetery Protective Association*, 795 F.2d at 701.
46. Speaking of the noise that could come off the road, Judge Beezer wrote: "While it is possible that . . . the road would impair religious and medicinal quests in the area adjoining the area, it is apparent that the high country is a large area. The Indian plaintiffs have not established that their quests can take place only in the area near the road." *Ibid.* at 703.
47. *Ibid.* at 704.
48. *Ibid.*
49. *Ibid.* at 699.
50. *Ibid.* at 704.
51. *Lyng v. Northwest Indian Cemetery Protective Association*, 485 U.S. 439, 99 L. Ed. 2d 534, 108 S. Ct. 1319 (1988).
52. Justice O'Connor was joined by Chief Justice Rehnquist and Justices White, Stevens, and Scalia.
53. *Lyng v. Northwest Indian Cemetery Protective Association*, 485 U.S. at 451.

54. *Ibid.*, citing the opinion of the Ninth Circuit Court of Appeals, 795 F.2d at 693.

55. *Ibid.* at 459–461 (Brennan, J. dissenting). Justice Brennan variously cited American Indian Religious Freedom, Hearings on S. J. Res. 102 Before the Select Comm. on Indian Affairs, U.S, Sen. 95th Cong., 2d Sess. at 86 (Statement of Barney Old Coyote, Crow Tribe); U.S. Federal Agencies Task Force, American Indian Religious Freedom Act Report 11 (Task Force Report); Suagee, *American Indian Religious Freedom and Cultural Resources Management: Protecting Mother Earth's Caretakers*, 10 Amer. Ind. L. Rev. 1, 10 (1982).

56. *Ibid.* (majority opinion) at 450.

57. *Ibid.* at 477 (Brennan, J., dissenting).

58. *Bowen v. Roy*, 476 U.S. 693, 696, 90 L. Ed. 2d 735, 106 S. Ct. 2147 (1986).

59. *Ibid.*

60. *Ibid.* at 699 (emphasis in the original).

61. Justice O'Connor, joined by Justices Brennan and Marshall, filed a dissenting opinion from that part of the chief justice's opinion that substantially lowered the burden of the government when challenged on a religious basis in the administration of its welfare programs. Chief Justice Burger argued that the government should not have to justify enforcement of the use of Social Security numbers as the least restrictive means of accomplishing a compelling state interest. Justice O'Connor contended that such a position was an abandonment of First Amendment religious protection and argued that "the Government must accommodate a legitimate Free Exercise claim unless pursuing an especially important interest by narrowly tailored means." According to Justice O'Connor, although the government could show a compelling interest in using Social Security numbers to protect against fraud, it failed to show how granting an exception for Little Bird of the Snow, a less restrictive measure of her religious belief, would do harm to its compelling interest. See *Ibid.* at 724–733 (O'Connor, J. dissenting).

62. *Ibid.* at 700.

63. *Lyng, Northwest Indian Cemetery Protective Association*, 485 U.S. at 449.

64. *Ibid.* at 450.

65. *Ibid.* at 451.

66. *Ibid.* at 448, citing the Theodoratus Report.

67. *Ibid.*

68. *Theodoratus Report, op. cit.*, pp. 105–106. Italicized phrases are those excerpted by the Supreme Court's reading of the passages.

69. *Lyng v. Northwest Indian Cemetery Protective Association*, 485 U.S. at 449.

70. *Bowen v. Roy*, 476 U.S. at 707–708.

71. *Ibid.* at 727–728 (O'Connor, J. dissenting).

72. *Lyng*, 485 U.S. at 451–452.

73. *Ibid.* at 453 (emphasis in the original).

74. *Ibid.* at 449.

75. *Ibid.* at 473 (Brennan, J. dissenting).

76. *Ibid.* at 476–477, quoting from the American Indian Religious Freedom Act.

77. *Ibid.* at 466, quoting with emphasis added *Wisconsin v. Yoder*, 406 U.S. 205 (1972) at 209.

78. *Ibid.*, quoting with emphasis added *Wisconsin v. Yoder* at 217.

79. *Ibid.* at 467.

80. *Ibid.* at 467–468.
81. *Ibid.* at 475.
82. *Ibid.*
83. See *Ibid.* at 468, fn. 4. Justice Brennan referred to Webster's definition of "prohibit" as including "to prevent from doing something." His concern was to show that the meaning of the Free Exercise Clause, that "Congress shall make no law . . . prohibiting the free exercise" of religion, included a prohibition against government action that frustrates or inhibits religious practice.
84. *Wisconsin v. Yoder*, 406 U.S. 205, 213 (1972).
85. *Ibid.* at 215.

Bibliographical Index

With one exception, all of the sources consulted and cited by this work consist of the case law that evolved on the subject matter throughout the 1980s. Included in this source material is the variety of federal and state statutory legislation upon which the respective parties in the cases relied for support. For each of the five main cases herein examined, the entire record was consulted as available, and variously consisting of complaints; responses; motions argued; affidavits submitted; reports; studies; correspondence and other print exhibits entered into evidence; appeals filed and briefed; petitions for rehearing when made; petitions for writs of certiorari when made; *amicus curiae* briefs when filed; the published rulings of the respective district and appellate courts; and the final disposition of the issue by the United States Supreme Court in its rendering of the *Lyng* decision.

Fundamental to the entire study and the ultimate legal principle upon which the various tribes sought to protect their ancestral sacred lands is the religion clause of the First Amendment to the United States Constitution: "Congress shall make no law respecting an establishment of religion, or prohibiting the free exercise thereof. . . . "

Adderley v. Florida, 385 U.S. 39 (1966).
Administrative Procedure Act, 5 U.S.C.A.§501 et. seq. (1946).
American Indian Religious Freedom Act, Pub. L. No. 95-341, 92 Stat. 469, 42 U.S.C.§1996 (Supp. III 1979).
Badoni v. Higginson, 455 F. Supp. 641 (D. Utah 1977), aff'd 638 F.2d 172 (10th Cir. 1980).
Bowen v. Roy, 476 U.S. 693 (1986).
California Wilderness Act of 1984, Pub. L. No. 98–425, 98 Stat. 1619 et. seq.
Cantwell v. Connecticut, 310 U.S. 296 (1940).

Committee for Public Education and Religious Liberty v. Nyquist, 413 U.S. 756 (1973).
Cox v. Louisiana, 379 U.S. 536 (1965).
Crow v. Gullet, 541 F. Supp. 785 (D.S.D. 1982), *aff'd*, 706 F.2d 856 (8th Cir. 1983).
Endangered Species Act of 1973 (ESA), 7 U.S.C.A.§§136 et. seq.; Pub. L. 93-205 §§2-15; 87 Stat. 84, as amended.
Federal Water Pollution Control Act Amendments of 1961, 33 U.S.C.A§1151 et. seq.; Pub. L. 87-88; 75 Stat. 204.
Frank v. Alaska, 604 P. 2d 1068 (Alaska 1979).
Hague v. CIO, 307 U.S. 496 (1939).
Hopi Indian Tribe v. Block, 19 ERC (BNA) 1215 (D.D.C. June 15, 1981) *aff'd sub nom. Wilson v. Block*, 708 F.2d 735(D.C. Cir. 1983).
Kleppe v. New Mexico, 426 U.S. 529 (1976).
Kunz v. New York, 340 U.S. 290 (1951).
Larson v. Valente, 456 U.S. 228 (1982).
Lemon v. Kurtzman, 403 U.S. 602 (1971).
Lyng v. Northwest Indian Cemetery Protective Association, 485 U.S. 439 (1988).
Matthiessen, Peter, *Indian Country* (New York: Penguin Books, 1992).
National Environmental Policy Act of 1969 (NEPA), 42 U.S.C.A.§§4321 et. seq.; Pub. L. 91-190; 83 Stat. 852, as amended.
National Historic Preservation Act of 1960, 16 U.S.C.A.§470–470w6, as amended.
Niemotko v. Maryland, 340 U.S. 268 (1951).
Northwest Indian Cemetery Protective Association v. Petersen, 565 F. Supp. 586 (N.D.Cal.), *aff'd*, 795 F.2d 688 (9th Cir. 1986), *rev'd sub hom. Lyng v. Northwest Indian Cemetery Protective Association*, 485 U.S. 439 (1988).
People v. Woody, 61 Cal. 2d 716 (1964).
Sequoyah v. Tennessee Valley Authority, 480 F. Supp. 608(E.D.Tenn. 1979), *aff'd*, 620 F.2d 1159 (6th Cir. 1980).
Sherbert v. Verner, 374 U.S. 398 (1963).
Tennessee Valley Authority v. Hiram Hill et al., 437 U.S. 153 (1978).
Theodoratus, D. J., J. L. Chartkoff, and K. K. Chartkoff, "Cultural Resources of the Chimney Rock Section, Gasquet-Orleans Road, Six Rivers National Forest" (1979).
Thomas v. Review Board of the Indiana Employment Security Division, 450 U.S. 707 (1981).
United States v. Lee, 455 U.S. 252 (1982).
West Virginia State Board of Education v. Barnette, 319 U.S. 624 (1943).
Wilderness Act of 1964, 16 U.S.C.A.§§1131-1136; Pub. L. 88-577; 79 Stat. 890, as amended.
Wilson v. Block, 708 F.2d 735 (D.C. Cir. 1983).
Wisconsin v. Yoder, 406 U.S. 205 (1972).

Index

Adderley v. Florida, 32
Administrative Procedure Act, 68, 75, 132
AIRFA. *See* American Indian Religious Freedom Act
Alaska, 34
alcohol, 52
American Indian Religious Freedom Act (AIRFA): and *Fools Crow v. Gullet*, 101, 102; and *Lyng v. Northwest Indian Cemetery Protective Association*, 125, 131, 136, 150, 172; and *Sequoyah v. TVA*, 16–18; and *Wilson v. Block*, 66, 68, 73–75, 91
Amish, 19–20, 34–36, 47–48, 81–82, 85, 164–66
Anderson, Aldon J., 44–50
Andrus, Cecil D., 21
archeology, 128–29
Arizona, 4, 40, 61
Audobon Society, 156

Badoni v. Higginson: and AIRFA, 73; background, 39–43; and *Crow v. Gullet*, 105, 107, 115–16, 117; in district court, 44–50; and *Lyng v. Northwest Indian Cemetery Protective Association*, 132–33, 141, 146, 166; in Tenth Circuit Court of Appeals, 3, 50–60; and *Wilson v. Block*, 70; and *Wisconsin v. Yoder*, 166–67
Baker, Howard, 12, 24
Baptists, 28
Bear Butte, 93, 94, 96–98. *See also Crow v. Gullet*
Beezer, Robert R., 140, 147–49, 187 n.46
Black Crow, Selo, 100. *See also Crow v. Gullet*
Black Hills, 3, 94–95, 96–97
Block, John R., 65, 131. *See also Wilson v. Block*
Blue Creek. *See Lyng v. Northwest Indian Cemetery Protective Association*
Bogue, Andrew W., 101, 103–8

Bovee, Harold, 96
Bowen v. Roy, 153–56, 159, 162, 188 n.61
Breitenstein, Jean, 50–60
Brennan, William J., Jr., 4, 150, 159, 163–66, 188 n.61
Bright, Myron H., 116–18
Bureau of Indian Affairs, 66
Burger, Warren, 154, 159, 188 n.61
burial grounds, 13–14, 131. *See also* Lyng v. Northwest Indian Cemetery Protective Association

California Wilderness Act, 140
Canby, WIlliam C., 140–49
Cantwell v. Connecticut, 28–29
Catches, Pete, 100. *See also Crow v. Gullet*
cathedral analogy, 109–10
centrality standard, 34–35, 37–38, 132–33, 141–42, 166
Chartkoff, Joseph L. *See* Theodoratus Report
Chartkoff, Kerry K. *See* Theodoratus Report
Cherokee, 9–10, 13–16, 22–23, 175; Eastern Band and Oklahoma, 24–25. *See also* religion
Cheyenne. *See* Tsistsistas Nation
Chimney Rock, 123, 125, 129, 130, 145, 150
Chota, 13, 14
civil rights, 101, 102, 108
Coconino National Forest, 4, 66, 72. *See also Wilson v. Block*
Colorado River, 39–41
Cometsevah, Laird, 101. *See also Crow v. Gullet*
compelling interest: in *Badoni v. Higginson*, 51, 55–56, 168; in *Crow v. Gullet*, 107, 113–15, 118, 167–68; in *Lyng v. Northwest Indian Cemetery Protective Association*, 135, 146–47, 151–53, 158–59, 165–66, 168; in *Sequoyah v. TVA*, 20–22; in *Wilson v. Block*, 81–83, 167–68; in *Wisconsin v. Yoder*, 167
cornerstone standard, 34–35, 37–38
Cox v. Louisiana, 56
Crow v. Gullet: background, 93–100; in Eighth Circuit Appellate Court, 109–18; in Federal District Court, 3–4, 100–108; and *Lyng v. Northwest Indian Cemetery Protective Association*, 132–33, 141; Ninth Circuit Appellate Court, 118; and *Wisconsin v. Yoder*, 166–67

dances, ceremonial, 122
Doctor Rock, 123, 125
Duncan, John, 12
Duniway, Benjamin C., 140–49
Durham, Jimmie, 38

Endangered Species Act: and *Sequoyah v. TVA*, 11, 17, 20, 25, 31; and *Wilson v. Block*, 68, 75, 91
Energy and Water Appropriations Act of 1978, 16–18
environmental concern, 41–42, 172–73. *See also* fish; National Environmental Policy Act; water
Environmental Defense Fund, 10–11
erosion, 124–25
Establishment Clause: and *Badoni v. Higginson*, 54–55; and *Crow v. Gullet*, 108, 109–10; and *Larson v. Valente*, 111; and *Lyng v. Northwest Indian Cemetery*

Index

Protective Association, 135, 142, 143; and *Wilson v. Block*, 72–73, 84–87
estoppel, 25–26

Federal Water Pollution Control Act, 132
First Amendment, 3–4, 13–14, 25–26, 45, 111. *See also* Establishment Clause; Free Exercise Clause
fish, 124–25, 138, 139, 143–44, 147
fishing rights, 132
flora and fauna, 65, 69. *See also* Endangered Species Act
Florida, 32
Fools Crow, Frank, 100. *See also Crow v. Gullet*
Frank v. Alaska, 34–35
Free Exercise Clause: in *Badoni v. Higginson*, 45, 50–51; in *Bowen v. Roy*, 153–54; and *Crow v. Gullet*, 101, 106, 109; language interpretation, 166, 189 n.83; and *Lyng v. Northwest Indian Cemetery Protective Association*, 135, 143, 146, 150–52; in *Sequoyah*, 16, 26, 28–29, 35–36, 37–38; and *Wilson v. Block*, 66, 68, 69, 71, 78–79, 80, 185 nn.26, 27
Friends of the Earth, 41–42

Ginsburg, Ruth Bader, 76
Glen Canyon Dam, 3, 40
God Committee, 20
government benefits, versus religion, 79–82
groundsel, 68, 75
Gullet, Tony, 98–100, 101, 103. *See also Crow v. Gullet*

Hague v. CIO, 57, 58
Hamilton, Walter, 101. *See also Crow v. Gullet*
healing power, 122–23
high country, 122–23
Hoopa Valley, 120, 121, 140
Hopi, 61, 63, 175. *See also* religion; *Wilson v. Block*
Horned Antelope, Grover, 100, 105–6. *See also Crow v. Gullet*
horses, 31–32
human rights, 101, 102, 108
Hupa, 120. *See also Lyng v. Northwest Indian Cemetery Protective Association*; religion

Indiana, 79–80, 82
indispensability standard, 34–35, 37–38, 132–33, 141–42
International Covenant on Civil and Political Rights, 101, 102, 108

Jehovah's Witnesses, 28–29, 53, 57, 79–80

Kachinas, 61–62
Karok, 119–20, 175. *See also Lyng v. Northwest Indian Cemetery Protective Association*; religion
Keith, Damon J., 37
Klamath River, 119, 120, 125
Kleppe v. New Mexico, 31–32
Kunz v. New York, 28

laches, 25
Lacota Nation, 93
Lake Powell, 3, 40–42. *See also Badoni v. Higginson*
Lakota Nation, 175, 184 n.1. *See also Crow v. Gullet*; religion

land: and AIRFA, 74–75; and environmental concerns, 172–73; productive use, 147–49; public use, 52–58, 83; sacred nature, 5, 13, 37, 44, 115–16, 122–23, 141–41, 145, 158. *See also* property; sites.
Larson v. Valente, 111
Lay, Donald P., 116–18
least restrictive means, 82–83
Lemon v. Kurtzman, 86–87, 143–46
Lincoln Memorial, 46
Little Tennessee River Valley, 13–16
Lively, Pierce, 37
Logan, James, 50–60
logging, 124–25, 133–35
Looking Horse, Arvol, 100. *See also Crow v. Gullet*
looting, 65
Louisiana, 56
Lumbard, J. Edward, 76
Lyng v. Northwest Indian Cemetery Protective Association: background, 119–32; District Court decision, 4, 132–40; in Ninth Circuit Court of Appeals, 140–49; repercussions, 171–74; in U.S. Supreme Court, 2–3, 5–8, 149–70
Lyons, Oren, 26–27

Marshall, Thurgood, 159, 188 n.61
McWilliams, Robert, 50–60
Merritt, Gilbert S., 37–38
Minnesota, 111
monuments, 40–41
Multiple-Use Sustained-Yield Act, 68, 75, 132, 139

National Environmental Policy Act: and *Lyng v. Northwest Indian Cemetery Protective Association,* 131–32, 136–38, 144; and *Wilson v. Block,* 67, 68, 75
National Forest Management Act, 132, 139
National Historic Preservation Act, 68, 75–76, 91
National Register of Historic Places, 130, 131
National Wilderness Act, 68, 91
Navajo, 41, 43, 62, 64, 105, 175. *See also Badoni v. Higginson*; religion; *Wilson v. Block*
Nelson, Francine, 100. *See also Crow v. Gullet*
Niemotko v. Maryland, 57
Northland Recreation, Inc., 63, 65–67
Northwest Indian Cemetery Protective Association v. Peterson, 4

O'Connor, Sandra Day, 150, 159–61, 188 n.61
Old Coyote, Barney, 27

Paiute Strip, 44–45
parades, 56. *See also* permits
paramount interest. *See* compelling interest
Peak 8, 123
People v. Woody, 34–35
permits, 107, 110–12
Peterson, R. Max, 65, 131
peyote, 34
political rights, 101, 102, 108
prohibition: definition, 189 n.83; and Free Exercise Clause, 51, 70, 71, 79, 80, 151; and Lakota and Tsistsistas, 100, 101. *See also* permits

property, land as: in *Badoni v. Higginson*, 45–46, 58–60; in *Crow v. Gullet*, 103–4, 107–8; in *Lyng v. Northwest Indian Cemetery Protective Association*, 2–3, 148–49, 152–53, 161–63; in *Sequoyah v. TVA*, 22–27, 29, 31; in *Wilson v. Block*, 71–72, 88–90
purification rituals, 106–7, 122–23

Rainbow Bridge, 40–41, 44–45, 105, 117. *See also Badoni v. Higginson*
Red Hat, Bill, Jr., 100–101. *See also Crow v. Gullet*
Red Shirt, Larry, 100. *See also Crow v. Gullet*
registration, 107, 110–12
Rehnquist, William, 161
religion: Cherokee, 13–14, 26–27, 36–38; government accommodations to, 53–54, 84–85, 108; versus government benefits, 79–82; Hopi, 61–62, 69, 77, 183 n.16; and land, 5, 13, 37, 44, 89–91, 103, 112; Navajo, 43, 44, 45, 47–49, 62, 69, 77; non-Indian, 177; in Theodoratus Report, 126–27; of Tsistsista and Lakota, 94–96, 98, 101, 106–7, 115–16; of Yurok, Karok, Tolowa, and Hupa, 122–23, 126, 128, 129–30
Richey, Charles R., 65, 68–76, 104, 108
Ross, Donald R., 116–18
Ross, John, 24
Roy, Stephen J., 153, 159

Sabbath. *See Sherbert v. Verner*
Salmon River, 120

San Francisco Peaks, 61–63. *See also Wilson v. Block*
Scalia, Antonin, 161
Schultze, Charles, 21
Sekaquaptewa, Abbott, 63–64
Senecio franciscanus, 68, 75
Sequoyah, Ammoneta, 9
Sequoyah v. TVA: and AIRFA, 73; background, 9–16; Cherokee arguments, 16–22; and *Crow v. Gullet*, 107, 115–16, 117; and *Lyng v. Northwest Indian Cemetery Protective Association*, 132–33, 141; Sixth Circuit appeal, 3, 30–38, 71; TVA response, 22–27, 31–33; U.S. District Court decision, 27–30; and *Wilson v. Block*, 70, 71, 88–90; and *Wisconsin v. Yoder*, 166–67
Seventh-day Adventists, 19, 53, 79
Sherbert v. Verner: and *Badoni v. Higginson*, 53; and *Crow v. Gullet*, 113–14; and *Lyng v. Northwest Indian Cemetery Protective Association*, 135–36; and *Wilson v. Block*, 79–82, 84, 87–88
Shuttlesworth v. City of Birmingham, 56, 111
Sierra Club, 156
Sioux. *See Lakota Nation*
Siskiyou Mountains, 122
Siskiyou Wilderness, 140
sites, religious, 126
Six Rivers National Forest, 124
ski resort, 62–63, 64–65
snail darter, 11, 17
Social Security numbers, 153–56, 188 n.61
South Carolina, 19, 53, 79, 82

South Dakota, 93, 96–100, 101, 106
Stevens, John Paul, 161
Stone People, 43, 45
summary judgment, 76, 103, 108
Summit Properties, Inc., 66
sweat lodges, 106–7

Tamm, Edward Allen, 76
Taylor, Robert L., Jr., 27–30
Tellico Dam, 3, 10–13
Tennessee Valley Authority, 3, 9–13, 22–27, 31–33
Tennessee Valley Authority v. Hiram Hill, 11, 17–18, 25
Theodoratus, Dorothea J., 126
Theodoratus Report, 126–32, 150, 156–57, 172
Thomas v. Indiana Employment Security Division, 79–82, 84–85, 87–88
Tolowa, 120, 175. See also *Lyng v. Northwest Indian Cemetery Protective Association*; religion
tourism, 52–58, 83, 97–100, 104–7. See also ski resort
trespass statutes, 32
Tsistsistas Nation, 94, 175, 177, 184 n.1. See also *Crow v. Gullet*; religion
Tso, Faye, 62

Universal Declaration of Human Rights, 101, 102, 108
U.S. Congress: and *Badoni v. Higginson*, 40–43; California Wilderness Act, 140; and *Sequoyah v. Tennessee Valley Authority*, 10–12; and *Tennessee Valley Authority v. Hiram Hill*, 17–18
U.S. Constitution, Property Clause, 31–32. See also First Amendment
U.S. Department of Agriculture, 65, 66, 131
U.S. Forest Service: and *Lyng v. Northwest Indian Cemetery Protective Association*, 124, 125, 126–27, 133–36, 138–39, 142, 145; and *Wilson v. Block*, 65–66, 67, 68, 73–74, 76
U.S. Supreme Court: *Adderley v. Florida*, 32; *Cox v. Louisiana*, 56; on Establishment Clause, 54; *Hague v. CIO*, 57; *Kleppe v. New Mexico*, 31–32; *Larson v. Valente*, 111; *Lemon v. Kurtzman*, 86–87; *Lyng v. Northwest Indian Cemetery Protective Association*, 2–3, 4, 5–8, 149–70, 171–72; *Niemotko v. Maryland*, 57; *Northwest Indian Cemetery Protective Association v. Peterson*, 4; *Sherbert v. Verner*, 19, 53, 79–82, 84, 113–14; *Shuttlesworth v. City of Birmingham*, 56, 111; *Tennessee Valley Authority v. Hiram Hill*, 11, 17–18; *Thomas v. Indiana Employment Security Division*, 79–82, 84; *West Virginia State Board of Education v. Barnette*, 53; *Wisconsin v. Yoder*, 19–20, 34–36, 47, 53, 84–85
Utah, 3

vision quests, 94–95, 104, 105, 184 nn.10, 11

water, 125, 132, 138, 139, 143–44, 147
water rights, 132
Weigel, Stanley A., 132–40

West Virginia State Board of Education v. Barnette, 53
White, Byron, 154, 161
Wilderness Society, 156
Wilson, Richard and Jean, 65
Wilson, Terry, 100–101. *See also Crow v. Gullet*
Wilson v. Block: background, 61–68; and *Crow v. Gullet*, 104, 108, 115–16, 117–18; and D.C. Circuit Appellate Court, 3–4, 76–91; and district court, 68–76; *Lyng v. Northwest Indian Cemetery Protective Association*, 132–33, 141

Winter, Joseph, 131
Wisconsin v. Yoder: and *Badoni v. Higginson*, 47–48, 50, 53, 166–67; and *Crow v. Gullet*, 166–67; and *Lyng v. Northwest Indian Cemetery Protective Association*, 135–36, 164–67; and *Sequoyah v. TVA*, 19–20, 34–36, 37, 166–67; and *Wilson v. Block*, 81–82, 84–85, 166–67
Wise Use Movement, 1–2

Yurok, 119, 120, 175. *See also Lyng v. Northwest Indian Cemetery Protective Association*; religion

About the Author

BRIAN EDWARD BROWN is Chairman and Associate Professor of Religious Studies at Iona College in New Rochelle, New York. He teaches classes in the Buddhist, Chinese, and Native American traditions; religious cosmology; and the Constitutional law of church-state relations.

HARDCOVER BAR CODE